Divine Science

Finding Reason at the Heart of Faith

MICHAEL DENNIN, PH.D.

Franciscan
MEDIA
Cincinnati, Ohio

Cover and book design by Mark Sullivan
Cover image © iStock | Andrew Ostrovsky

LIBRARY OF CONGRESS CATALOGING-IN-PUBLICATION DATA
Dennin, Michael.
Divine science : finding reason at the heart of faith / Michael, Ph.D.
pages cm
Includes bibliographical references.
ISBN 978-1-61636-947-7 (alk. paper)
1. Religion and science. I. Title.
BL240.3.D464 2015
261.5'5—dc23
2015027538

ISBN 978-1-61636-947-7

Published by Franciscan Media
28 W. Liberty St.
Cincinnati, OH 45202
www.FranciscanMedia.org

Printed in the United States of America.
Printed on acid-free paper.
15 16 17 18 19 5 4 3 2 1

This book is dedicated to my parents, wife, children, brothers, and sister, whose love and support for me have provided a mirror for the unconditional love of God.

Contents

Acknowledgments

This book—like all books—did not arise in a vacuum. It is a reflection on the questions and insights that have captured my interest over the years, and I owe a great debt of thanks to the many books, teachers, friends, speakers, and others that have influenced my thinking on this subject throughout my life. At the risk of missing someone, a few influences do stand out.

In my personal faith journey, I owe thanks to the Jesuits at Fairfield Prep; Prof. Elaine Pagels at Princeton University; Fr. Ken McGuire, C.S.P., Fr. Bill Edens, C.S.P., Fr. Frank Sabatte, C.S.P., and Harriet Burke at St. Mark's; Fr. Michael Crosby, O.F.M. Cap., Fr. Edward Hays, and Fr. Richard Rohr, O.F.M.; and colleagues Prof. Bill Heidbrink, Prof. Thorsten Ritz, and Prof. Clare Yu. In my scientific career, I am indebted to my advisers Profs. David Cannell, Guenter Ahlers, and Charles Knobler, as well as the many collaborators and friends throughout the years.

The writing of this book would never have occurred without the incredible help of my research assistant, a splendid intellect, Justin Colvin. Also, I want to thank the friends and family who read drafts of the book and provided helpful feedback: Peter Dennin, Kimberly Dennin, Harriet Burke, Ken McGuire, Cate Neuhauser, Sarah Novak, James Abowd, Dan McCurrie, Prof. Jonathan Feng, Fr. Michael Crosby, O.F.M., and Monica Wissucheck. Finally, as with so much of my life, this book has been accomplished in partnership with my wife, Jeni—her ideas, support, and love are woven throughout the book—and the patience of my children, Kimberly, Melissa, and Rachel, who let Daddy spend the time needed to complete this book.

Author's Note

Writing a book about God, theology, philosophy, and science presented some unique challenges in the use of language. When it comes to God, who is singular but with no gender, there is the challenge in the English language of which pronouns should be used. My approach to this issue was to avoid the use of pronouns for God in the text I wrote, but not to edit the usage in quoted sources.

Discussing theology, philosophy, and science presents the challenge of technical language. These are words that have developed to express complex ideas and concepts that occur regularly within the field. For experts, this provides an efficient shorthand. But as this book is intended for nonexperts, my goal was to find more common language, while still communicating the original complexity and depth of the ideas. However, at times, the technical words are sufficiently important and useful, so I have chosen to use them and at the same time to provide a definition for the nonexpert. Where it made sense, the definition is part of the text. If the definition would break up the flow of the text, I have provided it as a footnote.

Fallow Fields and Good Ground

I n February 2014, while I was writing this book, one of my research assistants sent me a Washington Post article that covered a so-called debate between Bill Nye, the renowned "Science Guy," and Kenneth Ham, founder and CEO of the Creation Museum and AnswersinGenesis. com. "They're at it again," my assistant's e-mail read. The debate ostensibly sought to settle the matter between evolution by natural selection and young earth creationism—all in the space of two and a half hours.

The debaters marshaled the same old talking points both for and against young earth creationism. Their theses were telling:

"I believe it's the creationists that should be educating the kids out there, because we're teaching them the right way to think," said Mr. Ham.

"If we continue to eschew science and try to divide science between 'observational science' and 'historical science,' we are not going to move forward, we will not embrace natural laws, we will not make discoveries, we will not invent," responded Mr. Nye.

Both participants performed deftly in the debate. But, they spoke exclusively from within their respective frameworks, leveraged the full weight of their perspectives into their arguments, and, accordingly, they were simply talking past one another. But then, really, I think that was the point of the debate. This debate was never intended to win one side over to the other; there never was to be any reconciliation.

Debates like the one between Mr. Nye and Mr. Ham attempt to prove definitive positions regarding philosophy and theology. This book starts from a completely opposite perspective and is neither intended to be one side of a debate nor is it an attempt to prove the existence or nonexistence of God. Its purpose is to share my experience of faith and science, which I believe can help clarify for people of faith the important role that science plays in our understanding of reality and encourage them to embrace science as a tool for enhancing faith.

How is it that in 2015 we're still "debating" faith and science in a spirit of antagonism? We've put a man on the moon. We've unraveled the human genome. We live with science in our daily lives, where each day provides incontrovertible evidence that the natural sciences work. On the other side, religious faith continues to provide a vehicle by which we can share our experiences of the infinite. Moreover, our faith communities provide for us moral guidance, practices for self- and communal improvement, and a framework by which we can understand our experiences of the transcendent. So, why do we persons of faith feel threatened by the sciences? Why do we not instead embrace the sciences as another glimpse into the infinite?

Debating apparent differences—even when supposedly gilded with a veneer of productive dialogue—will get us nowhere. At best, the true believers of both sides will continue to believe as they previously did; at worst, these debates inspire ill will in members of both sides. Really, we shouldn't even pay attention to events such as these because they are disingenuous in their offer of understanding and patently misleading in their offer of reconciliation.

All of this rancor overshadows a rather simple notion that is grounded in the implicit points of agreement that these two sides actually possess. Both Mr. Nye and Mr. Ham, I imagine, would agree with the following: were one to accept a literal reading of the Bible, such a reading would be incompatible with the natural sciences. Therefore, when Mr. Ham takes a literal position for Genesis, the only option is conflict. But, I think, such a literal position is actually at odds with many people's understanding of Scripture. On the other side, if you assume the only reality is *physical* reality, the reality that we access with our five senses or tools used to enhance our senses, it becomes equally difficult to imagine the existence of a meaningful, transcendent God. Understanding these two points, we see that the heart of the conflict is not really God's existence; the debate is between two assumptions about reality: biblical literalism and empiricism.[1]

If science and faith are not inherently in conflict, what are the other approaches? One approach is to view science and faith as focused on entirely distinct sets of issues. Such an approach maintains that science deals with explaining how the physical world works whereas religion deals with moral behavior and questions of purpose. This has its appeal, and I find it essentially correct. But my experiences point to a key element that is missing from this view. Faith is not just about moral behavior and purpose. A central element of my approach throughout the book is realizing that faith focuses on our attempts to understand the *fullness of reality*, which is arguably the most natural definition of God. Therefore, by definition, the study of physical reality—that is, science—logically should inform our faith. After all, physical reality is a subset of the fullness of reality, so the study of physical reality is part of our faith journey. One rational approach to the relation between science and religion starts with questions regarding the fullness of reality.

A key feature of my proposed starting point is that the questions we ask are almost more important than the answers we currently have. After all, we are all on a journey of exploration. A focus on fruitful questions will, I hope, provide for conversations among the sciences and all faiths from a universal perspective, and not result in a reiteration of positions already cast in stone. I want this book to achieve three related goals: First, I hope to demonstrate that the questions of interest to science and those of interest to faith do overlap in certain areas. Therefore, science and faith are not inherently in conflict or completely separate.

Second, by demonstrating how the sciences have actually enhanced my faith, I hope to provide a road map for others as to how science can enhance anyone's religious inquiry. Both science and religion wish to understand better the nature of *all* of reality. Faith specifically asks questions beyond physical reality, but the answers faith comes to must be consistent with the nature of physical reality. By definition, science is *limited* to studying physical reality, which may or may not be *all* of reality—a quantity I have already defined as the *fullness of reality*. Despite this limitation, the insights provided by science contribute to our deepening understanding of the fullness of reality, as it is the best way we know to gain knowledge regarding the physical world, and therefore, the sciences cannot undercut faith, and vice versa. Indeed, science actually enhances our understanding of faith experiences that are grounded in physical reality, even as we reach beyond to the fullness of reality.

Third, and finally, I hope this book contributes to the more productive conversation about the intersection of science and religion based on mutual regard, reciprocal respect, charitable consideration, and humility. This is a conversation that explores how advances in our understanding of the physical world can inspire a deeper understanding of theology. If this is your first foray into scientific understanding enhancing faith, then you certainly will want to explore other writers and thinkers involved in the conversation. If it has been a while since you studied science, you might also want to explore other popular books on science. To this end, I have included a list of further reading at the end of the book that you might find interesting. I do not necessarily agree with everything in the books I list, but I have found them thought provoking and interesting enough to recommend.

I should be clear at the outset that I am not a professional theologian or philosopher. So, why do I feel justified in writing this book? Well, for two reasons. First, I am a cradle Catholic who still regularly attends Mass at Saint Elizabeth Ann Seton parish in Irvine, California, where I have often helped teach the youth of the parish. My mother is Jewish and my father is Catholic, and though I was raised Catholic, this combination has provided particularly valuable insights into the breadth of faith experiences. I am the happy product of a Jesuit secondary education, and I received my undergraduate degree from Princeton University and my graduate degree from the University of California, Santa Barbara—both in physics. Second, I am a tenured professor of physics at the University of California, Irvine. I have been active throughout my career both in research and popular science education. My research has focused primarily on the mechanical and flow properties of foam and other nonlinear, nonequilibrium systems. I have appeared on a number of television programs, such as *Ancient Aliens* and *The Science of Superman,* in the interest of popularizing the sciences and scientific discourse. I see this book as uniting these two community outreach efforts.

On the one hand, I aim this book at inquisitive persons of faith who want to have a better understanding of how science can enhance their faith. I am hopeful that, by sharing how my vocation as a scientist has enhanced my own faith, I can accomplish this. Accordingly, I have endeavored to keep this book as untechnical as possible with regard to the sciences. I should be clear at this point that, because I use my life as a model, this book has an explicitly Christian perspective. But the aspects of science that bear on faith are general enough that persons of any faith—even humanists and atheists—are likely to find my questions of interest and relevant to their lives, though some translation to your own faith experience may be needed. As you will see, I do not see science as a vehicle for commenting on particular doctrines and moral teachings of a given faith. Because these questions are beyond the purview of the natural sciences, I will not focus on matters of morality and doctrine.

On the other hand, I write this book as an offering to demonstrate to scientists that persons of faith are not the sheeplike buffoons that the controlling caricature would imply. Instead, persons of faith can be as reflective, as critical, and as sophisticated as even the most technical of scientists. This is one reason why I have approached this subject using the voice and the perspective of an expository memoir; I hope that my experiences can offer some insight to the ways that I've found to make room for both my vocation and my faith.

Faith and *science* are words that conjure many images, and can mean quite different things to different people. Therefore, a key to this book is my approach to faith and science. This is outlined in the first chapter, Faith and Science: Why Ask Questions? Though not strictly necessary to the rest of the book, it provides the foundation for my approach and gives some specific advice to nonscientists on how to approach the sciences themselves. If nothing else, it highlights why I believe the key to both faith and science is asking the right questions.

Given the importance of good questions, I have structured this book around a series of key questions. I do not envision this book as articulating a specific philosophy, advancing a theological framework, or prescribing a scientific approach. Neither do I intend to prove anything by writing this book. Instead, I will start from core tensions between science and faith that are often expressed publicly, and show how focusing on key questions moves us away from these tensions and builds bridges between the two endeavors. The following question governs the entirety of this book: Can I accept findings generated by the scientific method and still accept the teachings of my faith? I emphatically argue yes—provided we are honest about our faith and approach this subject in a manner that respects both approaches, that is, a *consilient* manner, a term we will come back to later in the book.

The first three chapters form an introduction to bridging science and faith. Chapter one seeks to reframe the starting points from which discussions between the sciences and faith advance. The question of whether or not God exists seems to me to be neither the most fruitful starting point nor a quantity that can be investigated using the intellectual tools provided by the sciences. Therefore, I believe it is most fruitful to recognize explicitly that both science and faith are methods for developing a better understanding of reality, with the ultimate goal of understanding the fullness of reality. Sciences are particularly focused on physical reality, but, by definition, this is part of the fullness of reality.

In order to get to this initial position, persons of faith need to avoid two common assumptions regarding faith that are focused on in the popular media, but are not central to the faith journey. Namely, we need to move past our image of God as merely a physical being, even if we imagine God as a superbeing. We need to allow God to exist as something far greater than a simplistic, anthropomorphic being. Rather than simply a being, God is instead, I argue, a type of superreality—the ultimate superhero, and the fullness of reality that is the focus of this book. This will be the subject of chapter two.

In addition, I suggest we need to be clear about our relationship to Scripture. Such an intellectual move requires that we go beyond simple biblical literalism and embrace Scripture as truth. By doing so, we take seriously the perspectives according to which Scripture was written, and we invest Scripture not with fact (a quantity most at home in our own paradigm) but with truth (a quantity that would have been recognizable to the authors of Scripture themselves). This will be the subject of chapter three. Should a reader agree with these initial premises, the first three chapters will probably provide little that is explicitly new, but they will help the reader understand how I connect science with these initial issues.

After these positions are outlined, I will proceed through a number of questions and demonstrate the unity that can exist between the sciences and faith—if only we allow it to. Chapter four will consider ex nihilo creation (creation from nothing), a commonly held religious view of creation, as consistent with the cutting edge of particle physics and quantum mechanics. This is where we explore the Big Bang theory of creation. Chapter five will consider salvation theology as the ultimate expression of evolutionary biology. Evolution is not a moral system, and the actuality of evolution does nothing to disrupt the moral underpinnings of creation.

Chapter six will address consciousness and love from both a theological and scientific perspective, and demonstrate the relatedness of the two positions. In addressing the complexity underlying consciousness, we will explore the scientific concept of *emergence*—the idea that certain properties of a system can only be understood when considering the system as a whole, and not by studying the individual parts separately. Chapter seven will consider a potentially powerful view of miracles as God's actions in physical reality. God's laws are not just found in Scripture; they are woven into the very fabric of physical reality. Indeed, it seems to me that the regularity of physical reality itself provides a strong case for the existence of a reality beyond physical reality.

Chapter eight approaches the challenges presented by the concept of free will. Free will is the cornerstone of elective salvation, and the sciences are indicating powerful ways in which complexity allows for elective behavior. Predestination and its scientific cousin, determinism, would seem, then, to be misunderstandings of the theology of salvation, or *soteriology*, and the physical underpinnings of reality, respectively. Finally, chapter nine will address the question of the afterlife, which is the linchpin of most world faiths. The sciences have no definite word on this matter, but can indicate exciting possibilities for the ways in which we might conceive of the afterlife. Perhaps surprisingly, the afterlife posited by the three major Abrahamic faiths—Judaism, Christianity, and Islam— makes a lot of sense to the sciences!

Taken together, these chapters will forcefully argue that the sciences do nothing to threaten our understanding of core religious experiences and instead support some of our most hallowed truths. As Paul says in 1 Corinthians, "When I was a child, I spoke as a child, I understood as a child, I thought as a child. But, when I became a man, I put away the things of a child" (13:11). For me, science provides a welcome challenge to aspects of my faith, but always in a way that moves me to a more mature, adult faith, and never in a way that is in conflict with my core experiences and beliefs.

Chapter 0

Faith and Science: Why Ask Questions?

In my family, there was a very strict rule—you only ate two cookies at any given time. Now, I certainly could follow this rule—the words make sense taken at face value. If there are cookies being offered, you should only eat two of them. However, for a long time, I did not understand this rule. It made no sense to me; cookies were really good, so why not eat more than two? It was only as I gained more experience with eating—and, in particular, eating cookies—that I discovered potential negative effects of cookie eating (which, if my bathroom scale is correct, gets all the more negative as one gets older). It was the coming together of maturity and knowledge that resulted in understanding. The words themselves are insufficient; only accumulated experience has allowed me to really understand this cookie rule.

Arguably the greatest similarity between faith and science is that practitioners of both would agree that increased understanding comes with experience. So, before providing a more detailed look at these two ways of knowing, we should think about what it actually means to understand science. This book will offer many explanations of current ideas in science—and some inhabit rather abstract arenas, such as quantum mechanics and relativity. In my experience discussing science with nonscientists, I am often told by people, "I do not understand what you mean by that." At first, I thought, sure, science is hard—it makes sense that it is hard to understand. But I have realized over the years that what they really mean is, "I understand what you said, but it does not make sense intuitively or based on my experience." This situation is completely analogous to my experience with the two-cookie rule: the words are understandable but the rule does not match my intuition.

None of us has direct experience of quantum mechanics or relativity[2]—not even we physicists! Therefore, we have no point of reference that we can call *understanding*. Worse, quantum mechanics and relativity often appear to violate our experiences of the everyday world. And yet these two fields represent two of the most highly tested and highly confirmed sets of rules that govern the world around us. Every time you use your computer, cell phone, microwave oven, flat-screen television, or global positioning system, you are confirming that the rules of quantum mechanics and relativity are, broadly speaking, correct. Just as the two-cookie rule may have not made overt and intuitive sense, but my parents were still right.

As you read about the rules of science in this book, understand that at times you will need to let go of the desire to have the rules "make sense" and simply accept them as rules. Have faith in them; their constant validation through scientists' experimentation and your own experience with modern technology ought to be reasons enough to have faith. And this last step is absolutely critical. I am not asking you to accept the rules because scientists state that they are true; I am asking you to accept the rules because of the vast number of experiments that have confirmed them to be true. As a quantum mechanics professor of mine once said, "In this class, we learn how to use quantum mechanics; if you want to discuss what that those rules and understandings mean, that is best done over a beer at the pub."

What Is Faith?

Throughout this book, I will make reference to religious belief broadly using the term *faith*. Scholars have advanced many definitions of religion—ranging from Emile Durkheim's social model to William James's experiential model (Emile Durkheim is a sociologist/philosopher and William James is a psychologist, both from the early twentieth century).

I see the definition as lying somewhere in between. Religious experience undergirds religion more broadly, but these experiences are articulated and communicated according to the conventions of a religious society. Religion, therefore, is somewhat distinct from faith. Religion, to my mind, encompasses the confessional conventions erected to articulate religious experience.

This book is certainly written from a religious perspective. My own religious language has naturally been informed by my Catholic perspective. I was born into, raised according to, and continue to practice the Roman Catholic Christian religion. But my experience is also grounded in the fact that my mother is Jewish, and this played a major role in my faith development. Additionally, I have had the fortunate opportunity to study most major world religions over the course of my education, and I have cultivated this curiosity throughout my life. Therefore, while I expect my perspective to be consistent with Catholic teaching, I do not intend this book to be in any way a collection of Catholic teachings. This book is not intended to bring converts to Catholicism. However, within the limitations of my experience and according to the language I am most comfortable with, I have made an attempt to make the reflections in this book as broadly applicable as possible. I hope that my questions and conclusions are general enough that any person of faith can find resonance with their own experience, even when the language and references are explicitly Christian.

While we certainly have a social apparatus to discuss faith (i.e., religion) the stuff of religion is experiential. Religion begins with that individual experience—with that matter of faith. When we try to share these experiences with one another, when we try to find commonalities, when we try to move these matters of faith into the context of a community, then we have religion. I have come across many definitions of faith, ranging from blind belief to a gift from God. I would, however, like to offer a definition of faith that is, at its very core, a critical enterprise. Faith goes beyond simply accepting a premise that you have read or that you have been told.

To me, faith is a process, not an end point. If we are to define faith as having a relationship with the divine—which, it seems to me, is as good a definition as any—then we must understand that faith is fundamentally a process. All relationships must be dynamic or they wither. Faith involves the examination of experiences in a context of personal and communal experience, and, in the process of examination, we of faith accept or believe things that are not readily subject to examination by strict logic. An article of faith is, at its core, an assumption, but even these assumptions must be subjected to critical reflection. A vibrant, agile, critical faith is one that is constantly subjected to revision and reflection. A faith that is not subjected to these critical evaluations is not just a blind faith; it is a dead faith.

Sometimes faith seems to be the opposite of doubt. Yet, in my experience, the people I would describe as the most faithful can be so described precisely because of their struggle with and acceptance of doubt. Doubt is an important aspect of the process of faith. Faith must grow to accommodate the concerns raised by doubt. Now, by doubt I do not mean to suggest that we need to approach these important and foundational religious experiences with dubious circumspection; rather, faith, as a process, involves careful consideration of and critical incorporation of doubt. And this process of faith transpires by reconciling both the initial experiences and the process of incorporation in a communal environment. A healthy faith will grow through our struggle with doubt.

I can never share with you the totality of my faith experience—even despite the established channels at our disposal to do just that. I can never foster the same experience in you that I, myself, have had. And this failure is a result of our status as subjective individuals and to the limitations of our language. To borrow a phrase from Karl Barth, a twentieth-century theologian—who was, himself, borrowing from Soren Kierkegaard, a nineteenth-century philosopher and theologian—God and humanity are separated by an "infinite qualitative difference." We cannot possibly fully capture the divine—or experiences of the divine—using our linguistic technologies of description. We have, however, no alternative but to try. We must use delimiting, finite language to describe perceptions of the infinite. In this, I agree with Barth and Kierkegaard that these experiences of the numinous—experiences of the divine so powerful that they inspire not just fear but an overwhelming fascination—are indescribable by their very definition.

Rather than being dissuaded by the prospect of the indescribable nature of the infinite, I believe this is an opportunity. Only if we persist in trying to share these experiences will we be able to refine, reflect on, and grow our faith with critical questions. This, I contend, is the process by which we can enhance these experiences. Thus, our faith journey is equally personal and communal. People from the Judeo-Christian tradition only need to look at their faith heroes to see how people of faith are continually questioning—their situation, God, and God's commands. The end result is a choice, based on the best understanding of their experience of reality and the shared experiences of their community. As often as not, these experiences inspire persons of faith to follow God to the best of their ability. This exhortation may lack a logical proof, but it aligns with their core experience and intuition. And it is often surprisingly reasonable.

What Is Science?

If we are to trust Thomas Kuhn, a twentieth-century philosopher of science, then science itself has something like a religious underpinning. I do not mean to suggest that science is a religious enterprise in the sense that persons of faith would understand; rather, we scientists believe certain things about the world based on communal experience, and we use these understandings to make predictions about and measurements of the reality we inhabit. We believe that the world operates according to physical laws that can support and anticipate hypotheses and conclusions. We have a process by which we can elicit scientific experiences, namely the scientific method. A commonly misunderstood aspect of the scientific enterprise is the matter of objective proof. Science, as a rule, does not prove anything. Rather, science assembles a series of isolated results that are suggestive of a larger pattern that provides insight into the physical laws that govern events. Science, then, is belief in the aggregate. The findings of science are useless in isolation, and depend on three things: a scientific community, repeatability, and accordance with a logical framework.

If we think back to our high school science course—in whatever subject that course might have been—some of us might recall that we learned the scientific method. Some particularly enterprising souls might be able to recall the process. A scientist begins with a quantitative question: How does water purity affect surface tension? When is the optimal time to plant corn in Alaska for maximal yield? Which material conducts electricity most efficiently? What sugars can bread yeast consume? Where in the brain does the human ability to perceive color reside? We pose questions like these for two reasons.

First, they are quantitative, meaning they can be measured. We do not ask questions about why in a qualitative sense. That is to say, when scientists ask *why,* they mean, "by what mechanism?" or "under which conditions?" So, the question, "Why is the sky blue?" is a scientific question only in the sense that a scientist can conduct experimentation to ascertain its cause. The *why* in this case refers to natural mechanisms and conditions of blueness. *Why* here does not pose questions about purpose or quality.

Second, questions such as these lend themselves to an empirical metric.[3]

Simply put, we are able to observe the phenomena while we measure the parameters. We can add salt to distilled water and measure the time it takes to drip from the head of a pin. Or we can stagger the planting time in an Alaskan field by days or weeks and measure total production. We can send an electrical impulse through a variety of materials—controlling for width and length—and determine speed and strength of that signal. We can buy a tub of Fleischmann's yeast and produce solutions of a number of different sugars and measure the amount of alcohol they produce. We can test a subject with MRI, a CT, or EEG machine and ask him or her to look at color placards while we peer into the brain for areas of concentrated activity. These questions are able to be measured using the instruments and metrics at our disposal. But all of these phenomena are grounded in an empirical, observable reality that can support our objective observations.

The scientific method is bound to posing questions about observable, testable phenomena. This feature cuts both ways: On the one hand, this requirement negates the attempts of religious persons to impose a sort of creation science into science curricula. Science is not prepared to pose qualitative questions about God's love, or Jesus's resurrection, or the substance of the Holy Spirit. We cannot measure these realities. We cannot form observable, testable experiments about these realities. We cannot term these realities empirical or material to a degree that would support the scientific enterprise. Thus, articles of faith regarding the nonphysical world are not under assault from the sciences; we cannot measure the unphysical. On the other hand, scientists who make claims to the nonexistence of a deity simply by uncovering naturalistic explanations for phenomena are overstepping the bounds of science. Simply because we now have a working understanding of evolution by natural selection, for example, does not mean God is not involved with the world. The sciences simply cannot pose questions about the nonphysical. But, by observing physical reality, we do learn how God might interact with creation.

After we have our scientific question, we then turn to observation and experiments. Younger scientists might acquaint themselves with cursory and unstructured observations; professional scientists perform more detailed, controlled experiments supported by an exhaustive knowledge of prior scientific work. Initial observations and experiments serve as the basis of an initial explanatory hypothesis. This hypothesis is, perhaps, best thought of as educated guess. A hypothesis fuels even more careful experimentation and increasingly refined predictions—all with the goal of generating a highly verified model that can be used to predict as wide a range of phenomena as possible. Once sufficiently verified, scientists use the word *theory* for their models. The central feature of verification is repeatability; both the initial experimenter and subsequent others must be able to repeat and reproduce the outcomes of a given model or hypothesis for it to be considered confirmed. And the best models are being confirmed all the time. For example, every plane flight is a confirmation of the principles of aerodynamics and lift!

Another crucially important aspect of the scientific enterprise is the notion of falsifiability—the concept that it is possible to prove a given statement false. In order for a hypothesis to be legitimate, this hypothesis must be falsifiable by well-defined experiments. That is to say, an initial premise must be subject to the means of evaluation available to the community of scientists. The postulate that God does not exist is not really a falsifiable premise—especially the concept of a transcendent God—and it is therefore an unscientific position. The challenge of testing a sufficiently broad definition of an intrinsically infinite God is one of the main reasons that I argue that discussions of God's existence are generally fruitless. In contrast, concepts of God that have a sufficiently specific definition can be tested. For example, we now have the scientific tools to test the hypothesis that the sun is a god who possesses a humanoid form and drives a horse-drawn chariot through the sky. Careful tests of this hypothesis confirm that the sun god, as defined, does not exist.

Like religion, science transpires within the context of a community, and, like religion, one purpose of this community is to make experiences in the world understandable to a broader audience. The distinction, though, is that the scientific community is wholly predicated on the idea of repeatability of results. All things being equal, I can recreate a given scientific experiment and reach the same result as the initial experiment done by someone else anywhere in the world. That is the essence of science. And embedded into this community is the stated intention of refinement and revision. We view our data in aggregate in order to refine them; we assemble our data in order to revise our conclusions about them; we bring our data together in order to critically evaluate them. A hallmark of the scientific method—the methods according to which we have established the scientific community—is constant, critical doubt. Science is not about certainty, as some persons of faith and even some scientists would have you believe.

And it is here, I think, that there may be a misunderstanding between scientists and the general public—including persons of faith. Often, we hear from young earth creationists that evolution is "just a theory," and that other theories, equally plausible, could account for the variety of life on earth. But this formulation misunderstands what the sciences mean by the word *theory*. We derive this word from the Greek "θεωρία," which means "speculation," "reflection," and "contemplation." This word was originally an abstraction from the Greek "θεατής;," meaning "spectator." Ultimately, this word was a compound of two Greek words—"θέα," *a view* or *a sight,* and "ὁρᾶν," "to see" or "to look." We incorporated the word *theory* into English during the sixteenth century with the initial meaning of its Greek ancestor—a reflection or a consideration. From the seventeenth century onward, we see *theory* being used in the technical sense for which we now deploy it in the sciences: a coherent statement or set of ideas that explains observed facts or phenomena, or that sets out the laws and principles of something known or observed.

It was not until the eighteenth century that the word *theory* was deployed to refer to a conjecture (e.g., a detective's theory about an ongoing case). In the sciences, we use the word *hypothesis* (literally from Greek, "ὑπό," "below," plus "θεση," "to place"; so, something postulated before experimentation) to refer to something conjectural. *Theory* is reserved for a unified body of experimental results that indicates the predictive power of a principle or law. So, when a young earth creationist urges an instructor to "teach the controversy," there is certain degree of dissimulation at work. There is no controversy because the overwhelming body of experimental results strongly suggests the actuality of the process of evolution by natural selection. Evolution is not a hypothesis as the *theory* of common parlance might suggest; it is a scientific fact.

In the sciences, we speak of atomic theory (a very ancient idea), cell theory (Robert Hooke, 1665), the theory of gravitation (Isaac Newton, 1687), germ theory (Louis Pasteur, 1864), plate tectonic theory (Alfred Wegener, 1915), the theory of relativity (Albert Einstein, 1916), and many, many others. No sane, rational person now doubts any of the theories mentioned above. But the theory of evolution (Charles Darwin, 1859) is different; it seems uniquely able to inspire bitter disagreement. We will discuss this matter further in chapter five, but rest assured that evolution is a scientific fact. I bring it up here in order to address one of Mr. Ham's curious arguments about science—namely that there are distinct fields of historical science (evidently phenomena that happened long ago) and observational science (science that we can observe and that all persons agree on). The distinction is false. The predictive power of our theories and models of the physical world are robust and accurate enough that we can use them to predict past occurrences.

The truth is that our physics—the building blocks upon which both chemistry and biology rest—is always the same everywhere, and we have no reason to doubt that it will remain the same for all time as well. And if physics is the building blocks of our science, then our universal constants are the building blocks of our physics. The speed of light (c in Einstein's E = mc^2) is always 299,792,458 meters per second; Euler's number, e (also called Napier's constant), is always 2.7182...; the Planck constant, also called h (the physical constant that is the quantum of action) is 0.00000 00000000000000000000000000662606957 joule seconds; the ratio of a circle's circumference to its diameter, Π, is always and everywhere 3.1415.... We have no reason to believe any of the above constants have ever or will ever change. We have no good indication that so-called historical science is different in any way from observational science. To pretend that it is would negate much of the predictive power of the sciences—on which all of modern technology is predicated.

So, the term *science*, as I will use it in this book, is the habits of mind, the methods, and the social framework within which explorations about the nature of physical reality transpire. Science is a method based on empirical materialism, and it encompasses the systematized and inductive application of reason. As with *faith*, *reason* is a word that is used in many different contexts. At times, it is synonymous with empirically based logic and observation. These are certainly significant aspects of reason more generally, but reason suggests an extension from observation and depends on the application of a critical guiding framework that results in a logically sound conclusion. Logical arguments, as I will suggest in chapter one, are only as good as their initial propositions. If a logician starts with a false assumption, even the most perfect logical argument will result in an untenable or unreasonable conclusion. Reason, for the purposes of this book, will tend to reflect both aspects of the logical argument. It is the combination of testing initial assumptions against experience, experiments, and intuition, and then using logical arguments based on tested assumptions. Science is simply the institutional application of experimental testing of assumptions, but there are times we also need to rely on experience and intuition that fall outside of the experimental realm.

So, the goal of science is to make quantitative predictions regarding phenomena in the physical world. Fundamentally, science is about phrasing questions for which an experiment can be done in a well-defined and repeatable fashion. This is one way—an extremely powerful way, to be sure—to test assumptions about the nature of the world around us. Unfortunately, it cannot test every assumption. And that is where we come full circle to faith—or, if you do not like that word, *intuition*. As both a practicing scientist and a practicing Christian, I find no discomfort with the sciences because I understand the respective purviews of both ways of knowing. Persons of faith should understand the ways in which we marshal arguments in the sciences and understand the matters that sciences are equipped to address. Scientists, on the other hand, should understand and respect their evidence and refrain from making arguments that are indefensible given the tools at their disposal.

Intersections of Discourse: The Spiral Journey of Faith

We have seen the rancorous effects of framing the intersection between science and faith as a debate. Such a framework nearly eliminates the possibility of productive conversation. I will elaborate on this possibility in the next chapter, but I think it is prudent to mention here that the best way, to my mind, of spanning the chasm between science and faith is to dispense with the notion of the chasm. One step in this process is to subject our faith to a critical program like the one to which we subject scientific findings. Here, I do not mean that we should simply nuance our faith to accommodate the findings of science—although I am inclined to believe that such an exercise would result in a more robust, healthier faith. Rather, I think persons of faith can borrow some of the critical methods of science in order to facilitate such growth.

So, what would a critically engaged faith look like? What would the method and process of this faith be? I envision this process of faith takes as its point of departure the idea that, as in science, experience plays a crucial role. As the happy product of a Jesuit education, I am deeply moved by the notion of the spiral journey of faith. Faith, like scientific experimentation, is neither linear nor deterministic. On the contrary, the ideal faith journey comes back to problematic things repeatedly. But, thankfully, if life is going well, this faith journey is slowly moving forward. Many become preoccupied with the "known knowns"—to borrow an infelicitous phrase from Donald Rumsfeld, Secretary of Defense of the United States under President George W. Bush. Some focus on the truth that Jesus died on the cross once and for all, redeemed our sins, and the rest is done. Such a perspective is fine, but it doesn't mean that your relationship with God, your understanding of the world, and your relationship with other people are done. And therein lies the crux of this fitful spiral journey. An active, dynamic, living faith is one that is constantly subject to refinement. A faith not thought about, not critically evaluated, and not revised as part of a journey—that is a dead faith.

But this type of growing, waxing faith requires a great deal of humility; it requires an honest recognition of the limits of our understanding. Even for Christians who believe that revelation is complete in Christ, there needs to be a recognition that our *understanding* of revelation is not. We must be open to areas in which we need to grow in our faith and deepen our experience of the fullness of reality. We see the same type of humility in the sciences, when they are done well. The tools are different, but a key element of science is the ability to quantify what you do not understand. Scientists make the most progress when they recognize where old experiments can be improved upon and new experiments are needed.

Therefore, both faith and science require a comfort with doubt and uncertainty, as these are the starting points for increased knowledge. It is our belief—in either the possibility of deepening our relationship with the fullness of reality, in its most maximal articulation, or the power of

the scientific enterprise to deepen our understanding of physical reality—
that animates the journey of discovery through our doubts. But—and this
is a crucial point—both the faith and the scientific understanding that
sustained the investigation of our doubts must be allowed to be changed
by the very discoveries this investigation produces.

If either a thinking, faithful person or a scientist were not comfortable
in the midst of confusion, then this person would lack the confidence to
proceed forward in discovery. Faith is not about certainty of facts; it is
about certainty in one's relationship with God (or the fullness of reality).
It is about exploring one's relationship with the infinite to its fullest; it is
about having faith that the journey is even possible in the face of the great
unknown of the infinite; it is about dealing frankly with the doubts while
holding faithful to our core truths.

Not surprisingly, constant doubt is also a hallmark of the scientific
method. To be sure, scientists will use different terms: they have an inductive criteria of examination; they engage in an intellectual exchange that is
predicated on the notion of repeatability. But the uncertainty is the same.
Science is quite adept at defining the terms of its uncertainty. Faith, on
the other hand, often avoids uncertainty where it should be embraced.
Rumination, consideration, reflection—these are the hallmarks of a
dynamic, critically engaged faith.

Both faith and science are about evaluating information and moving
forward. This same self-reflective and self-reflexive process ought to guide
us in the interpretation and discernment of Scripture. We cannot use
Scripture as the basis for our science; that is too easy, uncritical, and incorrect. We should not even view Scripture as the science of its own time,
as folks like Baruch Spinoza, a seventeenth-century philosopher, would
have us do, and folks like St. Augustine, a fifth-century church father, have
warned us against. The authors of Scripture used a wide range of modes of
conveying truth; most of these are mythic and thereby radically different

from our own. We should focus on the challenge of incorporating the reality communicated by our scientific mode with the truths communicated by our Scriptures. One should never employ one to supplant the other. They should breathe as two lungs of a single body—animus and anima, mind and soul.

Chapter 1

Plenitudo Realitas: The Fullness of Reality

I am Who am.

—Exodus 3:14

I think, therefore I am.

—Rene Descartes, *Discourse on Method* (1637)

It was the fall of 1980. As summer faded into the year's twilight, taking with it memories of science camps, baseball games, and idle hours enraptured by comic books, I sat awaiting Fr. Egan's freshman religion class. Fr. Egan strode through the door, a smug half grin resting placidly above his frocked neck. Never tarrying, he seized the instructor's seat at the front of the class and turned it around so that the seat's back faced us. Down he sat, seat back between his legs according to the vogue of the time. He eyed our class, clearly taking special care to size each of us up; in such a presence, silence is advisable, and each of his students—I in the front row—sat perfectly taciturn and spellbound. This display suggested Fr. Egan was not a man to cross.

"How many of you," he intoned, "think that the story of Adam and Eve is a factual account of the creation of man and woman?"

A forest of arms sprang up, eager not to cross this man of God, who remained sitting, seat back between his legs, as if he were waiting to bowl, polishing a rifle in a barracks, or rapping (as they called it then) at a fraternity roundtable. Only my hand remained on my lap. He bristled with umbrage while he took careful stock of our sheepish responses.

And then he bellowed, "You're all wrong!"

Stunned silence settled all around me.

"That story is false. It is not a fact—at least not in the sense to which you're accustomed. That story, as it is told in Genesis, never actually happened."

My hangdog colleagues had by this point penitently withdrawn their offending arms.

Fr. Egan continued, "That story may be factually false, but it's a myth. And a myth can convey truths that are more important, more salient, and more applicable than any fact you might encounter. That story is better than factual; it's truthful."

My astonishment settled into satisfaction. First, as a studious pupil (no more cool a pursuit in 1980 than it is now), I felt confirmed in providing to my instructor a correct answer. Second, as both a science geek and a practicing Catholic, I now had an inclusive means of interrogating my experience—both in science and in faith. Fr. Egan that day confirmed for me that there was ample intellectual space to accommodate not only my scientific interest, nature, and thought, but also my religious faith. Yet, as satisfying as Fr. Egan's browbeating might have been, a cursory glance around our contemporary world would suggest that faith and science are incompatible. In many ways, this book seeks to redress the failure of that discourse. It seeks to establish an initial location—a starting point, if you'll allow—from which we can begin to have a constructive, meaningful dialogue about the things that are most important to us.

Probably, we can all conjure up a few of the points about which the media and vocal public discourse tell us that persons of science and persons of faith would disagree. There are those that gather the most press time: evolution, the age of the earth, the existence of the soul—this list could stretch on for pages. Then there are those that do not regularly make the press: ex nihilo creation, free will and predestination, the

Resurrection—this list, too, could fill the pages of this book. In no small way, the assumption of antagonism has become a self-fulfilling prophecy.

We hear from both extremes (scientific and religious) that science and religion are in conflict, and too often people feel the need to take sides. However, I think describing science and faith as opposing forces is a false dichotomy, and the fact is that both science and faith are tools that can enhance each other as we explore all of reality. This idea of bringing both science and faith together, or consilience, to borrow a phrase from Edward O. Wilson, a twentieth-century biologist, will be a recurrent theme in this book.

I recognize that many people, both in the past and currently, have articulated the view that science and faith are not in conflict, and there are many ways to approach the two working together. As I reflect on and share my experiences, it is critical to be clear at the outset that my approach starts from the basic assumption that God exists and that God loves me. In response, I desire to know and understand God better, and to improve my relationship with God, who is—to use a phrase that will recur often in this book—the fullness of reality.

If we get down to brass tacks, we can appreciate that both the sciences and faith are working toward ascertaining the fullness of reality. We may speak about that fullness with different dialects, but the language is the same. The idioms and vernacular may be different, but both the sciences and faith are focused on the same goal: the nature of the fullness of reality. The strategies of approach may vary, the apparatus of proof may not be uniform—and in this, they are focused on different aspects of reality— but in common they share an ambition to understand the world we occupy. I would even take it one step further and contend that in its quest to understand physical reality, science never can contradict true faith, but it can enhance our faith by deepening our understanding and awareness of those aspects of God, as the fullness of reality, that are experienced through physical reality. It is this enhancement of my own faith through science that I hope to express and share in this book.

Ontological Absolutes and the Absolutions of Ontology4

On some basic level, both the sciences and faith are about ascertaining the nature of reality. I believe that is the crux of both epistemologies—studies of knowledge and how we know. Freeman Dyson, a contemporary physicist, in his speech accepting the 2000 Templeton Prize, reminded us:

> Science and religion are two windows that people look through, trying to understand the big universe outside, trying to understand why we are here. The two windows give different views, but they look out at the same universe. Both views are one-sided, neither is complete. Both leave out essential features of the real world. And both are worthy of respect.

Reality, on some level, is then the object of focus for both the sciences and faith. The contours of this reality, the responsibility of and for this reality, and the proper tools for experiencing this reality are contestable; what is not, however, is the importance of this reality to the functional enterprise of both science and religion.

Both the sciences and religion seek to uncover, by various methods of discovery, core truths about this reality. However, these architectures of knowing—the disciplines of science, on the one hand, and religion, on the other—aim at the different aspects of reality. The sciences, by construction, aim exclusively at physical reality—the part of reality that can be directly experienced by the five senses and the tools we make to enhance those senses. Faith experiences aim explicitly at the fullness of reality—or, a better understanding of God. From this, I argue that, because physical reality is by definition an aspect of the fullness of reality, science, by definition, contributes to faith. In all of this, the phrase *fullness of reality*

19

presupposes, in its very formulation, that there exists a discernible, knowable, experiential reality.

The existence of reality may seem obvious, but considering the nature of this reality provides a good starting point for discussions about the intersection between science and faith. Though we experience reality every day, one can imagine that true reality is very different from the reality that we experience. In certain branches of epistemology there is a tendency to suggest a type of antifoundationalism with which I am uncomfortable. Essentially, antifoundationalism assumes that there is no direct access to understanding ultimate reality. One need only recall Plato's allegory of the cave, in which the reality we experience is mere shadows on the wall of a cave and not true reality. In many philosophical formulations, ultimate reality lies outside our ability to readily perceive and understand it. The really real and truly true stand outside of immediate, empirical discernment. These thinkers usefully caution us to come to terms with subjective experience, but when we make absolute their epistemologies, or systems of knowledge, we can be left with a sort of empty nihilism.

Radically antifoundationalist positions are esoterically philosophical, to my mind. One could say, "Well, how do you know gravity is not going to turn off in the next instant?" Such a mental exercise is surely interesting, but, to me, it is neither particularly useful nor practical. To be sure, I certainly understand why philosophers invest their energies in metaphysics and think carefully about the metaphysics of science. At the heart of these imaginations are critical and challenging philosophical questions. But, at the end of the day, as a practicing scientist, I recognize that there is no good evidence that the world does not obey laws and is not reliable.

Even among the philosophical positions that render problematic the empirical enterprise, methods exist that allow a person to transcend immediate apprehension and appreciate reality in its fullness, rather than from within the shades to which we are accustomed. We can imagine a circumstance in which all human agents are actually figments of some other being's imagination, or a computer program, or the result of some other construct that makes us not real. Descartes, often called the father of modern philosophy, for instance, imagined a malevolent absolute force, which he called the *dens deceptor*; or the *dieu trompeur*—the deceptive god, who is "as clever and deceitful as he is powerful, [and] who has directed his entire effort to misleading me." This deceiving force successfully presents Descartes with a completely illusory external world, such that no thing is ontologically absolute—nothing has undeniable, actual substance or existence. Descartes systematically unraveled this illusion and arrived at the one ultimate quantity that this deceiving god could not generate: his thought. "I think, therefore I am," Descartes maintained.

It is worth noting that even in the example of the deceptive god proposed by Descartes, something must exist that generates the thoughts that result in Descartes's "me." So, it is possible to conclude that the fact that I can think about whether or not I exist does not necessarily mean that I exist as a truly independent reality. It simply means something must exist to generate my thoughts. It is better to adopt, I think, a phenomenological approach to this formulation by recasting this famous saying as, "I think, therefore something is." I may be a brain in a vat and my consciousness may be the result of a computer program somewhere else. So, the fact that you are reading my thoughts right now suggests that something outside of you and me must exist. That existence does not necessarily have to be a real you and a real me. (You could be the result of a computer program, too!). But our thinking means that an irrefutable externality must exist, and therefore something must be real.

I am firmly convinced—even if absolute reality is not all it absolutely seems to be—that something real must exist. Those among us who can agree to the existence of reality can then be tasked with sorting out the nature of that reality. This is where both science and faith begin: the examination of the nature of reality. Science is well equipped to consider the nature of physical reality; faith explores the nature of nonphysical reality and its relationship, if any, with physical reality. But even this distinction may overstate the case, as there are many areas in which physical reality and nonphysical reality intersect.

In contemporary Western society, we often automatically connect physical reality as the only true reality. In this context, nonphysical realities that are viewed negatively include things usually referred to as supernatural or magical. Ultimately, we need to consider many other nonphysical realities, ranging from mathematics to what one might call serious mystical experiences of reality. From a faith perspective, serious mystical experiences seem to cause the most trouble for traditional Western thought. I would suggest that this consternation has two major causes.

First, there is the excellent track record of the scientific revolution and its ability to eliminate what is commonly called the god of the gaps. Throughout human history, physical phenomena that were not understood have been attributed to gods or mythical beings. For example, almost everyone is familiar with historical veneration of some form of the sun god; we now understand the basic physics behind the sun. We understand that it is a star; we understand the principles of its formation; we understand the mechanisms by which it emits light; we understand how the light that it emits is foundational to our experience of life on earth. We know a lot about the physical quantity that used to be a god.

As science progressed, more and more gaps in our understanding of physical reality have been filled. Rightfully, many people fully expect science to provide some level of explanatory power over all physical phenomena. Furthermore, as this process has eliminated magical or supernatural explanations of predictable phenomena in favor of scientific ones, it seems natural to assume that even unpredictable phenomena must have a scientific explanation that will one day threaten the viability of religious belief founded purely on not knowing. The problem arises if one takes this logic further and assumes that the success of predicting physical behavior justifies questioning all nonphysical reality, even mystical experiences. However, I do not see the logical connection between predictive success in the physical world and conclusions about the nonphysical. One would not use a screwdriver on a nail, after all.

Second, there are plenty of examples in contemporary times of outright fraud regarding nonphysical phenomena, ranging from ghosts to extrasensory perception to healing powers. A natural reaction to proven fraud is to mistrust all claims of a similar nature. This is the James Randi quandary: all parlor magic is chicanery and trickery, therefore no magic can exist that is not. It is a natural reaction, I think, to disbelieve the veracity of a thing in the face of previous demonstrations of its falsehood. Adopting greater suspicion and circumspection generally serves to prevent being subjected to additional fraud. However, even if each and every account of nonphysical reality were fraudulent, we cannot conclude conclusively that all claims to a reality beyond a physical reality are thereby ipso facto frauds as well.

In fact, as we will explore in greater detail in later chapters, quantum mechanics, one of the major triumphs of twentieth-century physics, gains much of its predictive power based on the reality of a fundamentally nonphysical quantity: the wave function. The implication of the nonphysical nature of the wave function and its reality are the basis of significant amounts of scientific research and philosophical investigation. But its existence points to the importance of taking the nonphysical seriously as we explore the nature of the fullness of reality.

When considering physical reality, the scientific process is equipped to distinguish valid models of physical reality from invalid ones. However, for many important questions regarding the nature of reality, current scientific methods cannot provide an answer. For some important questions

(Why are we here? What is consciousness? Where are we going?), science might not ever be able to provide an answer.

Because there are no easy criteria for evaluating nonscientific claims, a common fallacy invades the public debate: "Some ideas regarding God are clearly irrational; therefore, any belief in God is irrational and must be rejected by all reasonable people." Likewise, one might occasionally hear the statement, "If science cannot prove it, then it must not be true." But this is not a logically valid statement because the conclusion is no more than the underlying assumption that the only reality that exists is the reality established by science. So I encourage all of us not to simply reentrench into the worldview we find most comfortable; no true growth can sprout from that hard, fallow ground.

Persons of faith occasionally maintain that Scripture must be interpreted literally, even to the point of it being a science textbook. Scientists, on the other hand, can occasionally overreach their purview (and, indeed, outstrip their ability to offer evidence) by maintaining categorically that God cannot exist. At fault here are the ideologues: scriptural literalists, on the one hand, and empirical fundamentalists, on the other. Scriptural fundamentalists risk erring when the Bible becomes a science textbook, and when they claim any attempt at suggesting a reality outside that presented in Scripture must be wrong, in its most generous iteration, or must be a trick, in its most trenchant guise.

Empirical fundamentalists maintain that the only reality that may exist must be the one that can be perceived by the natural sciences. Physical reality, for these folks, is all that there is, and it is accordingly unnecessary to turn to Scripture to answer any question. These people would reduce all mental, spiritual, and experiential phenomena to neurology, and they would root the totality of existence in an objective, knowable, physical world. This may be true, but it is ultimately only an assumption. They risk erring when placing too much faith in the logical conclusion, from this perspective, that God does not exist, as this conclusion can only be as valid as the initial assumption.

Now, these two worldviews, as loud in the discourse as they may seem, fail to capture the plurality of the human experience. And, alas, there is generally no talking these people out of their opinion; put simply, both scriptural literalists and empirical fundamentalists make truth claims that cannot be substantiated by logical means, and are therefore not subject to refinement nor alteration. They are both faith claims in the negative sense: both perspectives negate the possibility of a reality or an explanatory model that exists from without their epistemology. Therefore, it strikes me that both are equally likely to be true, and either one may be the real nature of reality.

The problem with the two extreme worldviews is not really their potential truth or falsehood. Instead, I maintain that, because both views are ideologically rigid, neither can provide a truly solid foundation on which to build our edifice of knowledge. Both groups operate within a paradigm absolutely defined by a faith claim: the former takes as an article of faith biblical literalism; the latter makes a claim about the nonexistence of God that is not subject to inductive experimentation. Neither one really stands up well beneath the light of reason. So, what other avenues exist to pose questions about reality?

Science and Faith: The Range of Engagement

Scholars have spilled whole vats of ink attempting to reconcile the perceived quandary between science and faith. One need only think of such legal cases as *Tennessee* v. *John T. Scopes* (1925), *Epperson* v. *Arkansas* (1968), *McLean* v. *Arkansas* (1982), and *Edwards* v. *Aguillard* (1987)— all cases deciding science education—to take my meaning. Ideologues on both sides of these legal cases seem entrenched and intransigent, and they appear all the more bellicose in our adversarial system of law. It is telling that each of these landmark cases is an important battle in the culture war—we even frame the juridical eruptions produced by this divide in martial terms. How we can circumvent these vitriolic debates? If we begin by threatening "a day in court," how and why would we ever come to the table in good faith? Conflict has clearly obstructed the intersection of science and faith—legally, morally, and financially.

If discourse about these topics in an open forum has led to ingrained antagonism, has the academy fared any better? Sadly, the answer is no. But, as is often the case, the hallowed halls of academia have permitted a less rancorous permutation of this "debate." Let's consider a well-regarded thinker on the matter of the science-religion encounter is Ian Barbour.

Ian Barbour was a professor of religion and physics at Carleton College in Minneapolis. He served as the first chairman of the religion department there, beginning in 1955. Barbour's life was an interesting one, and it seems to me that he rather enjoyed sorting out difficult topics in a morass. After claiming conscientious objector status for the Second World War, he served as a research assistant for Enrico Fermi, a physicist at the University of Chicago, where he conducted his doctoral studies. There he pioneered research that culminated in the creation of atomic weapons—a bell he spent the rest of his life trying to unring. In addition to being a top-flight physicist, Barbour was also a deeply devout Christian.

When he accepted a research position at Yale in 1953, he also began work toward his divinity degree at Yale Divinity School. Barbour's project—creating a place of dialogue and integration for the sciences and faith—garnered him much praise worldwide. His Gifford Lectures, given from 1989 to 1990 at the University of Aberdeen in Scotland, were published as *Religion in an Age of Science* (1990). The book has been retitled twice and republished countless times, and it remains a classic in the field. For writing it, Barbour won the 1999 Templeton Prize. In this book, Barbour lays out four approaches for framing the science-religion encounter: conflict, independence, dialogue, and integration.

We currently find matters of religion and science publicly approached in a spirit of conflict. Not too surprising, as this generates the most money. Celebrity atheists on the one side and biblical literalists on the other side, to an untoward and unrepresentative degree, frame this discourse. Taking conflict as intrinsic to discussions of science and faith, per Barbour, treats as natural an inability to reconcile science to religion or religion to science. The aims, methods, discourses, and starting premises of science and religion are viewed as too dissimilar to make possible any attempt at mutualism.

Barbour's independence model focuses on the different realms of science and religion. Were we to approach matters of science and religion in a spirit of independence, we would recognize that the two epistemologies are provisioned to consider different questions altogether. Science can tell us how the sky appears blue, but cannot support questions of why it is blue. Religion can answer moral questions, but has no business in cosmology. The approach of independence eliminates conflict because it presupposes the different spheres in which these two epistemologies operate.

I find independence as a starting point better than conflict, but still incomplete. Dialogue, as an initial premise for the science-religion encounter, would allow the sciences and faith to inform one another mutually while still observing their separate spheres as inviolate. Science can bring us to a point where human cloning is possible, Barbour says, but religion can tell us whether this would be a good idea from a moral standpoint. Religion, then, serves as a moral check on science. Barbour maintains there is important work to be done in the realm of dialogue, but both he and I suggest that this starting point remains incomplete.

Barbour's final approach is integration, where the sciences and religion work toward goals with mutual respect, humility, and argumentative weight. Integration, which he believes would necessitate a "natural theology," a "theology of nature," and a "systematic synthesis" of science and faith, would refashion both the sciences and religion into tools that could be collaborative rather than confrontational. The project of reconciling science to faith is thereby complete for Barbour; when all engines of knowledge production work to advance the same vehicle, we have truly achieved parity and equanimity.

I find much to admire in Barbour's vision, and I think the work of full integration needs to be our focus. Neither conflict, nor independence, nor dialogue really moves us toward full integration. Integration must be our starting point. But we're not there yet, and I think we won't be there if we continue to view the sciences and faith as two completely separate spheres of knowledge. Until we tear down the walls that divide, we are stuck with an edifice. Embedded into the very notion of reconciliation is an implied articulation of conflict. We ought to reject any attempt to frame the interaction between science and faith as an adversarial debate—or indeed as a marriage of enterprises. I believe that viewing science and faith as mutually informative to each other will allow us to dispense with the problematic approach suggested by attempts at reconciliation. An approach of mutuality can, thus, eradicate the implied conflict between these two ways of knowing.

Reconciliation—and its inverted doppelganger, conflict—presupposes an antagonism that I do not believe is necessary; framing the relationship between so-called faith and so-called reason as an antagonistic one has a number of subtle, but destructive, effects. Viewing science and religion as fundamentally distinct and naturally at odds invariably leads to a discourse predicated on the false assumption that one must be right and the other must be wrong. In emphasizing distinction and setting in motion competition, we have, by means of our assenting to a discourse framed in these terms, made more difficult the task of allowing each way of knowing—or epistemological mode—to contribute its best features to our worldview, and this imposition threatens to undo what is best in both.

We have been conditioned by this rhetoric of antagonism to assume that there exists a division between science and faith. The distinction is problematic and the dichotomy is false. I contend that we must turn this dialogue on its head by first defining the terms we use. I propose that instead of discussing science and religion in necessarily adversarial terms, we should instead view the substantial commonalities between these two entities as contributive to a total worldview. This worldview, which I call the fullness of reality, is really at the heart of both the scientific enterprise and expressions and experiences of faith.

The Fullness of Reality

Whether or not God exists seems to be the obvious question that any debate between atheists and theists attempts to answer. And yet, when we listen carefully to the debate, we generally find that one of two things happen. Often, atheists are not questioning whether God in the ideal sense exists, but arguing rather that a particular definition of God does not exist. The definition in question could be one they were taught at some point in life that failed them. It could be a definition that they project onto believers. Or it could be any of a wide range of other options. Whatever the source, atheists reject the existence of God on the grounds that the chosen definition is viewed as unreasonable for any of a number of reasons. In contrast, theists generally defend their particular definition of God. This definition generally derives from their particular religious acculturation; theists typically defend the God that they were taught or have experienced. This experience of God may or may not align with the God rejected by any given group of atheists.

As I suggested above, this adversarial debate is doomed to failure by the faith-based postulates of both factions. But it is also doomed by the fact that the two sides often have different definitions of God! Were a believer to take the time and carefully consider the definition of God proposed by an atheist, that believer might indeed assent by concluding that the atheist's definition of God is untenable. Were believers to communicate their understanding of God to the atheist in a patient, understanding, and empathetic way, I am firmly convinced that there are experiences of God that even an atheist would agree are plausible, even rational.

Right away we see how this addresses a major issue in the ongoing debate of God's existence. Too often the God rejected by atheists is one that a subset of believers defined. Not surprisingly, it is often a limited definition that many other believers in God would also reject. To suggest too specific a definition of God is a fool's errand. Despite this, narrowly defining God can be a trap that anyone—but especially organized religions—can fall into when focused on proving God's existence. Instead, by focusing on developing a better understanding of who God is, we can advance considerations about characteristics of God and the nature of our relationship with God. Our understanding of God's characteristics starts when God, as the fullness of reality, reveals God's existence through our experiences. We can go even further. It is sensible to consider the characteristics of God, as suggested by experience and revelation, alongside lessons in physical reality as provided by science. This is one way to test if our *understanding* of revelation is reasonable.

Whether or not revelations provided by faith are reasonable is a valid concern. This is why I argued earlier that faith is a continual process. I hope here to convince you that science can provide one means to evaluate and enhance faith. I believe that science can actually improve our understanding of God, of how God works in the world, and, in the process, deepen our relationship with and to God.

Therefore, the question of God's existence is neither the best nor the most useful question on which to predicate a discussion of science and faith. Persons on both sides of this discussion invest their perspective with "fact" and believe it is incumbent upon them to convince others of those facts. Deductive reasoning has been used by partisans of both perspectives to conclude both for and against the existence of God. Anselm of Bee's ontological argument, advanced in his *Proslogion,* and Thomas Aquinas's *quinque viae* are examples par excellence of logically based proofs for the existence of God from two medieval theologians. Pascal's Wager and Voltaire's "invention of God" are arguments from the seventeenth and eighteenth centuries that present cases for God's existence. And the reductionist arguments of Ludwig Feuerbach and Sigmund Freud from the nineteenth and twentieth centuries are examples of argumentation predicated on logical proof that questions the necessity of God's existence.

Both theists and atheists, then, use logic as their instrument of proof. At the end of the day, logic is only as good as your initial assumption; that is, a syllogism[5] could be logically impeccable, but incorrect and unreasonable given the nature of the initial postulates. Reason here implies a type of logic, but it is an empirically based logic. Reason is not always strictly logical in the mathematical sense of logical formulations. We must, at times, use intuition to gauge whether or not a logical conclusion is reasonable. This intuition is empirical in the sense that it stems from reasonable application of previous experience. At some conclusions, intuition informed by experience tells us, "That is not reasonable." For, others, we will conclude, "That is reasonable," even if we do not have logical proof. Instead, the conclusion is an intuitive statement based on our experience.

Ultimately, it is quite impossible to infer from logic either the existence or nonexistence of a deity. I cannot dissuade an apologist from his initial postulates any more than I can call into question an atheist's initial principles. Using logic alone, there is no way to convince someone of the soundness of your starting premises and the lack of foundation of their own. This is the definition of starting assumptions—they are subjective. One's perspective ultimately derives from the experiences he or she has had, whatever they are, that make the individual think their assumptions are justified.

My own experience has led me to believe that the fullness of reality extends beyond the physical realm, and that starting premise is the subject of this book. What I have found in ruminating on the fullness of reality—both from a scientific and a religious perspective—has led me to believe that reality beyond the physical realm is both a rather rational and reasonable conclusion.

So, a discussion about the existence or nonexistence of God can be fruitless; a discussion about the fullness of reality, however, focuses on the experience we all have in thinking about and dealing with reality itself. I expect a potential complaint at this point will be that I am just playing semantics and replacing the word *God* with the phrase *fullness of reality*. On one level, this critique is warranted, but I believe the change in question is a critical step. Using neutralizing terminologies can provide a less contentious means of approaching a problem. When such a change facilitates constructive dialogue, then that shift is a useful semantic gesture.

But, in this case the change in language goes beyond facilitating dialogue to focusing on the correct question. In science, and I would argue our faith life, one of the greatest challenges is simply asking the right question. For example, at the turn of the twentieth century, there were many apparent paradoxes in the behavior of particles and light. These were often phrased in terms of the question—is light a wave or a particle? Once scientists were able to accept that this question was not the correct one, and reformulate the question in terms of "Why does light sometimes act as a particle and sometimes act as a wave?" then significant progress was made.

In every major faith tradition that I am aware of, the fullness of reality (or some other functionally equivalent statement) represents the best understanding of God. Now, you might argue that this is not true for the faith tradition that you, personally, understand best. But I am inclined to propose that the reason for this slippage is that most faith journeys focus on understanding the attributes of God rather than treating God in totality. Consequently, there is no reason, unless you are a professional theologian, to think about the definition of God. God simply exists, and your job, as a faithful believer, is to grow in your understanding and get to know God.

We often confuse the attributes of God with our definition of God, and unraveling the two will be the subject of chapter two. In this regard, it is important to distinguish between a definition of God and a description of God. Most debates over God's existence tend to be inordinately preoccupied with descriptions of God. The focus manifests as a debate about whether or not particular attributes of God are possible. Would an all-loving God allow suffering? Why would God answer some prayers and not others? How can the Almighty allow free will?

Though these are questions we will return to in the book, I would argue that these mysteries are part of the process of understanding the nature of reality in its fullness. In the Judeo-Christian tradition, we are accustomed to understanding God as this totality. In Exodus, Moses asks for God's name, and God resoundingly replies, "I am Who am" (Exodus 3:13–14). The awesome implications of this formulation cannot be understated. God here makes a claim to encompass existence across time and across space. God's purview expands from Moses alone to the whole of creation. Thus, God makes a direct claim to be the fullness of reality.

Bringing It All Together

When we dispense with debate and invite integration into the science-religion encounter, we turn the tables on our initial positions. No longer are we discussing the existence of God—a singularly useless enterprise; instead, we are discussing the fullness of reality—a quantity that encompasses both physical and nonphysical reality. Attention to the fullness of reality will necessarily raise questions that do not have answers, and so it seems prudent to admit frankly that this book will not attempt to systematically debunk either scriptural or empirical fundamentalism. In other words, it is not my goal to prove anything. Rather, this book is written for the plurality of persons (religious persons, humanists, agnostic folk, et al.) who want to take time and think critically about applying both personal and social experiences, either faith- or science-based, to their worldview.

I wholly believe that, in order to achieve a coherent set of experiences that can suggest an operable framework, one must be sensitive to understandings gleaned by both faith and science. But in order to facilitate integration of science and faith—and in order to see how the sciences can enhance faith—we must do away with the notion of a purely anthropomorphic, tangible God and understand our Scriptures to convey truths in a mythic voice. These two clarifying points, it seems, are prudent to put forth here.

The first point concerns the imaginative ways we conceive of God. Even readers from traditions that explicitly avoid representations of God are likely to have a mental image of God. We are all quick to conjure an image of a deity, when no such image is necessary to our appreciation of that deity's actual existence. Some adopt the controlling image of the wizened old man in white robes walking on clouds—Michelangelo painting the Sistine Chapel with God reaching out to Adam, for instance. But it is important to recognize that any image has power only in that it appeals to our tendency to relate to an objective reality. We are conditioned by our experience to relate to a physical entity; when considering an abstract notion, our brains—wonderful organs that they are—are predisposed to latch onto a pictorial mental image as a reference point. Even when people speak about ghosts or other phantasmic entities, we describe them in physical terms because that is how we communicate—by using our sensory perception.

To be sure, God is described in Scripture as possessing human physical attributes (the hand of God, for instance, is referred to forty-five times in the Pentateuch) and in other physical manifestations: God appears to Moses as fire (Exodus 3:1–22); God is a passing wind (1 Kings 19:11); God is a column of smoke (Exodus 34:5). Really, the authors of Scripture condition references to God's physicality depending on the narrative function God must fulfill at that moment. All references should be treated as what they are: metaphors meant to encompass the totality and mystery of God's existence.

Readers of Scripture ought not to become preoccupied with these images of the divine because so doing would by necessity divorce their meaning from the circumstance of their composition. Our scriptural authors meant to convey transcendent truths about the divine presence, not to record the actuality of physical being, or fire, or wind, or smoke. The issue arises when we rely overmuch on the explanatory power of finite language to explicate the infinite—which is what our authors were intending to convey. After all, it is the voice of God that describes God's being as the totality of existence: "I am who am," he tells Moses on Mount Horeb, and the author could mean nothing but God's reflection of absolute reality—the fullness of reality.

It is important, I think, that we are absolutely honest with ourselves: descriptions of God as a physical entity are fundamentally metaphorical and fall short of capturing the fullness of God. Our images of God serve many purposes, but they are not a reflection of actuality. In order to see how the sciences can enhance religious faith, we must be prepared to abandon our preconceived and inherited notions regarding the image of God. Indeed, I believe that doing so allows us to treat God—as the fullness of reality—according to the expansive definition that God suggests in Exodus. Breaking the habit of reifying our image of the divine also enables us to dispense with the problematic limitations that placing God in a confining linguistic box occasions. This point will be the subject of the next chapter.

The second—and, perhaps, more crucial—point is that Scripture is true, but not necessarily fact. Charlemagne was crowned Holy Roman Emperor on Christmas Day, 800, by Pope Leo III, and the acceleration due to gravity on earth is 9.81 m/s^2. These are facts. We need to distinguish between fact and truth.

In the contemporary West, we have a tendency to view all of reality according to a rather clumsy binary; something is either true or false. We have a tendency to lose the distinction between fact and truth; in almost every way, they are different quantities altogether. Fact is an incontestable occurrence in history—one which all authorities agree transpired; truth, on the other hand, is more slippery a commodity. Truth denotes significance and meaning. We invest both fact and fiction with a type of truth—one that can be wholly divorced from its factual content. We would never say, for instance, that Shakespeare's characters are completely factual, but we can all appreciate and empathize with their plights. There is truth in all of Shakespeare's plays, but no one would suggest that even the historical ones about Julius Caesar or the English kings are meant to be completely factual accounts of the actual occurrences.

Some branches of modern Christianity have lost the distinction between fact and truth. To reclaim it, we must understand the differences between the ways we encounter Scripture and the historical context that produced Scripture. In short, it is incumbent upon the critical reader of Scripture not only to historicize his or her text, but also to understand the style in which any given text is written. The authors of the Bible composed the Scriptures in a time of storytelling; stories, during this period, equally communicated and interpreted truths. This is the power of myth.

Some Christians are affronted at the word *myth* being applied to Scripture. In fact, humanity shares its deepest truths about reality through our stories and our myths. Earliest humanity did it in the shared stories around the campfire; modern humanity does it through our epic movies, and dare I say, YouTube. Despite this, we tend to celebrate facts over stories, and *myth* is now connected with *falsehood*. Sadly, we rarely connect the word *myth* with the stories we share to communicate the great truths about reality. Even when we use phrases like *Greek Myths*, the focus of "myth" is on the fact that they did not really happen, and not on the fact that the Greeks were communicating truths about the human condition as they understood it. So, we seek to fit the intentions of the authors of Scripture into our own preoccupation with fact. Really, we are the outliers in our discomfort with myth, and the focus on myth as a type of falsehood.

I argue that we need to embrace the view that myths convey an important type of truth. The people who composed Scripture often communicated their revelations regarding reality in figurative language, without deep concerns regarding the absolute facts of a matter. They concerned themselves with the truths that the matter could convey. For most of human history, myths were the stories we told each other that conveyed the most important truths. The truth content of these stories was not intended to be read literally; fact was incidental to the greater truths the authors of Scripture hoped to convey. The stories in the Bible give us truth, and some of them may have actually happened that way.

Really, this discussion is aimed against scriptural fundamentalism; I contend that to interpret the Bible literally—as the term *biblical literalism* would suggest—is to misunderstand our text. Also, by expecting our Scripture to convey facts rather than truths, we are imposing our own concerns onto Scripture and not treating scriptural authors according to their own conventions. Scripture is true in the sense that it conveys truths. There are scriptural passages that convey actual occurrence, but not all Scripture has to be factual. We would never read the Song of Songs or Jesus's parables as accounts of fact; similarly, we should not expect biblical authors to have been concerned with our own preoccupations with fact versus fiction. I will elaborate on this point further in chapter three.

I often reflect on the strange path my faith and my vocation have directed. But, really, the seeds of my thinking on matters of faith and the sciences were planted long ago. That is why I view this book as a type of reflective memoir. My memories and my reflections have paved this path. There is a power to memory that evades simple truth; reflection occasions significance. Many of the conclusions I will seek to make in this book are the product of careful consideration and rumination, but there are also epiphanies. I can't guarantee that all people of faith, or even all Christians, will identify with my experience, but I can say that my spiral journey of faith has been profoundly conditioned by my vocation as a professional and practicing scientist.

This book is largely about how I've been able to appreciate the explanatory power of both religion and science, and how these two modes of understanding enhance and enrich each other. In this regard, I join Paul, who, in his Letter to the Romans, states, "Ever since the creation of the world, God's invisible attributes of eternal power and divinity have been able to be understood and perceived in what God has made" (1:20).

Chapter 2

God in a Box: The Limits of the Controlling Image

For all people who were ignorant of God were foolish by nature; and they were unable from the good things that are seen to know the One Who exists, nor did they recognize the Artisan while paying heed to His works; but they supposed that either fire or wind or swift air, or the circle of the stars, or turbulent water, or the luminaries of heaven were the gods that rule the world. If through delight in the beauty of these things people assumed them to be gods, let them know how much better than these is their Lord, for the Author of beauty created them.

—Wisdom of Solomon 13:1–3

When I was a child, I spoke as a child, I understood as a child, I thought as a child; when I became a man I put aside childish things.

—1 Corinthians 13:11

In the 1920s, the scientists who pioneered quantum mechanics— the study of physical phenomena on atomic scales—encountered a problem. At the time, conventional wisdom held that, on this minuscule, atomic level, all things were either a wave or a particle. Experimentation, logic, and mathematics suggest that these two concepts fall short. Electrons and light are *both* waves *and* particles. The brilliant minds that broke this ground did not invent a completely new terminology to describe this state; rather, they called this new understanding "wave-particle duality" and recognized that, on the quantum level, events act like both waves and particles.

I recall the fall of my senior year at Princeton, when I was a young student exploring this understanding of the cosmos. The brilliant leaves on the sugar maples gave the appearance of wild torches blazing yet unconsumed against the slate of the sky, which signaled the coming of winter. Nestled between the windswept South Jersey pine barrens and a two-bore arctic funnel—the Delaware and Hudson River Valleys—Princeton always seems to shiver at the coming chill of winter.

My roommate, Josh Yamamoto, and I were attempting, vainly then for some months, to comprehend the complexities of quantum mechanics. That very evening we were puzzling over the notion of wave-particle dualities. You see, for a variety of very technical and complicated reasons—esoteric enough to mystify the most visionary mystic, not to mention a couple of junior scientists—that same light reflected by the sugar maples and striking my eye as symphony of oranges, reds, and yellows exhibited properties of particles, which are localized in space, and waves, which exist extended in space. For a beginning physicist, I can assure you, the idea that particles also have a wave nature is mind-bending.

"By God, you are lucky," Josh said, breaking the silence.

"Hmm?" I said halfheartedly, not looking up from my book. So monkish was my devotion to the matter at hand that I had no intention of prolonging an otherwise congenial conversation about my good fortune.

"I mean, this is just so unfair."

Looking up from my book, and realizing the ascetic austerity of our cell to be a thing of the past, I said, "What's that?"

"It's only...well, you're a Catholic, yes?"

"That's right."

"So you've already figured out the Trinity—three persons in one God. This wave-particle duality thing is easy for you."

I gave a wry grin, nodded, and returned to my contemplation. But Josh's words had settled on me. That evening at the campus pub, I pored over his words. Could it be that my faith predisposed me to a different, more sensitive understanding of the ways in which we categorize events, phenomena, and reality? And to what degree do the ways in which we teach these matters to ourselves and to others influence our ultimate comprehension of them?

The Value of Provisional Models

St. Paul tells us that there are understandings appropriate to being a child and those appropriate to being an adult. A good term for the things we teach children might be *provisional models*—ideas that a child can grasp that are not fully true but, rather, prepare the way for truth.

Those who teach introductory physics are no strangers to provisional models designed to acquaint students with difficult concepts. These models can be quite far from what we would hold to be true, yet they still convey important elements to junior students, just wetting their beaks in the mysteries of quantum mechanics. We teach these untruths as provisional truths. True, these truths must be untruthed later; but their utility as educational tools outweighs the futility of their admitted falsehood. To be sure, these models are provisional, and it is their provisionalism that makes of them both a foundation and a pitfall.

Take, for instance, the Rutherford-Bohr model of the atom. The Rutherford-Bohr model superseded British physicist J. J. Thomson's plum pudding model, which held that electrons—which he, himself, had discovered—floated as corpuscles in a positively charged "atom soup." Looking back on this now, the conceptualization can seem almost quaint. The Rutherford-Bohr model is superior in every way; it was first proposed in 1911 by New Zealander Ernest Rutherford, who posited that atoms held their charge in a very small, concentrated nucleus. This model was refined by Danish physicist Niels Bohr in 1913, who added to it the negatively charged orbital electrons that were stable and in fixed orbits about the nucleus.

The Rutherford-Bohr model is often called the planetary model of atoms.

This nomenclature arises because the best way to picture the electrons and nucleus is as a solar system in miniature. The electrons take on the role of the planets, and the nucleus—with its protons and neutrons packed together—is the sun. The key feature of this model for the development of quantum mechanics is the fact that the electrons can only exist in specific orbits that correspond to set energy values. However, they are allowed to switch between these energy levels, and, in the process, the atom emits or absorbs light. The emitted and absorbed light is known as the atomic spectra. The Rutherford-Bohr model accurately predicted key features of atomic spectra, as represented by the particular colors of light emitted by highly studied atoms, such as hydrogen.

You have almost certainly seen an image of this model; it is pervasive. This depiction of the atom has become iconic to such a degree that it has come to symbolize quantum phenomena more generally. Moreover, it has become ingrained in the popular consciousness to a degree unparalleled by other graphic depictions of physical models. It is symbolic of the atomic age. It has found its way onto the seals of the United States Atomic Energy Commission, the International Atomic Energy Agency, and has been enshrined by the United States Department of Veterans Affairs as an approved emblem of belief for government headstones (denoting atheism). It is the logo of the Springfield nuclear power plant on *The Simpsons*.

This model is a study in elegant aesthetics, and it explains much about how we conceptualize the world on the quantum level. Its very simplicity is the key to its success. The model clearly denotes the constituent components of the atom: protons and neutrons clustered in the central nucleus, and orbital electrons swirling around that core. It is a scalable solar system—a decidedly more approachable and familiar image in the 1910s, when it was first published and disseminated. Any student beginning to learn quantum mechanics has dreams and nightmares populated by this model. And if you ask the average person to picture an atom, it is the Rutherford-Bohr model that he or she will imagine.

The problem, though, is that this model is wrong; it turns out to be fundamentally flawed in a few ways. To be sure, the Rutherford-Bohr model correctly predicted a number of the measured characteristics of atomic spectra, but it fell short in key ways as experiments were improved and refined. Therefore, as measurements of the spectra of atoms continued, it was clear that the Rutherford-Bohr model needed to be improved.

As quantum mechanics continued to be developed in the mid-1920s, it became increasingly clear that the notion of electrons, which surrounded the nucleus of an atom, orbiting the nucleus in well-defined paths as particles was insufficient to describe the experimental data. Rather, the electrons behaved in ways not unlike *both* particles *and* waves, and thus exhibited what is now called wave-particle duality. Traditionally, a particle was described in terms of its position and momentum (the combination of its mass and velocity). These quantities were used to compute two other central quantities: energy and angular momentum. In the emerging theory of quantum mechanics, the position and momentum of a particle are no longer central. Instead, the energy of the particle plays a central role in defining its state. And given its energy, one can predict the probability of the particle having a particular position, momentum, or angular momentum. The particle is now described in terms of a probability wave, or the *wave function*.

This new view of how to describe particles as probability waves provided a completely new model of the atom. Now, the electron does not have a particular orbit around the nucleus. Instead, it has a definite value of energy. Given that energy, there is a cloud of probability—a whole range of positions—where the electron might find itself, were you to try to measure its location. Most important, as it changes this energy state, it is still predicted to emit and absorb light—the atomic spectra. The predictions of the atomic spectra provided by this new way of viewing the atom are some of the most accurate predictions to date in science. Interestingly, the model still retains many of the aspects of the Rutherford-Bohr model. We still talk of orbitals, and the full quantum model of the atom has yet to supplant the Rutherford-Bohr model in the popular consciousness. In fact, the latter still has use value.

Why was I one of the fortunate souls to be taught the Rutherford-Bohr model? And why do I continue to teach aspiring physicists the Rutherford-Bohr model? We know this model to be, in a sense, wrong, as it does not convey the fullness of quantum theory. Why persist in a delusion? Because, put simply, these inaccuracies are enormously useful from an educational perspective. Because of its simplicity and because it produces correct results for some selected aspects of reality, physics instructors still regularly teach this model to introductory quantum mechanics students. This model captures such important key elements and it is so much more digestible a picture that we still teach it, and we still use it.

The full picture of an atom, as suggested by quantum mechanics, involves the challenging concept of electron clouds that provide the probability of the electron being in a certain position. No longer do we assign electrons specific positions or orbits, as the Rutherford-Bohr model does. Electron clouds are hard to describe, hard to draw, and require more advanced mathematics. More advanced students use the full predictive power of quantum mechanics in calculations regarding particles at the atomic and subatomic level. But, in everyday discussion, even scientists will employ this first-order approximation of the Rutherford-Bohr model with the clear understanding that it falls short as a model, but sufficiently simplifies the concepts involved in order to facilitate discussion.

There is another sense in which physics uses models that are incomplete—both in education and in actual practice. For these cases, the model in question is not wrong in the traditional sense of the word. It is better to speak of the model as limited; the model still applies to certain behaviors and certain systems, but does not apply to all cases—and we understand precisely where those limits are. One of the best examples of selective utility is the relationship between Newton's law of gravity and Einstein's theory of relativity.

Newton's law of gravity is incredibly accurate for gravity on the scale of the earth and the sun, but it fails to accurately predict behavior under extreme gravitational circumstances (where it is superseded by Einstein's relativity). Similarly, we use the term *Newtonian mechanics*—also called classical mechanics—to refer to the system of physical principles that works on the scale of everyday life. This is the physics that describes items on the scale of my office desk, a baseball, a football, my car, an airplane, or an ocean liner. If I wanted to calculate anything about the things we experience in everyday life, I would use Newtonian mechanics.

Newtonian physics is an approximate representation of reality, but it is more than accurate enough to predict, calculate, or describe most everyday events. Where Newtonian mechanics has trouble is when the speed of an event increases, or the scale of an event shrinks, or the strength of gravity in the system becomes too large. The physics of the late nineteenth and early twentieth centuries focused on addressing these shortcomings of Newtonian mechanics and saw the development of new tools and models—quantum mechanics for extremely small systems, special relativity for extremely fast systems, and general relativity for gravity (the last two are often grouped as the single field of relativity). A common error is to assume that with the development of better models, the earlier Newtonian mechanics is now incorrect in the strict sense of right or wrong. In fact, in a very real sense, there is nothing wrong about Newtonian mechanics; it is only limited in its application.

In contrast to the Rutherford-Bohr model, which is simply wrong in a few fundamental features, quantum mechanics and relativity extend and modify Newtonian mechanics. Physicists still view Newtonian mechanics as a sufficiently accurate approximation of quantum mechanics and relativity under the right conditions. For example, Newton's law of gravity is still useful for situations where gravity is not too strong. To be sure, Einstein's general relativity is more accurate, but that accuracy is not measurable in most everyday applications. Moreover, it is substantially more complicated, so nothing is gained by using it instead of Newton's law of gravity. So, we use Newton's law of gravity all the time, even though we know Newton's law of gravity has been superseded by Einstein's general relativity. But in this case, Newton's law is a well-defined limit of general relativity.

These three fields—Newtonian mechanics, relativity, and quantum mechanics—are each tools best applied to their appropriate task. As one considers smaller and smaller objects, there is a point at which Newtonian mechanics stops offering useful predictions. Rather than behaving in accordance with strict Newtonian laws, something as small as an electron obeys radically different laws based on probability. But the foundational reality of quantum mechanics seems not to interfere with the perfectly acceptable physical predictions offered by Newtonian mechanics. Why does Newtonian mechanics work so well in a world where at its foundation is quantum mechanics? We still don't really know, but it does. And so there's an exciting question there to explore, and it is from these spaces whence something new may come. We still await a Unified Theory of Everything.

The Utility of Stereotypes

In the sciences, we can see that there is a relationship between models and images and the scientific facts they supposedly convey. While the truth-value of these models can be unclear, they are nevertheless useful framing devices for teaching and dialogue. We have these relationships between models and reality in our everyday life as well. We call an image such as the one I suggest a stereotype, a word we borrowed from the French in the eighteenth century, who in turn derived it from the Greek στερεός meaning firm, solid, rigid, or stiff, and "ῥίπτω" meaning "the thing having been struck, or cast." Therefore, etymologically, a stereotype is the tendency to hold firm to an invented notion regarding the general character of a thing or, less usefully, a person. As often as not, these notions take the form of images or models that we apply in anticipation of an outcome.

Now, by stereotype, I do not mean to apologize for the assembling of pejorative controlling images of a person or group of persons and then applying these images indiscriminately. Indeed, that element of stereotype has no redeeming qualities. Rather, I advance the argument that we all harbor images and models—either inculcated and inherited or derived from experience—that condition the ways in which we perceive the world we occupy. So, we apply the images that we formulate and apply stereotypes to subsequent decisions. Stereotypes, according to this definition, are devices that a person has learned some time in the past that serve the purpose of framing their expectations. They pervade every aspect of our interaction with the world. Stereotypes, when we resist the all-too-common tendency to treat these categories as essentially true, can be tremendously helpful tools for navigating the world that we inhabit.

We are accustomed to associating a sort of ignorance to the very notion of stereotype, and, indeed, if a benign mental image is taken too far, applying stereotypes casually can have profoundly negative consequences. Even so, it is an element of human memory to form defense mechanisms in a stereotypical fashion. Imagine, for instance, that you lost a considerable amount of money in the stock market speculating on pork bellies. This imaginary investment fails to turn a profit—indeed, it is a spectacular loss. It is unlikely that sometime in the future, even though this failure may have been a fluke, a person who lost money on this investment would again risk the recurrence of this loss. You have formed a negative stereotype against investing in pork bellies. The old adage holds true: "Fool me once, shame on you; fool me twice, shame on me." We are expected to learn from our experiences and subject our decision-making processes to these experiences. This expectation involves, in its very formulation, the invention of stereotypes.

But it is prudent to note here that stereotypes are by necessity a fiction, albeit one that serves an explanatory purpose. Put simply, they are not true in any real or factual sense. Productive stereotyping allows one to make quick decisions when he or she needs to forecast in such a way that is somewhat accurate. Despite this utility, when we stop to think about it, we recognize that stereotypes are fundamentally fictional: they only give us a predisposed assessment of a thing or event; they do not privilege us to the actuality of the thing or event. Were we to dispense with these stereotypes—which, I argue, govern our every interaction—we would recognize that the actuality of the circumstance often fails to accord with our prejudice in important ways.

We know that the approximation offered by a stereotype is ultimately incorrect. But applying a stereotype can be pragmatically useful, provided we acknowledge the foundational falsehood of the initial postulation. I argue that this provisionalism is similar to teaching outmoded and obsolete scientific models to initiates. These constructs serve to acquaint us with the earliest stages of decision making or calculation, but it is a certain mischief to treat them as predictive or actual in any meaningful sense. When we move away from these stereotypes or obsolete models, we graduate, so to speak, from initiate to practitioner.

The God of the Box

I discussed in chapter one the tendency of people to hold fast to a notion of the divine that derives from our mental precondition whereby we apprehend the divine as an extension of the objective, physical world with which we are most comfortable. When we hear God referred to, we each conjure an image of God—both believers and unbelievers—and, as often as not, this image takes on anthropomorphic qualities. God, in this formulation, is a superbeing, possessed of all the physical attributes that humans themselves have. We are inclined to imagine God in a manner not at all dissimilar to the way in which neophyte scientists encounter atomic theory and the way in which we assemble and deploy stereotypes while negotiating our social terrain.

People of faith will often refer to their experience of the divine, and these experiences have a very personal dimension. Having related to God in a personal way, our experience conditions us to frame this commerce as having happened between ourselves and another physical being. But for those of us that have had such an experience, we know in our hearts that God cannot be a separate physical being, but is instead a transcendent, complex reality that resists the easy definition of being an entity.

I argue that casting God as an entity with specific attributes (i.e., physicality, personality, agency, vector, direction, and magnitude) actually diminishes God into a series of controlling images. When we try to communicate this relation, we too often "put God in a box"; we confine this being—who is supposed to be infinite—in the poverty of our finite language. Doing so refashions the fullness of reality into just another superperson, admittedly one possessed of more potential and power than can be imagined. But we of faith must always remember that we have undertaken this provisional shrinking for a range of possible reasons—including educational. Like the Rutherford-Bohr model and like stereotypes more generally, the convenience of the image is not the reality of God. Our controlling image of God, whatever our personal image is, too often limits the divine such that God's transcendent nature becomes problematically confined in God's approximate attributes.

Here at the University of California, Irvine, I have had the happy fortune of teaching multiple iterations of my popular course The Science of Superheroes. This course investigates comic book characters and interrogates their exceptional abilities according to the demanding criteria of the sciences. Even though superheroes' powers are often explained within the pages of the comics using scientific principles, they almost all eventually break science by acting in impossible ways. And my students and I must suspend disbelief in order to be entertained. Teaching this course has allowed me to think deeply about superheroes—both from a scientific and cultural perspective—and, I believe, the concept of the superhero has much explanatory power here.

Were the majority of confessional Christians to think critically about their personal, mental image of God, they might recognize the comparison to an all-powerful superhero—a transcendent Superman or a moral Doctor Manhattan or a good Apocalypse. I do not mean to propose that we think of God in a domino mask, flying from place to place righting wrongs (although mystery of identity and moral action in the world are elements of a popular conception of the divine). When I say, "superhero," I do not mean a square-jawed do-gooder in a cape and tights. I advance the word as a more generalizing term that acknowledges exceptional persons, entities, concepts, or agencies.

Superheroes are people or entities that have some power or control over the natural world that goes well beyond what we are used to. These exceptional agencies are wholly beyond human ability. Superheroes act to help and intercede on our behalf. Superheroes are not necessarily the denizens of the funny pages, but they epitomize and characterize the valorous ideals that we hold collectively as a society. Superheroes, according to this formulation, are beings of exceptional power that are clearly physical and can do amazing deeds.

I am anxious about a God who is simply another—admittedly more powerful—superhero. Modern superheroes, in no small way, are the intellectual progeny of primitive nature gods, spirits, and mythical creatures. Societies that revered such supernatural beings saw some regularity in nature—seasons, day and night, regular, unchanging constellations—and they personified these elements and erected explanatory mythologies about these phenomena. The seasons changed, for the Greeks, because Hades seized Persephone, and Demeter laments half the year, thus killing nature cyclically. These gods, who possess personalities and are relatable by means of icons, statuary, and the narratives themselves, were pressed into explanations of other extraordinary natural phenomena, such as floods, fires, storms, and so on. The development of these gods offered the possibility of control through description. Relating to these beings suggested a type of access that comforted otherwise destitute persons adrift amid the unsettling proposition of the then poorly understood natural mechanisms in place. But even beyond explanation and control, access to these gods allowed a satisfying means of prediction.

These nature gods monopolized one or another aspect of the natural world, over which they exercised absolute purview. Thus, Thor is the Thunderer, Artemis the moon goddess, Manannan mac Lir the sea god, and so on. These gods exercised their office departmentally, not universally. And even in the epoch of these gods, learned men (and they were almost always men, alas) questioned the actuality of the gods. Euhemerus posited that the gods were historical persons, whose deeds became amplified by retelling. Followers of Buddha maintained that the existence of gods was incidental to breaking the cycle of *samsara*—birth, death, and rebirth. Epicurus maintained that the universe was governed by chance without the need for divine intervention. Aristotle proposed mechanisms for the movement of the heavens that obviated the necessity for the gods.

The Sophists continued this critical work. As the naturalistic explanations for natural phenomena waxed into certainty, the purview of these gods diminished into nothingness. These are the gods of the gaps. As ancient thinkers began considering the nature of reality, the conceptual latitude allocated to these gods' agency shrank.

Fast-forward two thousand years: the superheroes of the comic books begin to fill the roles of these gods. Rather than being undone by naturalistic explanations, naturalistic explanations ostensibly form the intellectual defense of their powers. The idea of limited purview remains. Superpowers—with the notable and significant exception of telepathy—tend not to be reduplicated within a publishing company's extended universe. But the superheroes of the twentieth century are formulated out of our scientific culture and in a much more scientific way. They are our scientific superbeings.

Like the gods of old, superheroes solve problems for us: they beat the bad guys; they intercede in our interest. Their powers, when considered at face value, seem to be rooted in the sciences. Consider Superman, for instance. His powers derive wholly from his Kryptonian heritage. Were Krypton's gravity stronger than that of Earth, it is not unlikely he would be able to appear to defy gravity in flight. Were his bones a different density and muscles assembled differently than those of humans, his feats of invulnerability and superstrength could be explicable to science.

Indeed, science seems to be the inspirational underpinning to explain the phenomena of superheroes in their own universe. The key element here is that the core properties of superheroes make scientific sense; indeed, many superheroes' powers seem ripped from the pages of science journals. These powers, however, are taken to such an extreme that they violate physical principles.

To be sure, there are aspects of this universe that are scientifically correct and relevant to actual fields of inquiry. But by and large, any host of scientific disciplines must ultimately reject the powers these superheroes possess. We know superheroes such as these are not and cannot be real. The extreme versions of the powers in comic books, television, and movies are, for the most part, ruled out by science. So it seems reasonable that the degree to which we equate our image of God too closely with the image of the superhero will, in part, determine our level of comfort—as religious persons—with the sciences.

We have seen that sustained consideration of the natural sciences has lessened the purview of not only the gods of the gaps, but also of contemporary fictional superheroes. Any image of the divine that circumscribes God's power by making God an entity will ultimately be undone by the sciences. We know the gods of nature and superheroes are both categorically unreal; if our image of God is too much like that of a superhero, we are rightfully nervous at the possibility that this God, too, is unreal. God as a physical entity is akin to the provisional untruths represented by the Rutherford-Bohr atom and stereotypes more generally.

Therefore, I think it is safe to say that one of the major discomforts of people of faith is the knowledge that the sciences have systematically overthrown both nature gods and superheroes. If one's image of God is strictly that of a celestial superhero—one who solves problems, answers prayers, or judges people—then that person will be uncomfortable about the eventuality of his or her God being debunked. A transcendent God who is the fullness of reality cannot be one that exists in the relatively impoverished purview of a superhero; we must move God out of this mold into a more transcendent one; we must consider God, then, the ultimate superhero.

God, the ultimate superhero, goes beyond quotidian interaction with reality and becomes reality itself—the true "I am who am." Rather than conflicting with science—as a smaller God, confined by one's images of God, necessarily would—the existence of a transcendent God, who is the fullness of reality (a point that scriptural authorities seem to make regularly), would not be threatened by science. For Christians, the contemporary theologian Ilia Delio makes a similar point regarding the nature of Jesus in her book, *Christ in Evolution*. She points out that a challenge for modern Christians is that we have "locked the mystery of God into a single, individual human person, Jesus of Nazareth, so that Jesus Christ has become a single, individual *superhero* and we are mere spectators to the divine drama." (I have added the emphasis on superhero.) She goes on to state that "Christ is the power of God among us and within us, the fullness of the earth and of life in the universe"[6]—a concept worthy of further meditation.

Breaking the Box

Now, I do not want to suggest that mental images of God are without merit. Indeed, images of God can do very positive spiritual work; praying to God the Father, or Jesus the Son, or the Holy Spirit, provides us with concrete reference points that ease our relation to the larger whole. We must always recognize, however, that any given image or model or icon must, by necessity, capture only part of the more magisterial whole. In the sciences, we are constantly moving and pushing our models, modifying our theories, and extending our boundaries; as we measure and experience more, we constantly refine and revise. So, too, in faith communities must we always refine, redefine, and revise the relationship of our mental images to the fullness of reality that each of the aspects represent. This is the essence of the spiral journey of faith. If we are not constantly changing our relationship to the object of our prayers, and the relationship of the object of our prayers to the fullness of reality, then our faith is not a growing, moving, living thing. And really, then, what's the point?

We often teach children by inculcating images of the divine that are comprehensible to young minds. The point here is not that we teach the God in the box simply to unlearn it later. Rather, St. Paul in 1 Corinthians 13:11 reminds us that, as we develop, so too must our faith. We teach the appropriate image of God for the developmental age of the person, but by emphasizing one aspect of the divine that is, perhaps, more palatable to young minds, we have placed the infinite in a finite sphere. But these finite slices must always be a *pars pro toto*; we must not forget the aspect's relationship to the larger whole. We must never forget that the images and icons on which we meditate are metaphors, images, and approximations of the fullness of reality. God is so transcendent, so all encompassing, that any aspect of God cannot be anything but a reference to the total whole.

Inaccuracies and provisional images have their place in both scientific and religious education. My students, at college age, no less, will often ask me to supplement my lectures with pictures or to describe physical phenomena pictorially. One image I have conjured for them is an electron decked out in a racing helmet, a la A-ha's "Take on Me" music video. It's a joke, naturally. But imagining a little guy in a racing car, whizzing through a given field at close to the speed of light, trying desperately to stay on the track and to resist forces that seek to distance him from that track, is illustrative. It's absurd, but it plays an educational role. Were any student to write that metaphor on an exam, I would laugh, but it would probably be an incorrect answer. This image is heuristic, an aid to learning; it is not an analytical model, and it would be quite inappropriate for quantitative problem solving.

The same goes for images of the divine. During moments of careful thought, I think we all realize that thinking of God as an individual, physical being obscures God's nature as transcendent. Whether our picture is the old guy with a beard or something equally approximate, we have to be careful not to treat them as actual in any existential or essential sense. We have to remember to release ourselves from the desire to cleave to the physical, our locus of comfort, and recognize that all metaphors of divine physicality, divine appearance, and divine attribute are simply instances of figurative language designed to assist in our meditation. For God cannot and will not be confined by these images. These images are Rutherford-Bohr; God is quantum mechanics.

Chapter 3

Approaches to Scripture: The Multidisciplinary Necessity

All Scripture is God-breathed and is useful for teaching, rebuking, correcting, and training in righteousness, so that the servant of God may be thoroughly equipped for every good work.

—2 Timothy 3:16–17

Often a non-Christian knows something about the earth [and] the heavens...and this knowledge he holds with certainty from reason and experience.... To hear a Christian talk nonsense about such things—claiming that what he is saying is based on Scripture—[is offensive and disgraceful]. We should do all that we can to avoid such an embarrassing situation, lest the unbeliever see only ignorance in the Christian and laugh to scorn.

—Augustine, *De Genesi cid litteram libri duodecim*, Book 1, ch. 19, § 39

And yet it moves.

—Galileo Galilei, possibly apocryphal

We should not be surprised that academia often seems like a proverbial ivory tower, set apart from the so-called real world. Universities, as a cultural entity, arose from monasteries and cathedral canons in the twelfth century. As the institutional inheritors of these arcane and esoteric communities, initiation into the ranks of the professoriate can often seem just as esoteric. Indeed, I have labored the better part of my career to tear down the distinction between the ivory tower of the academy and community at large, but I still frequently encounter the very wall that I hope to tear down.

I remember first feeling the telling twitch of induction. Chuck Knobler, my postdoctoral adviser at the University of California, Los Angeles, extended an invitation to me to present my findings at a conference at my alma mater, the University of California, Santa Barbara. With Chuck, I investigated two-dimensional flow problems using Langmuir monolayers—but I won't bore you with the details; just rest assured that watching foam flow is substantially more riveting than watching paint dry.

Now, this invitation was doubly significant: not only was it a mark of approval from Chuck (and one that, like all students laboring in the shadow of an esteemed mentor, I desperately wanted), but it also was a chance to return to Santa Barbara to show Gunter Ahlers and David Cannell, my doctoral advisers, that I had made good on the investment of their time. Looking back, now that my waistline has waxed and my hairline has waned, I don't remember the title of the colloquium. I don't even remember the title of my talk. I don't remember whether how it was received by the audience. And, frankly, in hindsight, I don't care. But I keep with me a much more cherished memory from that conference; I simply remember the sickened excitement of the feeling that I had made it.

But I also remember this conference—far above the hundreds I've attended since—in large part because of a curious conversation that fastened indelibly in my mind. Strange that, nearly twenty years later, I often return to reflect on this memory.

I had just finished my talk, and a few colleagues—senior to me but junior to the rest—had stolen away to the veranda overlooking the Pacific. A more picturesque vista cannot be found in academia. In midafternoon, the scene is striking: the Santa Barbara sun casts an ever-changing mosaic over the breaking waves. We stood contemplating. "My God, that's gorgeous," one of us opined. And, turning to me, he asked, "You spent seven years here?"

"Sure did. And still I'm struck by all this beauty."

"Do you ever stop to think of the purpose of all this?" He swept a horizontal x-axis with his arms. "I mean, we can measure this; on a long enough timeline, we can figure out, neurologically, why this view is so appealing. But have you ever considered—in the face of all this beauty—why?"

"Of course," I answered. "I'm a Catholic." Their faces turned quizzically toward me. "I can't but believe that there's a purpose to this beauty. There's a reason, and we can use the tools of reason to pose questions about it."

The conversation continued; my response elicited the usual jibes and rhetorical questions, but I simply countered that I felt it was curious that people (both religious persons and irreligious scientists) feel a compulsion to take the Bible literally—the former to bolster, the latter to disparage. We talked about my views of creation, evolution, and cosmology, and most especially about the fact that I see no inherent conflict between my work as a Christian and my faith as a scientist. This conversation lasted the shuttle ride back from the venue; it continued through the vestibule of the hotel; it settled in the lobby. No longer facing any constraints of time, we were free to explore these concepts.

Just then, I heard over my shoulder, "Excuse me, may I join your conversation?"

I turned around to see a bookish man, late twenties, whom I recognized from the conference earlier. "Sure," I answered, "have a seat."

As he settled into a free lobby chair, he continued, "I couldn't help but overhear your conversation about faith and the sciences, and I think I have something to say." As he talked, as he told his story, we all listened intently. A child of pastors, rooted in the upper Midwest, this young man was essentially raised in a cloister. "Science was the enemy. Science was a threat. Science was wrong." Real pain rang from his voice, and it was hard to resist the temptation to pat him on the shoulder in comfort. All the milestones of his life—high school graduation, college selection, dating—had a decidedly fundamentalist inflection; his choice of vocation, however, did not.

This young man spoke of the way he trembled before announcing to his parents his choice of college major: physics. This young man spoke of being deeply troubled by the prospect that he might have to move beyond the scriptural hermeneutics[7] of his childhood in order to accommodate his study, afraid that doing so would somehow also loosen his grip from everything he had previously held. "In no way," he said, "was it an obvious or easy decision to study the sciences. But now, I'm pursuing my doctorate in physics."

From the hundred or so conferences I've attended since this one, I can say without fear of contradiction that when this young man finished his story, never was such a silence so profound in such a normally collegial setting. "My God," I said, "how is your faith now?"

"Really, it's as strong as ever. But my road to the sciences had no Damascus moment.[8] It was all a process. And the process was extremely painful; it struck at a lot of core tenets and bedrock foundations of who I thought I was. But when you come out on the other side, your faith ends up stronger, more flexible, more vibrant, and more dynamic."

There and then I gained a respect for biblical literalists. These people are often caricatured as Bible-thumping types—bombastic, ignorant, and irrational. They, most certainly, are not. But a faith grounded only in a literal understanding of the Bible too often lacks a strength, a flexibility, a vibrancy, a dynamism that can only come from sustained critical engagement and reflection.

To be sure, there is a challenge to moving beyond literalism; but the dangers of literalism, I think, are a certain rigidity of focus and fixity of the point of reference. Should something happen to disturb a faith of this type, it shatters. Material that is the most rigid, when struck just right, shatters into the most pieces; it is the least capable of resisting destruction. Kevlar, on the other hand, is produced of interwoven fibers that stretch and give, and that's what people use to protect themselves from bullets.

There is a benefit to moving beyond literalism, and that benefit is an agile faith. Faith is like a muscle; it craves dynamic interaction. The more you work this muscle, the more you introduce it to new actions, behaviors, and undertakings, the more this muscle develops, the stronger this muscle gets. But this process can be very painful.

The parents among us will empathize: consoling a child racked with growing pains is a desperate task. I think back to my own experience holding my three-year-old daughter, unable to comprehend the pain she was in. I remember rocking her back and forth, shushing her more for my comfort—I think—than her own, and cursing the pain she was in. But in retrospect, I think I have to thank those growing pains; they are responsible for the healthy, robust young woman my daughter is today. The pain, as invidious and intolerable as it seemed then, served a purpose.

I think I finally understand what that graduate student twenty years ago felt, and while I don't envy him, I empathize with him. Leaving behind inflexible rigidity for a more inclusive view of Scripture is hard, but it is necessary. We can still embrace Scripture as the foundational document for all our experience, provided we don't ignore fact to preserve fiction. Scripture can be transformative even if metaphorical, and it can furnish attentive readers with insights about the nature of reality. But, perhaps most fruitfully, embracing all you learn—from both Scripture and the sciences—allows religion and reason to become compatriots collaborating to conceive a Weltbild—an image of the world.

Literalism and Inerrancy: Literally Erroneous

Persons of faith, I think, are rightly uncomfortable with the notion that Scripture might be falsified or simply false. If I cannot trust in the inerrancy of the written word, how am I to believe in the living word? But this reasoning is mistakenly premised. Fact, as an epistemological quantity, places the event being described in a rather narrow box; it is, to be sure, a comfort zone. But it is by transcending this comfort zone that real growth and real understanding take place. The veneer of objectivity—and its gilt, objective fact—can and, I suggest, must be supplanted by attempts to ascertain truth. Scripture is not a science textbook, and we should not use it as one. Scripture is concerned with truth, and we should let that voice sing loudest in its harmony. Caesar Baronius, an ecclesiastical historian and friend to Galileo, reminds us, "The Bible teaches us how to go to heaven, not how the heavens go."

To be sure, biblical literalism is a straw-man idea. Were we to take the literalism suggested by the term *biblical literalism* absolutely literally, we would be led to rather uncertain terrain. The stereotype of the literalist—however inaccurate this image might actually be—is a rural or suburban political conservative, clinging to God and guns. A literalist hermeneutic—this reading strategy—would appear, according to the *Car Talk* guys, "unencumbered by the thought process." We would read the page, and we would think that what the page said must be factual by virtue of its being in this most special of books. But, at the end of the day, even the most literal of literalists recognizes that there are passages in the Bible meant as poetry, imagery, and story. If nothing else, the parables of Jesus, embedded in the Gospels, are stories not meant to be taken as accounts of literal occurrences.

I am not deaf to the very good reasons why we expect parts of the Bible to be factual, but I bristle at the notion that we must, because of its nature as inspired word, read the Bible as categorically factual. The world we occupy is not, after all, erected on pillars or set into a foundation (cf. Psalm 93:1; Psalm 96:10; 1 Samuel 2:8; and Job 9:6); the sky above us is not, after all, a vast body of water suspended above a spread-out, tentlike firmament (Genesis 1:6–9; Genesis 7:11; Isaiah 24:18; Isaiah 40:22; Ezekiel 1:22); the earth is not flat (Deuteronomy 28:64; 1 Samuel 2:10; Job 28:24); the earth docs not have corners (Job 37:3; Isaiah 11:12; Ezekiel 7:2; Revelation 7:1; Revelation 20:8); and the earth is spherical and thereby not viewable in its entirety at a single moment in time—no matter the altitude of the observer (Job 28:24; Daniel 4:10–11; Matthew 4:8). We have it on very good, scientific consensus that these passages cannot be factual in any sense that we would understand.

As an example, consider one vexing—and impossible—element of biblical cosmology: the geocentric model of the heavens that the authors of Scripture evidently labored within. Few people today—biblical literalists included, I would argue—seriously doubt the cosmological fact that the earth revolves around the sun. But for much of human history, this was actually solid science given the observational tools of the time. And this is reflected in description, such as this one from the Battle of Gibeon:

> Then Joshua spoke to the Lord, in the day that he delivered up the Amorites in the sight of the children of Israel, and he said before them, "Move not, toward Gibeon, nor thou, O moon, toward the valley of Aijalon." And the sun and the moon stood still until the people revenged themselves of their enemies... So the sun stood still in the midst of heaven and hastened not to go down the space of one day. (Joshua 10:12–13)

Joshua does not command the earth to stop its rotation, nor does the author seem to suggest that the sun simply appeared to stand still; rather, the whole celestial rotation was paused at Joshua's behest. The passage also implies that the east-to-west course of the sun through the heavens was arrested (Aijalon is west of Gibeon, which is itself about five miles northwest of modern Jerusalem). We see echoes of this geocentric perspective in Habakkuk, whose author writes, "Sun and moon stood still in their habitation in the light of thy arrows, they shall go in the brightness of thy glittering spear" (Habakkuk 3:11), and also in Ecclesiastes, whose author reminds us that "The sun rises and the sun goes down, and hastens to the place where it rises" (Ecclesiastes 1:5). We also see the agency of God moving the sun through the sky in unexpected ways. In 2 Kings, the prophet Isaiah counsels the recovery of King Hezekiah:

> Now Hezekiah said to Isaiah, "What will be the sign that the Lord will heal me, and that I shall go up to the house of the Lord the third day?" Isaiah said, "This shall be the sign to you from the Lord, that the Lord will do the thing that He has spoken: shall the shadow go forward ten steps or go back ten steps?" So Hezekiah answered, "It is easy for the shadow to decline ten steps; no, but let the shadow turn backward ten steps." Isaiah the prophet cried to the Lord, and He brought the shadow on the stairway back ten steps by which it had gone down on the stairway of Ahaz. (2 Kings 20:8—11; an account of this recovery is also found in 2 Chronicles 32:24 and Isaiah 38:1)

The sun, if this passage is interpreted literally, recedes in its path and accordingly lengthens a shadow in the stairway of Ahaz (who, not incidentally, is Hezekiah's father). The sun, the ultimate author of the prodigious shadow, is in motion here, not the earth itself. Accordingly, we again see it is not the earth that moves but rather the sun.

I do not list these examples to suggest that the authors of Scripture should have known better. The authors of Scripture did not have the tools of advanced astronomy. They dealt in a geocentric universe, as did everyone at that time. Also, I do not expect that God or the authors of Scripture were terribly concerned with the scientific accuracy of these passages. Rather, their goal was to communicate the importance of their subjects, not to communicate an accurate cosmological vision. Consequently, they

communicated these truths as clearly as they could, but they were naturally working within the cosmological worldview of their time.

We can see how these passages suggest a geocentric "geosystem" (as
opposed to a solar system), and, I think, this causes problems for the
rigid literalist. First, the texts of these passages literally state that the sun
stopped in or altered its path through the sky; second, it is the sun, as
opposed to the earth, that is in motion through the heavens; and, third,
the previous two points must by necessity imply that the sun orbits the
earth. If we were biblical literalists, we would have no choice but to read
these two episodes as indicating a geocentric cosmology. After all, in both,
it is not the earth's movement that is arrested, but the movement of the sun
through the sky. But most literalists do not demand a geocentric worldview, and most understand these episodes in their compositional context.

Why, the question must be asked, would we allow these episodes to
stand as literary flourishes—or even as reflections of the cosmological
mentality of the biblical authors—and persist in affirming young earth
creationism or the literal truth of the Genesis creation stories? If we were
to interpret the Genesis account of creation literally, and if we were to
be consistent in deploying that literal hermeneutic, then, in order to be
intellectually honest, we would have to describe the reality we inhabit as
geocentric. Now, we have it on very good authority, indeed, that our solar
system is heliocentric. So, either the passage must be read figuratively (i.e.,
heliocentrists are right), or, sometime since creation, God inverted the
orbital system of our stellarsphere (i.e., the sun used to revolve around
the earth), or, despite the enormity of the data that argue against it, the
sun still does revolve around the earth (i.e., the description of Battle of
Gibeon proves a geocentric universe). I am inclined to believe the first
proposition.

If we read these passages literally—that is, when we persist in the belief
that our stellarsphere is geocentric—we miss the point that the authors

of these books were intending to convey. This does require more effort on our part. Perhaps the author of Joshua wanted to emphasize the Providence of God in the Israelites' victory over the Gibeonites. Perhaps the author wished to suggest the extraordinary fortune of their victory at that battle? Perhaps the author wished to suggest that the people victorious at the battle were a very special group? Any or all of these authorial intentions could be explained by this literary device.

I doubt very seriously that the author actively sought to posit the actuality of this occurrence, and I am doubly certain that the author's cosmology is incidental to the message being conveyed in telling this story. But a literalist would be stuck with a single interpretation—one that is quite unsatisfactory, to my mind, from an intellectual point of view.

Now, I do not mean to pick on the authors of Scripture by disparaging their worldview. My intention is to point out that it often does a disservice to Scripture to focus on the factual nature of a given scriptural matter. And, alas, our past has witnessed moments at which a crisis of fact has incommodiously silenced persons laboring to enhance the Scriptures with the sciences and vice versa. I am reminded, here, of Galileo Galilei, that intrepid and pious soul, and his attempt to confirm and disseminate the understanding that Nicolaus Copernicus first articulated in *De revolutionibus orbium* (1543).

We all know the story: Galileo, at the beginning of the seventeenth century, began confirming the mathematics first advanced by Copernicus with empirical observation using early telescopes. After coming to the attention of the Inquisition in 1615, and after a theological advisory committee determined heliocentric theory to be incompatible with Roman Catholic biblical interpretation in 1616, Galileo was forcibly silenced—but not convinced: "And yet it moves," later authors alleged he maintained. The extent to which his censorship was actually enforced is debatable (he resumed publishing on the matter ten years later), and the degree to which the Roman Catholic Church viewed his support of this theory as a threat is a matter for historical consideration; what is known incontrovertibly, however, is that subsequent thinkers—both Protestant apologists, eager to portray the Roman Catholic communion as a medieval throwback, and early scientists, who took umbrage at the thought of a researcher being silenced for violating tradition—lionized Galileo, and his persona assumed a more mythic and representative character. Indeed, we are inclined to forget the pious man, father of two Roman Catholic nuns, who framed his investigations as attempts to better understand the nature of God:

> This I hold to be necessary and proper to the same extent that divine wisdom surpasses all human judgment and conjecture. But I do not feel obliged to believe that that same God who has endowed us with senses, reason, and intellect has intended to forgo their use and by some other means to give us knowledge which we can attain by them.[9]

Biblical literalists are the modern-day equivalent of the intransigent, inflexibly rigid, and outmoded bureaucracy that silenced Galileo.

Even the Church realized their error: In 1718, Galileo's works were printed with papal approval; in 1758, his works were lifted from the *Index of Prohibited Books;* in 1835, the last traces of institutional opposition to heliocentrism was dropped; in 1939, Pope Pius XII described him as a great researcher; in 1990, Pope John Paul II expressed regret over the Church's role in the censorship; and in 2008, Pope Benedict XVI formally apologized.

On the issue of biblical inerrancy—the notion that the Bible must be free from error—I am somewhat less critical. Literalism should not be conflated with inerrancy, though they are related concepts. While literalism takes Scripture both as literally factual and as truthful, inerrancy really only insists upon the latter. Biblical inerrancy—a step away from literalism in the right direction—still allows for a notion of truth to guide our reading. On the one hand, I would never accuse biblical authors of lying or dissimulating in an intentionally deceptive way. Rather, these authors were exponents of their own cultural moment and, accordingly, subject to the prevailing norms and controlling mentalities of their eras. On the other hand, the Bible, as mentioned above, does contain certain factual inaccuracies that render problematic the inerrantist's position if one adopts too narrow a definition of error.

Pope Paul VI summed up the post–Vatican II Catholic perspective on biblical inerrancy in 1965, when his encyclical *Dei Verbum* was promulgated. Because Scripture was inspired by the Holy Spirit, according to the encyclical, therefore "it follows that the books of Scripture must be acknowledged as teaching solidly, faithfully, and without error that truth which God wanted put into sacred writings for the sake of salvation (Chapter III, §. 11). The late Daniel Harrington, a Jesuit and professor of theology at Boston College, maintains that [this] statement suggests that the Bible's inerrancy consists primarily in its being a trustworthy guide on the road to salvation."[10] This inerrancy, then, is not a defensive posture, but rather a positive inerrancy that indicates the direction and appropriate application of Scripture. Scripture, then, is squarely focused on truth—especially as this truth relates to our relationship with God, namely the possibility and process of salvation. Scripture is not concerned with facts—at least according to the contemporary definition of that term.

The Bible can err in fact, but, I contend, it does not err in truth. Though we would never hold a memoir to the strict rules of fact, we understand the author's view of truth. Likewise, we cannot let a focus on facts interfere with understanding the truth contained in the experiences related by Scripture. Ultimately, Scripture is concerned with conveying the truth about experiences of God and wholly unconcerned about science or history. The authors of the Bible composed their works in history, and even though Scripture is inspired, that historical contingency leaves an impression on the finished product.

The authors of Scripture were clearly conveying—or seeking to convey—an experience that profoundly transformed them, and it is incumbent upon the reader of Scripture to recognize these transformative experiences. And, naturally, the ways in which they expressed these experiences accorded with the conventions of storytelling and written intercourse available to them at their cultural moment. We are used to this in other writings. The two Greek "Fathers of History," Herodotus and Thucydides assume different criteria for inclusion of material in their respective *Histories.* Or consider the choices made by Shakespeare when writing his historical plays. None of these examples would pass as scholarly history according to the definition of the modern, professional academy. But we understand that they convey both history and truth in various measures. Why would we think the biblical authors' understanding of how to tell a story that conveys their message in the most effective way possible would accord in any way, shape, or form with our notion of fact? And so, I think it's useful to question what we mean by truth, falsehood, fact, and fiction.

Were you to ask any average Christian whether there is fiction in the Bible, my suspicion is that too many would answer, "No." Fiction, because of a strong cultural association with it being "false," doesn't seem at home in the biblical paradigm of storytelling. But there is not one among those Christians who would take any of Jesus's thirty-three parables as factual accounts of actual occurrences. No, the parables are useful stories (i.e., fictions). They are didactic fictions. They are fictions that intend to convey a message greater than could be accommodated by the vehicle of fact. And Jesus himself gives us a hermeneutic for reading and ruminating on these extended analogies. "Why do you speak to the people in parables?" his disciples asked.

> The knowledge of the secrets of the kingdom of heaven has been given to you, but not to them. Whoever has will be given more, and he will have an abundance. Whoever does not have, even what he has will be taken from him. This is why I speak to them in parables: Though seeing, they do not see; though hearing, they do not hear or understand. (Matthew 13:10–13)

Allegory, then, was Jesus's preferred mode of teaching. Why should we assume that the authors of Genesis were any less allegorical or any less analogical when describing the creation of the world? Rather, it seems to be altogether most likely that those who treat creation and biblical cosmology literally are those who see and do not see and hear but do not hear, because they fail to understand the teaching conventions of the time.

Toward an Interpretive Strategy

So, how ought we to interpret the Scriptures? What's at stake? What's right and what's wrong from an interpretive perspective? First, I think we need to do away with the all-too-blithe equation of fact and correctness. There are, I contend, truths that far outstrip fact, which itself is a rather impoverished quantity. In a Western framework, we are accustomed to think about things in dualities: something is either right or wrong, full or empty, and so on. We are trained and educated to revere fact in the same way that we are trained and educated to arrive at the right answer, which is itself the answer best supported by the facts. It is not hard to imagine, however, something that is true but not factual. A poem conveys truth. Paintings convey truth. And yet the experience of these works of art is so subjective and experientially contingent as to resist easy distillation into fact. To be sure, these may have factual elements, but their truth is contingent on their circumstance and their situation. Truth is multipolar and relational. Fact is impersonal, singular, and intransigent.

Now, when reading Scripture, it can be challenging to uncover these core universal truths, communicated as they are through a particular idiom. Moreover, the collective understanding of these truths is subject to change in time. For example, most people are struck by what has become the stereotypical Old Testament God—that vengeful, spiteful figure, seemingly overeager to beset creation with cataclysm. In contrast, the common image of the New Testament God is one who "so loved the world, as to give his only begotten Son; that whosoever believeth in him, may not perish, but may have life everlasting" (John 3:16). Now, did God really change over time, or did our individual and collective experience and awareness of God evolve over time, as any good relationship will?

Clearly, the breakdown between an Old Testament God who is vengeful and a loving New Testament God is specious. After all, the Old Testament opens with a God who loves creation (in Genesis, God declares it to be "good" a number of times), and, though the writers of the Old Testament do communicate God's vengeance, a careful reading reveals a God constantly reaching out to people in love.

It is not surprising that the early authors of Scripture, whose experience is grounded in a world of uncertainty, would find it difficult to communicate clearly their shocking experiences of a God of love. After all, across most cultures, early civilizations' experience of reality often produced stories of gods who were somewhat arbitrary and potentially vengeful. This collective experience would color the early Hebrews' experience of a fullness of reality, the "I AM" revealed to Moses that desired relationship with people.

As the individual and collective experience of a loving God grew, the message of God as love would be clarified in the Scriptures, producing a work that mirrored the experience of the people. A work that moved in fits and spurts from the common experience of uncertainty to the common experience of relationship. In other words, Scripture is the ultimate romantic comedy in which God, the ever faithful lover, is constantly being thwarted in every attempt at a deeper relationship with us, the incompetent lover, by our blindness, clumsiness, and inability to understand what is really going on!

Second, and related to the first point, I think we have to understand Scripture as historically constructed. Scripture must, by necessity, bear the marks of its historical construction. And the markers of construction may not occur only in the realm of genre (i.e., the way in which a story is told), or in the realm of authorial intention (i.e., what the author hoped to convey)—they are found in the ideological underpinning that can be gleaned only obliquely by viewing the author's perspective.

A geocentric cosmology is one example; a discomfort with kings, but a resignation toward their utility, is another (Judges and 1 and 2 Kings). Sometimes there is even the projection of elements of the author's current time into past situations.

In February 2014, the *New York Times* published an article summarizing recent archaeological discoveries using radiocarbon dating that placed the earliest introduction of camels to the Levant at around the tenth century B.C., centuries after the patriarchs and decades after David. But recall, according to Scripture, the patriarchs, their wives, and the early Israelites had full access to camels. If one is deeply concerned about facts, the apparent contradiction between archaeology and the Bible might cause problems. The fact is that the early parts of the Bible were written long after the events they purport to convey. Only by frankly dealing with this fact can we understand the presence of camels in the early stories. The author simply decorated his account of Abraham's world with elements of his own world. But the camels, of course, are not the relevant part of the story. Embedded within this narrative is a timeless truth, and the authors are attempting to share that truth using the intellectual tools they have at their disposal.

The ways in which we interpret Scripture, too, are historically bound. My uncle is a chemistry professor at Texas Tech, and he shared a story with me regarding a minister he knew. The minister maintained that the Genesis account of the Fall of Adam must be historically true; otherwise, there would be no reason for the redemptive sacrifice of Christ. But even this idea—as foundational as it may appear to be in Western Christian theology—is not communicated by Scripture itself. Original sin, the theological defense for Christ's sacrifice, is the historically contingent product of a fourth-century North African cleric, St. Augustine. Augustine bequeathed to us his notion of original sin, but not even he requires a literal interpretation of Genesis. St. Augustine himself wrote a treatise warning against the dangers of taking Genesis literally when it clearly contradicts known science.

Biblical literalism, in its modern guise, dates back to the nineteenth century. Martin Luther, John Calvin, and others were avowedly not literalists. I would suggest that scriptural literalists adopted their strict reading of the Bible in response to a fear that scientific facts would require a rejection of essential truths in their faith. But, I would also suggest that this fear is the result of a misunderstanding of what science can and cannot do, and resulted in demanding of Scripture, particularly the Genesis accounts, more than their original intent can support.

Finally, I think we must embrace the Scriptures for the truths they contain, rather than for the facts they do not. If fact is a problem for literalists, and I believe that it is, then truth is their solution. And in order to understand this truth, we must be both sensitive to the presence of allegory and cognizant of the power of myth. Jesus himself taught by means of analogy; who are we to press his truths into clumsy fact—a quantity more at home in our world than in his? To be sure, fact, in this case, limits the interpretation of the Bible and causes not only logical but also rational problems. It is incumbent upon persons of faith to understand their Scriptures as vehicles provisioned to convey the most profound of truths—not the simple, uncritical facts we deal with in our quotidian experience.

As ponderous as the Bible may be, we ask too much of it, I think, to suppose that it will bear fact according to our desires. It speaks in its own idiom of truth. Like the great fantasy epics of the twentieth and twenty-first centuries—J.R.R. Tolkien's *The Lord of the Rings*, C.S. Lewis's *The Lion, the Witch and the Wardrobe*, and J.K. Rowling's *Harry Potter*, to name a few (Christian allegories, all)—we must allow the Bible to speak to us its own truths according to its vernacular mode. To encumber it with fact and to freight it with objective reality asks of it too much and misplaces the authors' concerns for storytelling with our insatiable thirst for certainty.

Conclusion

I remember when my youngest brother, David, was born. My mother and my father called the three older kids—my sister, Elizabeth, my brother Peter, and me—into the dining room. My mother announced, calmly, evenly, that David had Down syndrome, and she explained what that meant. Elizabeth, Peter, and I were permitted to ask questions about David's syndrome and about how life would be—both for him and for us.

The exact words used by each person vary according to whom you ask. But we all agree on the substance of our answers. Each of these reactions fit our personality. The facts of the story change depending on the teller, but the truth of the story remains true for each of us. I, being the most academic of the three older kids, wanted to know how he would learn; I wanted to understand the mechanism behind his syndrome. Elizabeth, being the most protective of the three older kids, preemptively threatened to physically accost anyone who ridiculed him. Peter, being the pragmatist among us, maintained that there was no problem because there was no negative impact.

Now, my mother tells this story differently from any of us—and even David has a version of it (despite the fact he was a newborn). And while the attributed quotations and exact verbiages vary with the teller, each account of the story features the core personalities that participated in the event. The facts are contestable and, in truth, irrelevant; the truth of our reactions, however, is not. Truth, to my mind, is much more potent than fact. If we were so inclined, we could squabble over the precise phrasing, or we could belabor boring points about actuality. Instead, we are content that the truth of the matter is the same for each of us. We can adorn our truth with any facts we like, but it is truth that binds our accounts together.

Chapter 4

In Principio Creavit Deus: Scriptural and Scientific Narratives of Becoming

In the beginning God created heaven and earth. And the earth was void and empty, and darkness was upon the face of the deep; and the spirit of God moved over the waters.

—Genesis 1:1–2

I beseech thee, my son, look upon heaven and earth, and all that is in them: and consider that God made them out of nothing, and mankind also.

—2 Maccabees 7:28

In the beginning was the Word, and the Word was with God, and the Word was God. The same was in the beginning with God. All things were made by him: and without him was made nothing that was made.

—John 1:1–3

"C'mon, hon. Just imagine it!"

"But Dad, it's ridiculous! It's not even a likely scenario."

"So use your imagination. That's what metaphors are all about." I had agreed, with no small amount of pleasant coercion, to serve as a cate-chist at my local parish, Saint Elizabeth Ann Seton Parish, here in Irvine, California. "You can teach," they said. "You teach college physics," they said. "Teaching ought to be a cakewalk," they said. I can say now, teaching fact is much easier than teaching truth.

My daughter Kimberly was a very bright eleven-year-old, and she was to be my guinea pig. After all, it was for her sake that I had agreed to serve in this capacity. On the dinner table between us were my catechal materials, graciously provided in case I misspoke—even teachers need a crib sheet occasionally. The materials asked me to present the students with a simplified proof for the existence of God. This proof, as I found out later, has its intellectual heritage in *teleological* arguments, also called arguments by design, for God's existence. An example of a teleological argument that has been made popular in this day and age by proponents of Intelligent Design is the classic analogy to a watchmaker, first made by the eighteenth-century philosopher William Paley. Essentially, the argument states that just as the design exhibited by a watch clearly implies a watchmaker, the design exhibited by the world implies a Creator God.

More broadly, the teleological argument is an example of *a posteriori* reasoning—knowledge or justification dependent on empirical experience. This argument is one of the *quinque viae*—five proofs for the existence of God—offered by St. Thomas Aquinas (d. 1274) in his *Summa Theologiae* (1265). This argument begins by asserting that all natural objects obey laws and behave in accordance to rules of conduct. This behavior is true even of objects that do not possess intelligence. A rock dropped from the roof of a five-story building will accelerate at 9.81 m/s^2; this is not a decision made on the part of the rock but is instead a natural force to which the rock is subject. Aquinas then argues that laws of conduct—such as the gravitational force of earth—are indicative of intelligence. Therefore, we must posit an intelligent designer that set in place the physical laws that govern bodies. This designer, according to Aquinas, we call God. The idea behind this argument is that we can observe God in the very details of existence and conclude that God exists.

We are all familiar with some variety of the deistic notion of the watchmaker god, who sets the world into motion and then refrains from worldly interference. As Voltaire (d. 1778) eloquently framed it in 1772: "The universe troubles me, and much less can I think / That this clock exists and should have no clockmaker." This argument suggests that, logically, the universe requires the existence of a creator, but that the physical laws imposed by this creator are sufficient to ensure the smooth running of the universe. The universe requires minimal intervention, apart from creation, but cannot have come into existence except by God's agency.

I had decided to offer to my students a simplified version of the proof of a creator. I decided to ask my students to imagine coming upon an oven in the woods with chocolate-chip cookies baking inside. I reasoned that most students have had the experience of baking cookies at home. Indeed, over the past six years that I have served as a youth ministry volunteer, many of my students have been able to offer specifics about the process. Most students will recognize elements of the process (combining eggs, sugar, flour, butter, salt—if you're doing it right—and the chocolate chips), and most students will recognize the intelligent application of heat as the key to the process of transformation from dough to cookie. But—and I think this comes as a surprise to some students—the existence of baking cookies suggests the presence and agency of a baker.

"So, just imagine it," I continued. "What would you do if you came across an oven full of cookies baking in the woods?" I was waffling even though I was talking about cookies.

"OK, so if I saw some mystery oven in the woods with cookies? What type of cookies?"

"Any type of cookies. I don't know...chocolate chip." Now she was being clever. My teaching experience had braced me with the Socratic method; they had drilled me with the constructivist approach to teaching; they had made sure I knew my showmanship and could summon it at will. They did not, however, prepare me to teach to my daughter the finer points of our faith in our dining room. One can't learn motorcycle maintenance without an engine block in front of them.

"I guess if I saw mystery cookies, I'd have to wonder how they got there..."

"...right..."

"...and whether or not I should eat them."

"...and, for the record, you shouldn't..."

"But, I guess, I'd have to think that there was a baker..."

"Yes!"

But my daughter was right; I feel that both this simplified version and the original proof of God's existence fall short. They are reasonable, but I have never felt confident in them as strict proofs. Recently, I realized that my problem was less with the proof than with the image of creator assumed by the proof. When asking my students to imagine creator-creation binaries, I generally receive similar lists: chairs and carpenters, or a painting and an artist. Some enterprising young souls will even get as abstract as an automobile and an engineer. Or an advertisement and a copywriter. Or an iPod and Steve Jobs.

But, as often happens when you teach, I wound up pushing the boundaries of my own comprehension. In asking children about their images of creators, I realized the power of an alternative metaphor for a creator: an expectant mother with a child in the womb. You see, all these other images, when translated into metaphors for the creator—including the creator of my simplified cookie proof—are predicated on what I will call the artisanal model of creation: that the creator creates a creation wholly separate and distinct from the creator himself. I believe that the artisanal model treats as natural, ordered, and right the notion that creator and created must be distinct quantities. In contrast, our own tradition teaches us that God is the fullness of reality, and therefore, creation can no more be separate from God, the creator, than the fetus in the womb is separate from the mother.

With this realization, my mind immediately flicked to my wife, Jeni, and our three daughters, Kimberly, Melissa, and Rachel. The fortunate among us who have had the experience of anticipating parenthood will recognize the awesome power of the image of a mother and a child in the womb. The worry, the joy, the trepidation, the celebration, the planning, the executing—all are part and parcel to the emotional conundrum of pregnancy. It is magic—emotionally, spiritually, and physically; your unborn child seems to materialize as if by some divine mystery as its nine-month home begins to swell. To be sure, we understand quite a bit about the biological, chemical, and physical processes of pregnancy, but even our cold, sterile science does nothing to subvert the ineffable richness of this experience. I have never been more totally convinced and entirely convicted of the existence of a loving, providential creator than when prompted by seeing my smiling, expecting wife.

While I was writing this book, I was invited to speak at the Diocese of Orange on sciences and faith. It was here that I unveiled this metaphor as a robust explanatory model. My whole family was there to see me speak—including Kimberly. After a series of penetrating questions from the audience, the panel broke to applause. Out of the corner of my eye, I saw my daughter approach me. "Dad, it all makes so much more sense now."

"Better than the cookies?"

"Better than the cookies."

The metaphor is a tidy one; God—the mother here—is everything. And all creation—the fetus here—depends on God. The child would not and could not exist without the mother; the mother is fully invested, active, and engaged—even if just on a physical level—in the growth of this fetus. This child is fully integrated as part of the mother, even though it exists as a notionally independent entity. It is created in the image of the mother—even on a genetic level. But—and this is crucial—the child is physically integrated while still being functionally separate. The baby is not a full human—at least not yet; it is not fully conscious. It is unable to exercise its own will. It is quite confined in its uterine home. But there is a demarcation between the individual that will become the newborn and the mother. Even so, for nine incredible months, the mother and the unborn child are a universal system; they exist in a cosmic and existential symbiosis.

Now, imagine you were inside this child doing experiments as it was growing in the mother's womb. I contend that there is essentially no experiment you can do that is the analogue of a scientific, physical experiment that would tell you that there was a mother there. You would discover the laws of biology, chemistry, and physics. You would have to contend with the fact that your universe—the baby—was expanding rapidly. You might wonder where this material was coming from; you might send manned spacecraft (wombcraft?) to investigate; you might even find the umbilical cord and follow it to the placenta, but nothing about this enterprise would determine conclusively the existence or nonexistence of the mother. Your universe, such as it is, would be that child, and no inductive, experimental strategy could result conclusively in an argument for or against the existence of that mother. The child is your empirical, perceptual reality; the mother, though, is the fullness of that reality.

Our science is much the same way. On the one hand, some will say that science explains creation without necessary recourse to an agentive creator. We've figured out predictive mechanisms that work within our perceptible purview, so why do you need God? On the other hand, some will maintain that they've read and learned God is the creator, and they feel an anxiety about squaring that received knowledge and the knowledge provided by the sciences. One cause of this consternation, I believe, derives from our limited view of creator.

Our usual choices for creator models are the abject lack of a creator, or a type of superbeing that magically zaps the universe into existence. We have very limited vocabulary to speak about (let alone understand) the creation of things that are intimately part of ourselves, which I contend is exactly what God—as the fullness of reality—created. However, if we limit our understanding of creators and their creations to the traditional image of the baker, the carpenter, the artist, the engineer, the copywriter, or Steve Jobs—all of these people who create consumables outside of themselves—we fail to appreciate and fail to apprehend important elements of God's creation.

I encourage us to mediate on this metaphor, because according to an analogy such as this one—one that allows God to exist as the fullness of reality—we mutually accommodate both transcendent reality and observable reality. We must distance ourselves from the idea that creation was a process of production in an external, objective sense. Creation was not the production of items and beings of this world by a being outside of this world. Only then can we see how creation according to the sciences fits snugly with our biblical accounts of creation and creator.

Now, it may scandalize some—though, I know, not all—to suggest a feminine aspect to the creator. But as we consider metaphors and images for God, it is helpful to recognize, I think, that any image of God that is exclusively masculine limits God overmuch and does not appreciate God's actual position as the fullness of reality. God is beyond sex, and God is beyond gender.

The *Catechism of the Catholic Church* states, "God's parental tenderness can also be expressed by the image of motherhood, which emphasizes God's immanence, the intimacy between Creator and creature" (239). Moreover, we see in Scripture (Matthew 23:37) that Jesus himself self-identifies using maternal imagery: "Jerusalem, Jerusalem, you who kills the prophets, and stones them that are sent unto you, how often would I have gathered together thy children, as the hen gathers her chickens under her wings, and you would not?"

St. Paul also understands his vocation in the maternal sense when he writes to the Galatians, "My little children, of whom I am in labor again, until Christ be formed in you" (4:19). This maternal metaphor has an ancient antecedent in the Old Testament (Numbers 11:12), when Moses describes his task to God, "Have I conceived all this multitude, or begotten them, that you should say to me: Carry them in your bosom as the nurse is wont to carry the little infant, and bear them into the land, for which you have sworn to their fathers?"

The maternal metaphor of mother and child is, to my mind, rich and textured enough to occasion and to sustain deep contemplation. I would like to extend it to the role of the creator. There is an appreciably different creative sense implied by the maternal model when compared to the artisanal model. The latter, I contend, limits God's agency to the moment of creation, while the former allows for sustained and interested engagement with creation. The maternal model thereby suggests a more powerful, compassionate God. Also, perhaps ironically, the maternal model is the model that best fits the process of creation as suggested by the sciences. Of course, as with all metaphors, it is critical to not treat the mother-child image literally; no metaphor can accord with all aspects of our understanding of either physical reality or God. But I propose it all the same because I believe it is one of the best creator-created metaphors for God and physical reality that we have at our disposal.

Creation Science (No, Not That Kind...)

I think it is useful here to think about what we mean when we say matter, nature, and creation. Matter, a structural component of the universe, which has both mass and volume, is a substance made up of particles. The word itself descends from Middle English mater, which in turn was derived from Old French, materie, by way of Anglo-Norman, and ultimately originates in the Latin word materia. Materia, it may be unsurprising, is related by derivation from the word mater; meaning "mother," but used in the sense of source. Therefore, matter, in our sense, is derived from a word for mother, which is surprisingly suggestive of my maternal model.

Nature, or, that which preexists human craft, intervention, and design, is an elastic concept that can encompass all biological, chemical, and physical states, processes, and events in the universe. The word itself descends from Middle English *natur*, which in turn derives from Old French *nature*, and from Latin *natura*. *Natura* is an adjective formed from the future active participle from the verb *nator, nasci,* a verb meaning "to be born." Like our English phrase *to be born,* the Latin verb is, in a sense, defective; like English speakers, Latin speakers could conjugate the verb only in the passive voice: one could only "be born," one could not "born." (This is the same in English, in which we furnish the active sense by using other verbs, such as "to bear," "to birth," or "to have children," etc.) Therefore, nature, in our sense, is derived from a verbal idea for making a person into a mother, which, again, is suggestive of my maternal model.

Creation, or, that which is the product of an agent, who stewarded the item into being, is a nominalization of the verb "to create," which denotes an agent causing something to be put into existence. The word itself descends from Old French *creation,* and ultimately from Latin *creatio. Creatio* is in turn an abstract nominalization of the verb *creo, creare,* meaning "to make grow." This word is of ancient origin and finds cognates in other ancient languages: Old Armenian ծնանիմ, "to be born"; Attic Greek κόρη), "a girl"; and, perhaps most tellingly, in the name of the Roman goddess Ceres, the goddess of agricultural harvest. Therefore, even creation, in our sense, descends from a word with an originally feminine ambit.

While grammatical gender is a poor indicator of perceptual gender, in Latin, all three of these nouns are of the feminine gender—a sparkling and effervescent coincidence. These etymological explorations serve to underpin my maternal metaphor. When we speak of the creation of matter in nature, we are using three terminologies that are most at home in a female, generative sense.

I encourage us to view God's creative capacity as one of integrated generation. That is, if we can accept God as the fullness of reality, and if what God created was physical reality, then there must exist some sort of sustained relationship between the creator and the created. Also, we see that physical reality comes out of no thing—in other words, it is creation ex nihilo, creation of matter from nothing. This is because physical reality, in the view I propose, does not come from an initial physical state, but a state that explicitly has physical reality absent—a great definition of nothing. In contrast, a more artisanal model of a creator suggests creation of one physical entity by and from other physical entities. Conveniently, the sciences support and accommodate my proposed maternal image and creation ex nihilo. As we will see, science even has its own sense in which the nothing from which physical reality emerges is actually something (the vacuum state), just as in my proposed image of God, the nothing before creation is also something, just not anything physical!

From our maternal metaphor for God, nothing is the emptiness of the womb, which itself is immanent to, or intimately within, the creator. Creation itself is immanent to God (the child within the womb) and continues to transpire instead of being a discrete, finite event. We shall see below that this is exactly the type of creator that Scripture and exegesis would suggest.

We in the sciences are quite comfortable with the notion of ex nihilo creation. To understand why, we need to look at how science treats creation. First, physics can identify the processes by which the current structures in the universe have formed out of the initial state of the universe. We start with the origins of physical reality approximately fourteen billion years ago. To get to the beginning, we trace history backward by looking at the far reaches of the universe. Because light travels at a finite speed, when we look at great distances we are looking at light that started traveling in the distant past. The farther away we look, the further into the past we are observing. Then, using predictions from a range of disciplines—including quantum mechanics and general relativity—we can calculate the state of the universe at extremely early times.

Following these calculations to their natural conclusion, we find that there is a point in the far past where we expect the universe to consist of an infinite density of matter, what is known as a singular point or singularity. This singular point is now called the Big Bang. We declare this point the birth of the universe. From this singular point, the universe came into being so quickly that it is difficult to comprehend the rate. Starting after the first 10^{-36} seconds and lasting until 10^{-33} or 10^{-32} seconds—the time frame known as the inflationary epoch—the universe expanded at least by a factor of 10^{50}. Therefore, assuming 10^{-32} seconds to create a universe, if I held a flashlight perfectly vertical and turned it on, by the time the light from it hit my roof, approximately 10^{24} universes could have been created.

The rapid expansion of the universe caused an equally rapid decrease in density and temperature. Though we have good models of inflation, the exact details are still unclear. However, within about 0.000000000001 seconds after the Big Bang, we are significantly more confident in the predictions that physics makes. Just a few minutes after this event, the ambient temperature of the universe was one billion degrees Kelvin. After about three hundred and eighty thousand years (a mere blink of the cosmic eye), conditions cooled enough for radiation to decouple from matter, which existed mostly in the form of stable hydrogen atoms. After a few billion years of steady expansion, the expanding universe began to accelerate. We do not know why, exactly, such should be the case, but the most likely candidate for driving this accelerating expansion is so-called dark energy. We know dark energy exists from its effects on the expansion of the universe. We understand how it acts like a pressure force that opposes gravity, but what, exactly, dark energy is remains one of the great mysteries of science going forward in the twenty-first century.

This moment of creation, from an incomprehensibly dense singularity, is indeed dramatic. And it accords perfectly with the theological perspective of ex nihilo creation. Explaining exactly how this happened, however, is one of the contemporary challenges of modern physics. One problem is that within this gravitational singularity, both general relativity and quantum mechanics would be required for making predictions. Within our current understanding of the universe, space and time are objects themselves that have a dynamic structure. They bend and curve, stretch and expand, shrink and compress. Imagine, if you will, space as a sheet of rubber, and you will have a reasonable picture for our current understanding of space and time. General relativity is the theory we use to describe these dynamics of space and time, and it becomes particularly important as space shrinks in size and becomes the initial singularity.

Now, the term *singularity* ought to suggest something very small, and there is no doubt that at and near the singularity of space and time, everything was indeed very small. Therefore, quantum mechanics is necessary for any discussion of the creation of the universe. But, for a variety of reasons, quantum mechanics and general relativity are two theories that are essentially incompatible, and so far we have failed to use quantum mechanics to make detailed predictions about the earliest stages of the universe. But the lack of detailed predictions does not prevent us from making decent guesses, given our robust, though lamentably separate, understandings of quantum mechanics and relativity.

From the perspective of quantum mechanics, the state without a universe (nothing) is described as a vacuum state. Now, before going any deeper into what the vacuum state really is and our ruminations on quantum mechanics and relativity, it is important to recall the two-cookie rule discussed in chapter zero. Your intuition may fail as you read my descriptions of the physics, because the physics is very nonintuitive. But you can trust to a large degree in the literal images the words evoke and take this as reality. And then, as your interest in the subject is piqued, I encourage you to continue exploring these concepts with additional reading and discussion, and by doing so, slowly increase your intuitive understanding of these ideas.

In physics, the vacuum is a way to describe the lowest energy state of a system. In a very real sense, a vacuum is the state of there being nothing. However, within the context of quantum mechanics, this nothing can fluctuate. Applying this idea to space and time itself, it is reasonable to expect that these fluctuations can spontaneously create bubbles of space and time that start as incredibly small, dense regions of space, and then expand. These bubbles, we think, appear, for all intents and purposes, ex nihilo. Understanding the creation of these space-time bubbles (and the corresponding creation of matter and energy in the process) from nothing is deeply connected to developing an understanding of how quantum mechanics and relativity are connected. Therefore, it is a very exciting area of current research.

But, to be sure, we do not know how quantum mechanics and relativity work with each other—yet. And, accordingly, we do not have a detailed model of the creation of the singularity. But we know that this singularity existed and that some catastrophic creation event occurred. We have two methods for exploring this event, namely mathematical models and observational evidence. Mathematical models allow us to apply current knowledge to the past and provide a logical argument for creation through a space-time singularity. As our telescopes continue to improve, the observational evidence for a singular catastrophic event only increases.

The underlying mathematical model for the evolution of space and time is general relativity. It is able to describe a universe in which the very fabric of space itself can expand or contract. One of the best examples for this is to imagine our universe as a two-dimensional sheet. One of the questions for cosmologists—those physicists who study the evolution of the universe—is whether or not our universe is best described as a flat sheet (open universe) or the surface of a balloon (closed universe). The most compelling evidence seems to suggest that the universe is flat and expanding forever. Modeling the structure of matter in the universe now and tracing the processes described by general relativity back through time, both suggest strongly a point at which our models cease to generate predictive results—a singularity. There is the Big Bang. Understanding the nature of singularities, like the Big Bang, is one of the areas where Stephen Hawking and other cosmologists focus significant effort.

Through extremely high-powered telescopes, we can observe faraway bodies in space. These are the experiments of cosmology. Many of these celestial bodies are millions and billions of light-years away; in some cases we are seeing light that is more ancient than the earth itself. As these objects move either toward us or away from us, the hue of their light changes due to the Doppler effect. It's the same principle that allows you to observe when a fire engine passes you: first, as the engine approaches you, the siren is higher pitched; as it passes you the tone evens; as it moves farther away, the pitch descends. Now, when we talk about the pitch of the sound, what we are referring to is its frequency; when we talk about the color of light, what we are referring to is its frequency. And, just as with sound, the frequency of light shifts—relative to a stationary point—when it is emitted by moving objects.

For light, low frequencies are red (i.e., infrared) and high frequencies are blue (i.e., ultraviolet). If something is what we call redshifted, that means it's moving away from us, and the frequency of the light is decreasing. The majority of these heavenly bodies are redshifting, indicating that the universe is expanding. An expanding universe would suggest an initial stationary point of origin, and there is your singularity. But, really, there are many other astronomical observations that, when taken together, point strongly to an expanding universe that began with the Big Bang.

This mechanism is the definition of ex nihilo creation; in fact, in 1951 Pope Pius XII declared that there was no obstacle in accepting the Big Bang theory of creation.

The idea of a Big Bang also accords neatly with immanence—creation from within God. The cutting edge of theoretical physics suggests that spontaneous generation may not necessarily be confined to singular events such as the Big Bang. Consider a vacuum. In physics, the vacuum state refers to the lowest energy of a system under consideration. When we think of the universe, the system under consideration is space-time itself. Space-time is the merging of space and time, which, in the context of physics, are a single quantity—the very fabric of our universe.

One of Einstein's greatest contributions was recognizing that the best way to describe motion is to combine the three dimensions of Euclidean space with time. We are perfectly comfortable with the fact that directionality (e.g., up-down, right-left, and front-back) can mix relative to the observer. If I stand facing north, I will describe east as being to the right and west being to the left. If you stand facing east, you will disagree and tell me that south is to the right and north is to the left. Because we are used to these situations, we know that this is just a matter of our relative point of view, and we know how to translate between these two perspectives.

Time and space can be mixed just like the different directions of space. In our example, we mixed directions in space by rotating the body. To notice the mixing of space and time, however, you need to be traveling close to the speed of light—a situation, I reckon, patently unfamiliar to many of us! But our global positioning systems only work properly because they correctly account for this mixture. It is only when we understand that space-time is a single structure that we begin to understand ex nihilo creation.

The second piece in understanding ex nihilo creation is our current view of the vacuum state based on quantum mechanics. We physicists use the tools of quantum mechanics to peer into the smallest scales of physical behavior, but it also appears to be the fundamental way the universe operates. So, even though we do not yet have a complete quantum mechanical theory of space-time, we expect the basic features of quantum mechanics to apply even to space-time. We have already alluded to one consequence of this: space-time can fluctuate. To get a better understanding of this, it is worth exploring the concept of a vacuum state in more detail.

At its core, the vacuum in physics is what you expect—a state devoid of stuff. But it differs from our standard definition in that the vacuum is actually a state of constant fluctuation. Though we often think of a vacuum as the definitional absence of anything at all, it is actually the site of enormous creative activity, with pairs of particles constantly fluctuating into existence and nonexistence. We scientists are very confident that key elements of quantum reality are involved in the vacuum that existed before the Big Bang. These quantum fluctuations, as they are named, have been measured, studied, and predicted. For example, experiments have demonstrated that, when two metal plates are placed close together, we can measure attractive forces due to quantum fluctuations. Apropos the Big Bang, it seems that these fluctuations can also result in bubbles of space-time itself.

It helps to imagine the vacuum of nothingness before creation of our universe as a bubbling foam. Think about the surface of the ocean (granted, the surface locks this metaphor into two dimensions, but bear with me). The bubbles on the surface of the ocean are constantly appearing, disappearing, and collapsing back into the ocean. Think also of your soda, which has CO_2 dissolved into it. In a state of equilibrium, you don't see the bubbles, but shake it a little bit and bubbles will appear and pop. In the vacuum state of space-time, we have inherent vacuum energy that creates the fluctuations of space-time. And given the right conditions, one of those bubbles continues to grow instead of collapsing back.

With this, you have the creation of a physical universe from nothing, but also within the nothing it came from.

Now, naturally, not all of these bubbles of the space-time foam are destined to become universes—but some do. Think of the problem of blowing up a balloon at your kid's birthday party. Out of the package, it is stiff and noncompliant. Attempts to blow up the balloon result in it collapsing again. But when you stretch it enough and loosen up the balloon, you get past a certain critical point, and then the balloon inflates just fine. Space-time in a vacuum can fluctuate, but—barring a circumstance called a nucleation event, where a bubble reaches a critical size— most of these fluctuations simply go away. Still, every now and again, you get a bubble that goes beyond the critical size and it starts growing. And now you've generated a physical universe. You've actually generated a piece of space-time.

So we have a new and exciting lead in our investigation of creation. But there are two points to emphasize here. First, creation is immanent—in this case, from within the vacuum. But, when we conceive of God as the fullness of reality—God encompasses the vacuum and creates in an immanent fashion. And, second, that creation continues at the quantum level. This creation is ex nihilo, immanent, and continual. Now, it is a matter of faith to conclude that God encompasses and drives all of this creation; the only thing that exists before the existence of the universe is the fullness of reality in the nonphysical sense, which is God. And this nonphysical sense can, and, therefore, must encompass this idea of the vacuum—the nothing that is actually something.

According to this understanding of the fullness of reality, the sciences do nothing to contradict the idea of a creator, and, indeed, it seems that an integrated creator best satisfies the questions of cosmogony. A long-standing aphorism in physics is that physical laws must be the same everywhere and at all times. That is to say, with all conditions being equal, the speed of light, to use just one example, is a constant that is the same everywhere in the universe. Therefore, we should expect—and indeed we find—that ex nihilo creation was not a discrete event, but, instead, still occurs, albeit on the quantum level.

It is altogether likely that these new directions in physics will lead us to the conclusion that material creation is a natural course of events that happens all the time. But what we can all agree on is that these phenomena transpire in reality, and that, as the fullness of reality, there is an ineffable quality to the spontaneity and design of creation. Were we to call this unknown quantity God, I do not think we would be far from the mark.

Creation and Scripture

We have seen how the sciences support the concept of ex nihilo, immanent, continuous creation. The sciences do not require that an agentive God be responsible for this process, but the sciences do nothing to negate this concept. Indeed, the sciences can give us an indication about how this process occurred on the physical level. So, what does Scripture say about the process of creation? To be sure, Scripture is quite taciturn on the subject of this process—perhaps unexpectedly so.

I do not mean to suggest here that God is, anywhere in Scripture, not described as the author of Creation; God most certainly is. Scriptural authors, though, are not univocal on the nature of God's process. If we were to read Scripture literally, we would have to accept and resolve conflicting accounts that simultaneously maintain that God created ex nihilo and ordered preexisting chaos; we would see a figure that both emanates reality separate from God's reality and in whom reality is immanent; we would see creation as a discrete historical event and as a continual process.

These apparent contradictions are not really a problem. First, we concluded our discussion of the science of creation with the concept of a creation that both initiates creation ex nihilo and remains active by means of *creatio continue*—continual creation. Therefore, God both created ex nihilo and ordered this creation. We should, as I argued in the last chapter, allow Scripture to speak in the allegorical mode in which its authors intended it to be read. Therefore, we should not expect metaphorical consistency over time, and we should not force scriptural consistency to serve as a precondition for faith.

Different interpretations of God's creative process reflect the authors' concerns with specific truths regarding reality and God—and these concerns are determined by the authors' cultural moment. These different accounts do not reflect actual, substantive concerns with the details of the creation process. Therefore, what is important, I think, is to identify the figurative and literary devices scriptural authors employ, as well as the narrative function that these devices were meant to serve. My maternal metaphor satisfies these requirements; it does not dissent from scriptural metaphors, and it does not violate science. What we see from a figurative reading of Scripture is an ex nihilo creator, in whom reality is immanent, and who is in the process of *creatio continua*. None of these propositions conflict in any way with our understanding of creation as provided by the sciences.

It was the church fathers—most especially Irenaeus and Augustine—who first formalized the systemic theological understanding of God as an ex nihilo creator. Irenaeus, in his *Adversus Haereses* (Against Heresies), wrote, "God, in the exercise of his will and pleasure, formed all things... out of what did not previously exist."[11]

Augustine maintains this ex nihilo perspective in *Confessions*. "It was that—in the beginning, and through your wisdom, which is from you and born of your substance—you created something out of nothing."[12] In addition to the first chapter of Genesis, church fathers used a few scriptural supports for ex nihilo creation, such as 2 Maccabees 7:28, John 1:1, Hebrews 11:3, and other similar passages.

There are also Scriptures that support an understanding of God's creation as a process of ordering, pointing to God's continued involvement in creation. Opinions supporting creation ex nihilo departed from earlier, principally Greek beliefs, that matter—called chaos—must have preceded the event of creation, owing to the Aristotelian notion *ex nihilo nihil fit* "nothing is made from nothing." Some use this to point to an ordering that is in place of creation from nothing. Both Justin Martyr, a second-century theologian, and Origen, a third-century theologian, maintained that God's creative capacity simply imposed upon matter order and direction.

Some Scripture would seem to support this view. Isaiah 40:26, for example, says, "Lift up your eyes and look to the heavens: Who created all these? He who brings out the starry host one by one and calls forth each of them by name. Because of his great power and mighty strength, not one of them is missing." The bringing out and calling forth mentioned by the Isaiah author would seem to suggest preexistence, but it does not necessarily have to be interpreted in this way.

Indeed, there is no reason to suggest that creation ex nihilo and the grand-orderer model are mutually exclusive. God, it seems to me, is most likely to have both created and ordered, and, by combining these two creative capacities, we can see that there is no intrinsic conflict between the two scriptural and exegetical understandings of creation. To square this circle, I suggest we view creation as it comes to us in Scripture as a process of fabricative immanence, whereby God both creates reality within and emanates that reality.

A grand-orderer model of Origen and Justin Martyr as a mode of creation has some interesting aspects. It completely depends on how we view the matter being ordered. If matter is truly separate from God, then God is no longer the fullness of reality and less than infinite. This reintroduces the problem of the creator and created as separate. But, if God's ordering is a part of the fullness of reality (say, for instance, the chaotic fluctuations of the vacuum state), then we are back to creation from within God, and really the only difference between ordering and ex nihilo creation is semantic.

The statement that the creation of physical reality takes place within the fullness of reality, which is God, should not be seen as advocating a blithe pantheism here. Quite the contrary: the fact that the fullness of reality is greater than physical reality eliminates pantheism. And the metaphor of child in mother is simply a metaphor. But there is a sense in which creator models that treat creation as an artisanal quantity miss important aspects of creation. And, I contend, only when we are sensitive to the intrinsic nature of God and God's creation can we appreciate the profundity of this relationship.

As Paul writes in Colossians, "For in him were all things created in heaven and on earth, visible and invisible, whether thrones, or dominations, or principalities, or powers: all things were created by Him and in Him" (1:16). The choice of prepositions here is telling. Paul supports my notion of the fullness of reality by arguing for God's transcendence and immanence in the context of creation. Creation is not only "by Him" but also "in Him." Creation, then, is part of the creator.

Physical reality is both immanent in and emanates from the fullness of reality, which encompasses both the physical and nonphysical.

Now, both to fabricate and to make immanent creation would necessarily require a type of *creatio continua*—continual creation—and we see support for this notion in Jeremiah 18:1–6:

> The word which came to Jeremiah from the Lord saying, "Arise and go down to the potter's house, and there I will announce My words to you." Then I went down to the potter's house, and there he was, making something on the wheel. But the vessel that he was making of clay was spoiled in the hand of the potter;

so he remade it into another vessel, as it pleased the potter to make. Then the word of the Lord came to me saying, "Can I not, O house of Israel, deal with you as this potter does?" declares the Lord. "Behold, like the clay in the potter's hand, so are you in My hand, O house of Israel."

We see a similar notion of continued creative agency in Isaiah 29:16:

This thought of yours is perverse: as if the clay should think against the potter, and the work should say to the maker thereof: "You did not make me": or the thing framed should say to him that fashioned it, "You do not understand."

God, then, creates in clay; the potter must form the clay incrementally, building the structure slowly and according to a design. Both the Jeremiah author and the Isaiah author suggest this type of processual creation.

One might make the argument that these passages would seem to stand in contrast to Genesis 2:3, which relates that when God rests on the seventh day, God completes creation, thus consecrating the Sabbath. We see there is an apparent tension between a finite, discrete, historical event and creation envisioned as processual. But again, I would encourage us to understand that these visions need not exclude one another, and, indeed, are enhanced by one another. Continual creation, such as we see from the sciences, does not militate against a discrete initial point, nor does momentary, spontaneous creation need to be a contained, reducible event.

Creation, according to Scripture, should and must be viewed as the allegory that it is. So, what does an allegorical reading of creation Scripture suggest to us about the points the authors want to convey? Turning to the Genesis creation narrative, we see that after each of the days of creation, God considers God's day's work to be "good" (or even "very good"). What does "good" mean? Is it a moral evaluation? Is it a reflection on the nature of this creation?

I contend that part of the goodness of creation is its unique ability to support positive assertion. Reality is the only quantity that can support empirical, quantitative experience, and therefore, it is the only feature of creation that can sustain qualitative consideration of its goodness. We can pose questions about reality, and we can gather positive proof from our experience of it. That is some of the goodness God saw in the Genesis metaphor. Creation is both explicable and sensible, and therefore, in God's estimation, good.

We also get a sense of God's relationship to creation from the creation narratives. God's estimation of creation as good suggests that God positively regards this creation; the author of John famously writes, "For God so loved the world, as to give his only begotten Son; that whosoever believeth in him, may not perish, but may have life everlasting" (3:16). In light of the Gospel, the Genesis author—in deeming God's estimation of creation as good—is conveying a sense of love and positive regard.

That's an important point, I think. The infinite considers the finite worthy of a relationship, which is wholly without necessity or predication on merit. Who are we to expect God's love? But we receive it still, owing to the nature of reality as God's creation.

Consequently, because of this love, we get a sense that God wants to cultivate a relationship with us. It is only after humans are created on the sixth day (according to the first creation narrative in Genesis) that God recognizes creation as very good instead of simply good. There is a sense in which God is attentive to creation and wants the best for it; this optimal status is a relative one, in which proximity to and relationships to God are the highest good.

The nature of this relationship is enhanced further by the understanding of humankind as being created in *imago Dei*—according to the image of God. *Image* is a complex word, and it is no less contestable as we examine the terminology in the various languages of translation. The Biblical Hebrew original is הַנּוּמַת, which means literally *image, sight,* or *visage.* But how is the notion of an image even possible in an aniconic tradition such that biblical Judaism was and modern Judaism is? There is a profound sense in both Kabbalistic literature and Talmudic literature that implies that even the act of seeing something was not an apprehension of reality but a reflection of that reality. The sight of a thing and the thing being seen are dissimilar quantities.

This sense of the word was carried over into Greek by the translators of the Septuagint as εικόνα, literally *likeness* or *image.* Here we seem to be another step of remove from the image as actuality when we consider the meaning of *likeness,* like *resemblance* and *similarity,* this word preserves the non-coterminous nature of object and object referent.

The Vulgate renders this word as *imago,* and this might perhaps be the most etymologically complex and fraught of them all. Originally, *imago* implied a sense of similarity or resemblance; it is cognate with our English word *even* (a word, to be sure, that resists all but intuitive definition). But over the course of development of the Latin language, this word became more elastically applied until it could convey the sense of imitation, apparition, likeness, comparison, conception (in the philosophical sense), semblance, appearance, shadow, echo, statue, representation—all in addition to the word that Modern English derives from Old French, *image.*

What we see in the use of these words is a notion of likeness and similarity, but not a likeness or similarity that would be conflated with the original. So, what is the nature of this likeness? Well, according to Millard J. Erickson, there are three manners of understanding this formulation: the substantive, the relational, and the functional. The substantive mode of understanding suggests that God and people share the capacity for understanding, free will, and reason. Our minds are the *imago Dei.*

The relational mode suggests that God and people share an ability to cultivate a relationship with one another. Perhaps this ability to relate to God is even unique to humans of all species on earth. These relationships are far more complex and intricate than any other between creator and created. The final mode, the functional, means that God and people share the role of stewardship over the earth (whether or not that stewardship is discussed as dominion is another matter altogether). So, we see that the Genesis authors packed a good deal of conceptual freight into a rather concise formulation. But in each of these three manners, the point is that we are to feel special about our relationship to God. That is the thesis of the Genesis author. That is the linchpin of the story.

The biblical stories cannot tell us about the process of creation, but they can tell us about why creation was important to a conception of God as a participant in daily life. Creation allows us to contemplate on our own human importance according to our relationship to the divine. I would imagine that Scripture is equivocating on the question of the process of creation precisely because it was not central to the importance of the matters the authors wished to convey. Really, the stories advanced to describe creation are especially designed to support a sense that God maintained an extraordinary connection to creation. As the fullness of reality, creation is, in fact, a distinct extension of God's own existence. Reality—that is, creation—and the fullness of reality—that is, God—are but degrees. In the process of creating, God created not only the matter to be apprehended but the tools best equipped to decode, make sensible, and communicate about that matter. And God created us, in God's likeness, with the means of apprehending that matter: reason, intuition, and sense.

Conclusion

We see popular heroes who also have these creative capacities, but even these heroes are creating externally. If we break the mold of creator as artisan, we see God as a new type of ultimate superhero. Any Google search of the most powerful superheroes will serve up a list of heroes who channel in energy. To be sure, you have your brawlers (Superman, the Hulk, etc.) and you have your brains (Thanos, Darkseid, Galactus). But, really, the most powerful heroes are those who either conduct or consume energy and then create from that energy. Jean Grey as Phoenix, Green Lantern, Doctor Strange, and Doctor Manhattan are all energy conduits and each have the power to fashion from this energy and create in reality.

Were we to maintain that God is an artisanal creator—rather than the maternal creator I propose—we would have to locate God alongside these fictional heroes. Rather, I suggest we break our mold of creator and allow God to demonstrate the awesome power of actually creating the universe—complete with all the physical laws and natural mechanisms required to sustain it. Thereby, God becomes the ultimate superhero. Anything less would be unduly confining.

Chapter 5

God Changes Times and God Changes Seasons:
The Evolutionary Science of Scripture

There is a time for everything, and a season for every activity under the heavens.

—Ecclesiastes 3:1

An intelligent heart acquires knowledge, and the ear of the wise requires knowledge.

—Proverbs 18:15

The one who conquers will have this heritage, and I will be his God and he will be my son.

—Revelation 21:7

C oventry, Connecticut, is a small hamlet in Tolland County in the northeastern corner of a northeastern state. The birthplace of Revolutionary War hero Nathan Hale, it is a slice of small-town America nestled in the BosWash urban conglomeration—a city, more or less, from Boston to Washington, DC. It, however, remains one of those idyllic places more at home in literature than in reality. Towns just like that one contain the universes of *Leave It to Beaver*'s Mayfield or *Andy Griffith*'s Mayberry. The tableau is bucolic, and the mise-en-scene pastoral. It was here that I spent my early life, acquainting myself with the reality I would later examine as a professional and as a Christian. In the early seventies, Coventry did not bear the scars of the cultural upheavals of the few previous years; it seemed more a Green Acres than a Berkeley.

We lived on an acre of land, in a big red house on the top of a hill. The shoulders of the hill bristled with woods. When our Connecticut winter arrived, we would strike a deal with the snowplows: if it snowed enough on a given day, we would close the street leading up to our house. The plowmen would wave to us as we careened down the street on our sleds, resolved to come back later, after our fun, to do their work. Coventry was the place suburbia was supposed to be—not, alas, what it became.

I must have been about eight, and, like most eight-year-olds in large families, I spent significant time playing with my siblings. To be sure, there were quarrels and contests, but there was also quality cooperation. One of these cooperative moments set the scene for my "lost summer." It all started with a seemingly innocuous game of duck, duck, goose. Summer had just arrived, and my brother, my sister, and I were seated there in a circle with a clutch of the other neighborhood kids. I had just elected my brother Peter to become the goose. As if by second nature, our healthy rivalry engaged; he chased me with abandon. We had marked our spots with rocks. And as I landed in the spot he had just vacated, my shin slammed down on the knife-edge of a stone. As I fell to the ground, blood gushing from my shin, my brother ran to get my parents.

A five-hour trip to the emergency room—and twice as many stitches in my leg—later, I saw my summer slipping away before I had even possessed it. Swim lessons, strenuous activity, and other anticipated summer events shattered before their memories could be made. It would be a boring, tedious extension of the rest of the year. But, then as now, I was an optimist, and I was resolute that I could make the best of it.

I took no small solace in my science day camp. I have always been keenly interested, over and above my siblings, in the natural world around us, and intellectual pursuits were one of the few extraordinary activities available to me in my lameness. We were at the community pool, where my brother and my sister were splashing with glee, oblivious to my jealousy—or perhaps reveling in it. Peter, the author of my condition, taunted me, "Come on in! The water's fine!" I smiled sourly and turned back to my science workbook.

"All life began in the seas and, in its primordial condition, was simple when compared to the complexity of modern organisms," this workbook told me. *That sounds familiar*, I thought. "As evolution by natural selection conferred heritable traits from parent to progeny, life became more complex, resulting, in turn, in photosynthetic organisms, plant life, complex terrestrial animals, mammals, and, finally, mankind." I had read that story before—in Sunday school.

When I was eight, I was over the moon about dinosaurs—as many eight-year-olds are. I couldn't get enough information about brontosauruses. But I was also a Catholic. And I saw no conflict between dinosaur day camp and Sunday school. I remember clearly that day reflecting on the story of creation as laid out in Genesis. We know the story from our youth and it brings us comfort. But, with small modifications, that is evolution in a nutshell.

My eight-year-old brain reeled. How did these sandy authors—not even aware of the notion of natural selection, speciation, and heritability—invent out of whole cloth a process by which animals arose that increased in complexity in sequence? James Joyce would have called this moment an epiphany.

Later that day, after we had returned home, I hobbled to my room and opened my Bible alongside my workbook. In Genesis, light is created the first day. Then earth the second day. Then life the third day. Then creatures—first in the water, then in the air—on the fifth day. Then terrestrial animals, including mankind, on the sixth day. Provided we resist the easy, uncritical mischief of taking the Genesis author's literal word as some incipient science textbook, there need be no contradiction between evolution and the narrative of creation. When you're eight years old, a simple, noble discovery can change the contours of your world.

As eight-year-olds are wont to do, I passed over the points that did not accord with my neat little momentous discovery, but still, almost forty years after my personal revelation, I remain confident in both of my disciplines. I remain resolutely convinced that the sciences have enhanced my faith, and I know that critical faith—my spiral journey of faith—has underpinned my vocation as a practicing physicist. My eight-year-old keel had shifted, and no current could sweep me from the double mooring of my faith and my science.

As I discussed in chapter three, scriptural literalism has poisoned the biblical well for too many young, inquisitive Christians by insisting on a peculiar interpretation of the Genesis narrative. There are, I believe, a good number of people who tacitly accept young earth creationism simply because doing so does not outweigh the benefits they extract from their religious participation. However, to reject the science of evolution is to occupy a dangerous terrain; we have seen firsthand science fiction become science fact, and those among us who possess a self-reflective and self-correcting faith have learned to read our Scripture for the important elements it can convey—not the scientific understandings it cannot. St. Paul reminds us, "Bad associations spoil useful habits" (1 Corinthians 15:33); young earth creationism engenders a "bad association" that can lead the faithful to a precipice.

When we understand scientific theories like the Big Bang and evolution, we realize that God goes beyond the limited concept of a supreme being that creates a world external to himself—and us along with it—as if by magic. We are freed to embrace the full depth of God's self-revelation to Moses ("I am who am")—the fullness of being itself. In contrast, an emphasis on a being, in the classical, objective sense of the term (which was the subject of chapter two) limits our view and experience of God. Through the revelations of cosmology and the study of evolution, we are invited to embrace both a transcendent and engaged God that is best understood as the fullness of reality—encompassing all that is physical and nonphysical.

The Science of Evolution

It is difficult to stress exactly how deeply our biological and medical sciences depend on a strong articulation of the veracity of evolution. The only analogue I can muster is the theory of gravity. Like gravity, evolution is foundational to the sciences it supports. And, like gravity, no serious scholar now doubts its reality. And, like gravity, any number of observations about the world around us would be invalidated if the theory were contradicted. All biological investigations, on some level, either take evolution for granted and reinforce our understanding of evolution or demonstrate the process of evolution.

Simply put, there is no way that evolution did not occur. Yet, even for people who "believe" in evolution, the popular presentation of the phenomenon often lacks key elements.

If we are to take evolution seriously and reflect on how the actuality of this phenomenon impacts our view of and relationship to God, it is worth reviewing some of the history of the science of evolution. I think it's prudent to admit frankly, however, that my own field of research as a physicist does not privilege me to an intimate understanding of evolution in all of its multifaceted and variegated details. However, my occasional intersections with biology have given me enough knowledge of evolution, I hope, to speak about it intelligently. And, as the focus of my own research is on understanding complexity, the physics I study has direct implications for the study of the complexity that is life.

In 1859, British naturalist Charles Darwin published his seminal *On the Origin of Species*. The book proposed that the variety of life then extant arrived at its modern form by means of a common descent through a branching pattern of evolution. He termed the mechanism by which the forms of life developed in different species natural selection. Natural selection suggests that those individuals that are best adapted to their environments have a statistical likelihood to pass on their genetic material over and above that of individuals that are not as well adapted. By the process of heritable traits, these individuals' preferable traits become more common to the population, thus becoming the progenitors of future generations. Over a long enough timeline, environmental pressures would result in speciation—the making of new species (i.e., more adapted individuals) from the genetic material of the old.

Darwin intended the mechanism of natural selection to contrast with artificial selection, or the process of breeding for preferred traits. You see, even in the mid-nineteenth century, naturalists had a very good understanding of the concept of heritability. Offspring and children, for reasons we now know to be genetic in nature, bear many of the same traits as their parents. Just as we can artificially select—that is, selectively breed—desired features and traits into, say, dogs, so too does nature select for traits that are more suitable to the circumstances, environment, and situations of other animals—free from human agency.

Darwin's work was met with harsh criticism on the part of philosophers, theologians, and religious persons more generally upon its publication. Philosophers, especially ethicists, feared that a notion of randomness was incompatible with a purposeful, moral universe. Theologians feared that the competition intrinsic to Darwin's theory negated the necessity to build community in the religious sense. Other religious thinkers—most especially Protestants—bristled at the suggestion that creation could have transpired through natural means alone—let alone the potential that the theory had to destabilize the creationist worldview of an ex nihilo, historical creator. But Darwin's ideas represented a synthesis and extension of ideas that had found purchase for two millennia prior to his work.

Aristotle, summarizing the thinking of the pre-Socratic Sicilian philosopher Empedocles, considered the mutability of phenotypes as governed by heritability. Empedocles maintained that external factors such as heat and cold could influence the manifestation of traits. Aristotle referred to this theory in both his *Physics* and his *Generation of Animals*. Al-Jahiz, a ninth-century Arabic scholar attached to the Abbasid caliphate and centered at Baghdad, extended Empedocles's thought in his compilation *Book of Animals*. In the struggle to gain a competitive advantage, al-Jahiz maintained, the development of new traits could be bred. Darwin's own grandfather, Erasmus Darwin—a British polymath and exponent of the Midlands Enlightenment—also made investigations into evolution. A trained botanist, E. Darwin published a poem in 1789 entitled "The Botanic Garden" that posited a process similar to evolution, presaging the younger Darwin's research by seventy years!

Charles Darwin's principal contribution was to consider the well-known field of artificial selection alongside a geological timescale. If we see mutability of phenotype—selective breeding—in the short term and under the influence of genetic guidance (on the part of man), then, in a time frame of millions of years, we should expect processes of speciation by natural selection.[13] Darwin had his detractors, to be sure, but he also had his immediate supporters, among them Herbert Spencer, a nineteenth-century naturalist and philosopher, who coined the phrase *survival of the fittest* to describe Darwin's idea.

This famous phrase *survival of the fittest* emphasizes the brutal elements of Darwin's thesis and does not consider the substantial elements. I contend that it misrepresents Darwin's thesis in a few fundamental ways. First, the phrase views natural selection as a completed process rather than an ongoing process. Therefore, no organism can be "fit," but only adapted successfully or not—a case of survival of the *fitted*, perhaps. Second, the phrase is far too generalizing to be usefully applied in an analytical sense. An organism that is fit to survive in one ecosystem is unfit in another; no such attempt to understand the necessarily environmental condition of the survivor has been made. Third, and perhaps in uncharacteristic accordance with the Victorian social mores of his time, Spencer's formulation places an untoward amount of emphasis on the vicissitudes of life and death (i.e., survival) to the neglect of Darwin's more substantial proposition, namely reproduction, as the driving force in evolution. Success, if such a word could find purchase in a Darwinian paradigm, is about procreation—not survival.

Perhaps most perniciously, the simplistic phrase *survival of the fittest,* which made easily digestible a complex concept, allowed its tenets to be divorced from the natural sphere and applied to the social sphere. Social Darwinism is a perversion of Darwin's theory, which has nothing intrinsic in it to suggest an amoral world system of hypercompetition and, admittedly, un-Christian lack of charity. When we consider Darwin's thesis as a naturalistic, biological theory instead of a moral one, we allow evolution by natural selection to comfortably exist in the context that Darwin intended. But to understand Darwin's thesis, we need to understand what its effects were in the world.

What Darwin did was to precipitate and reconcile Mendelian genetics— a field that postdates the publication of *Origins* by seven years—with the idea of an ancient world. Gregor Mendel, a Silesian monk, cultivated pea plants for his community at St. Thomas Abbey in Austria. Through an exhaustive breeding and hybridization research, Mendel articulated the laws of genetic heritability that still serve as an entry into genetic research today. To be sure, Mendel's work went largely unnoticed to his contemporary peers, owing largely to the lack of institutional academic support for his work. His work was fortunately rediscovered for its ability to introduce laws of heritability to neophyte biology students in anticipation of more rigorous genetic analyses at a higher level. Darwin's thesis allows the work of heritability to transpire over the truly *longue duree* and to feature such variation as to constitute speciation.

Darwin's thesis also accomplished another elusive goal, namely the unification of biology into a discipline in its own right, which occurred during the 1930s and 1940s. Prior to Darwin's theory, geneticists (biologists who study heritable characteristics), cytologists (cell biologists), botanists (plant biologists), zoologists (animal biologists), bacteriologists (biologists of bacteria), virologists (biologists of viruses), epidemiologists (biologists of disease), ecologists (biologists of ecological systems), paleontologists (biologists of ancient species), and practitioners of other disciplines existed in an often fraught relationship to one another. Darwin allowed these people to talk to each other in the common vernacular of evolutionary biology. Darwin's theory created, as it were, a unified system of everything alive. If common descent were a reality, the thinking goes, then, really, these varied groups of scientists were all talking about epiphenomena: the study of biology is that of evolution by natural selection.

In the unification of the biological sciences, three main points emerged: First, known genetic mechanisms (i.e., DNA, both sexual and asexual reproduction, etc.) explain all evolutionary phenomena; if phenotype is the expression of sufficient adaptation to an environment, then genotype is the mechanism that underlies that expression. Second, even if evolution is, on the whole, quite gradual, small genetic changes—being the condition of natural selection—accumulate over time. Evolutionary events— the appearance of new taxa in accordance with the laws of natural selection—need not be rigidly gradual nor do they need to enjoy a constant rate; conditions requiring adaptation can occur, in a sense, by isolating populations or placing populations in new environments. Within this time frame, macroevolution (the constant process of adaptation by natural selection) and microevolution (the variability of individuals through processes such as mutation and gene drift) coexist as equally contributing to the rise of new species. Third, biologists need to think in terms of populations in addition to individuals; genetic diversity can confer advantage on populations by ensuring that their members have at their disposal a wide variety of genetic materials. Therefore, we should expect (and indeed we find) community and mutualism as natural outgrowths of natural selection—that is, natural selection selects for society and coexistence. Genetic diversity ensures adaptability and dynamic population development.

But despite the unification of these disciplines into a larger field of biology, proponents of Darwin's thesis initially lacked a common language of exchange. Sure, from a scientific perspective, we knew the process of natural descent was beyond reproach. But we did not know the mechanism by which generations conferred their traits to their progeny. My kids looked like me simply because that's the way the world works. But in 1869, Friedrich Miescher, a German physician, placed some discarded, pus-covered surgical bandages under his microscope. There he found a substance residing in the nuclei of the pus cells, which he termed *nuclein*. Nine years later Albrecht Kossel identified the five base nucleic acids of this substance. Forty-one years later, Phoebus Levene identified the base acids, the sugar superstructure, and the phosphate bonds of this substance, now being called by its contemporary name, deoxyribonucleic acid—DNA, in acronym. Eighteen years later, William Astbury demonstrated that the structure of DNA was regular and uniform, but could not say what that structure was.

The problem for cytologists at this point was clear: they knew that this substance was important, residing as it did in the nucleus of the cell, but they could not guess what this structure actually did. But an important corollary field at this time was molecular biology; Nikolai Koltsov, in 1927, argued forcefully for a molecular base of genetic information that passed on heritable traits from one generation to the next. The mechanism, he reasoned, had to be molecular as no overt biological system governed the random allocation of heritability. Theories ranged; was it a protein that contained this information? A yet undiscovered mechanism? An energy?

It was not until 1952 that Miescher's nuclein—our DNA—was recognized by two American bacteriologists, Alfred Hershey and Martha Chase, as the medium by which genetic information was transmitted. It resided in the nucleus of the cell and it was somehow responsible for coding proteins for use in the cell. Common perception maintains that DNA was discovered whole cloth by James Watson and Francis Crick in 1953. They did not; Watson and Crick simply described accurately the structure of DNA and demonstrated how the molecular mechanism worked in the transference of genetic material.

The great successes in the sciences, generally speaking, have had a tendency to be strongly reductionist. Physics has occupied itself with looking for the smallest blocks of matter, looking for the simplest laws of physics, and ascertaining the most minuscule features of reality. The understanding goes: if we comprehend everything we can about the electrons, protons, and neutrons in the atom, then everything else above that follows. But along comes either experimental data or mathematics that suggests an even smaller scale—quarks, leptons, and the like. The idea is to search for the fundamentals on which you build everything. DNA is no different; now that we understood the mechanism of heritability, we could fill in the hypothetical and postulative features of genetics prior to that point. DNA was a fundamental building block that was missing from the foundation of evolution by natural selection. We could describe the effect (i.e., speciation), but we had no means of ascertaining the mechanism until that final block slipped into place. Is it a keystone? Not being a biologist, I can't say, but I can say that it is as close to a keystone as anything yet discovered in the sciences.

Genetics: The Proving Ground of Evolution

Too often, evolution meets with the facile dismissal that it is "just a theory." Yet I claim that it is, quite simply, an experimental fact, and one that is foundational to our understanding of biology and, most important, genetics. The first way in which the modern understanding of genetics supports evolution is what I will call the functionalist argument.

We live with the benefits of genetic research every day. Gene therapy, gene screening, forensics, epidemiology...the list of contributions bequeathed to us by genetics could go on. Genetic research has furnished us with a window into an extremely infinitesimal scale—and it is on this scale that we can most directly improve the lives of people through medicine. Harvesting the body's own stem cells to treat—and, sometimes, cure—cancers? That's a direct gift of genetics. Counseling betrothed couples on the possible negative combination of their genetic profiles? That's a direct gift of genetics. Bringing murderers to justice based on a single hair left at the scene of a crime? That's genetics. Beating the next superbug by figuring out its genetic vulnerabilities? That's genetics. Sequencing the human genome to demonstrate the 99.9-percent commonality all humans share, thus scientifically rendering atavistic racism and racist ideologies? That's genetics. But genetics, as a field, depends totally on the veracity and predictive quality of evolution by natural selection.

Consider just one case: methicillin-resistant Staphylococcus aureus, or MRSA. This bacterium is among the most dreaded infections world-wide, and it perfectly encapsulates the importance of taking evolution seriously. In 1959, methicillin was approved in England to be adminis-tered to patients who had developed a particularly fatal strain of staph infection caused by bacteria that were resistant to penicillin. Within two years, though, the first cases of MRSA were confirmed. What happened? Simply put, the bacteria evolved. Antibiotics are wonderful drugs that have saved lives worldwide, but they are but a stopgap safeguard in a natural system. When the Staphylococcus bacterium encountered a more effective drug—in this case, a drug that itself was necessitated by the evolution of the bacterium previously—an advantage was conferred to those strains of the bacterium that carried the genetic information that allowed them to resist methicillin.

Now, this may seem to be a rapid development of such heritable traits, but the development of these antibiotic-resistant strains only seems rapid from a human perspective. It took two years for the Staphylococcus bacterium to respond to the change in drug regimen. But the average growth period of a laboratory-cultured staph colony is forty-two minutes. That means that the population of bacteria in the petri dish will double in number every forty-two minutes. That means that within two years, 25,028.6 generations would have transpired, giving ample time for natural selection—the means by which preferable heritable traits are isolated, preferred, and conferred—to develop a response to that regimen.

Just to give you a sense of scale, twenty-five thousand human generations, assuming twenty years per generation (owing to sexual maturity, cultural mores, etc.) would reach five hundred thousand years back, well into the Pleistocene era, when *Homo erectus* and *Homo rhodesiensis* dominated the cultural landscape, three hundred thousand years before the dawn of anatomically modern humans, before the Isthmus of Panama and the state of Louisiana even existed. I would imagine that is ample time to develop traits.

So why is evolution important to population genetics—in this case, the genetics of Staphylococcus aureus? Because, I argue, genetics gives us the best chance of beating this nasty bug. We have seen that when we make the environment (i.e., the human body) less habitable for this bacterium, it changes into something far more unmanageable. Because we know how it developed, we are provisioned to make educated guesses about how it will develop. Our best chance to beat it is on the genetic level. Because genes develop in a more or less predictable way, we can outpace this bug with enough brainpower and resources. But in order to end this scourge, a healthy acceptance of evolution must be brought to bear on the problem.

The second reason genetics is so important is the personal argument. Genetics—and its parent field, evolutionary biology—can tell us about ourselves. Like all other organisms, human beings are subject to genetic drift. By looking into our gene pool, we can see the ways in which we are different, yes, but we can also see the ways in which we are profoundly identical. Since the Human Genome Project—a multinational research initiative—published its findings in 2003, much work has been done by population geneticists to figure out the heritable traits that we know by intuition and perception so well. I have my father's eyes; I have my mother's nose; my kids have my smile and my wife's hair. Now we can answer why that might be the case. But we can also answer other questions: Why can Fuegians in Patagonia resist immersion in colder waters for a longer period when compared to, say, a Muscovite? What is the demographic mechanism that confers epicanthic folds around the eye? Why are the descendants of sub-Saharan Africa less susceptible to certain skin cancers? Why are they predisposed to sickle-cell anemia? These questions and more are free for the asking now that we have a working prototype of the human genome.

We can even pose historical questions to these data: At what point did Fuegians take to the water? How long would it take this trait to develop? When did East Asian, Native American, and some sub-Saharan African populations need an adaptation to accommodate reflective glare—an advantage conferred by epicanthic folds? At what longitude would dark skin be most advantageous? How long would it take to develop an immunity to malaria, the original advantage conferred by the sickle-cell gene? Genetics divorces these questions about human difference from their socially constructed home in race and race politics and locates them neatly in a venue of objective—and charitable—inquiry.

Also, we can see from the Human Genome Project how shockingly similar we all are as members of a single, albeit extended, human family.

All human difference resides within 0.1 percent of the genome; to put it another way, humans are 99.9 percent genetically identical to one another. But within those twenty-one hundred genes that differ between individuals lie the secrets of our lineage. For example, Bryan Sykes, a human geneticist at the University of Oxford, has headed a research initiative for some years now dedicated to unraveling the genome of Britain and Ireland.

The migration of peoples around the world is preserved in their genes, so, Sykes's thinking goes, every man, woman, and child carries inside of them their family history. What Sykes has found is shocking initially but intuitive upon reflection. The populations of Britain and Ireland are almost wholly identical; there are no appreciable differences among the English, the Scots, the Welsh, the Cornish, the Manx, and the Irish. The only differences that survive are cultural, not genetic. Sykes also carries his analysis onto the European continent, finding that—despite bloodshed and war fought to solidify these distinctions—the nation is itself a cultural concept, not a natural quantity. These findings serve to underscore the profound commonalities among humans and indicate a relatively recent common ancestor. We are all brothers and sisters.

Human geneticists like Bryan Sykes dive into their field by looking for the most recent common ancestor, a figure or couple from whom multiple lineages spring. An example, taken from Irish mythology, is that of Niall Noigiallach, or Niall of the Nine Hostages—a legendary character who supposedly lived in the northern part of Ireland in the fourth and fifth centuries. Making the leap from mythology to history, Sykes's research determined that, in the fourth and fifth centuries in the northern part of Ireland and the western part of Scotland, there was one extremely fecund man.

All men inherit their Y chromosome directly from their fathers; all people inherit their mitochondrial DNA from their mothers alone. By looking at these two genetic signatures and applying the rules of statistics, we can ascertain the age of these two markers. You see, genes mutate randomly but in accordance with well-defined probabilities and at a constant rate. Therefore, by comparing the Y chromosome of, say, one thousand men—as Sykes has done—he can triangulate the date at which these one thousand men shared a common ancestor. In modern northwestern Ireland, 21 percent of all men can be traced back to this single man who lived around County Antrim in the fourth century. Now, is this Niall of the Nine Hostages? I'll leave you to decide, but the proposition is tantalizing.

More than simply a search for our ancestors, this statistical feature of population genetics—affectionately referred to as a genetic clock—is totally predictable and totally sensible. And when we unwind this clock, we find incontrovertible evidence for the reality of genetic drift, itself a foundational feature of evolution. We are all evolving, all the time; it just happens outside our ability to perceive it. Our genetic clock is so attuned that we know that "Adam" lived fifty-nine thousand years ago and "Eve" lived about two hundred thousand years ago. The former is the most recent common paternal ancestor for all men on earth, and the latter is the most recent common maternal ancestor of all people on earth. What we have to countenance is that all of our physical clocks—radioactive decay, axial precession, even sidereal time lapse—indicate that the universe is much older than a literal reading of the Bible would support.

Randomness and Order

The other common criticism of evolution is that random processes could never produce the order and complexity we see in living systems. Often, the second law of thermodynamics is quoted to support this idea. The second law of thermodynamics tells us how a system at constant temperature (or, in sciencespeak, in thermodynamic equilibrium) would behave. The disorder inherent in such a system always stays the same or increases.

We all experience this in our daily lives as we struggle against entropy to keep our surroundings clean! At a more fundamental level, it is this increase in disorder that makes the gas molecules in a room spread out. If spontaneous order was possible, the molecules could all move to one corner of a room, leaving you in a vacuum and, lamentably, dead. Luckily, the second law of thermodynamics assures us that this will not happen.

Though the example of the gas in the room does suggest that the second law of thermodynamics would prevent the spontaneous ordering of molecules required for life, this argument against evolution misses an essential fact. The earth is not in thermodynamic equilibrium, as the sun constantly bathes the earth in light energy. Because of this, our intuition regarding random processes and the development of complexity and order fails us. In fact, a better understanding of complex systems and evolution reveals deep truths about the fundamental nature of reality and the emergence of order.

What we see in evolution is a steady process that generates life-forms that are more complex physically and more complex socially. Indeed, a critical aspect of the study of evolution is the study of the processes by which cooperative organizations arise in nature. DNA organizes into a nucleus; the nucleus organizes into a cell; cells organize into organisms; organisms organize into complex social relations. Complexity and cooperation are hardly accidents of random events, but are deeply intrinsic to the structure of reality.

The first idea to clear up, from a scientific perspective, is that randomness doesn't preclude order. For example: go to your kitchen and place a thin layer of oil in your frying pan and heat it from below. All things being equal, the surface of the oil will break into a beautiful pattern of hexagons because the fluid convects in nice, organized rolls that, when viewed from the side, look like little doughnuts, but when viewed from the top, look like hexagons.

Nowhere in the process of heating the oil have you forced the oil into a hexagonal shape; every molecule is in perfectly random motion. The probability of getting hexagons out of all these trillions of molecules moving randomly is effectively zero. And yet, every time you reach a critical temperature difference, you will get hexagons. It is completely predictable; it is unavoidable. It is built into the fabric of the universe. The feature you will have observed is called spontaneous symmetry breaking. And all it takes is the appropriate application of energy to the system such that it reaches a critical value determined by physics.

The earth, too, is a giant system driven by energy. The sun is heating the earth constantly. And so, it is completely consistent with the principles of physics for one to expect life, as a fundamentally ordered structure, to arise naturally from underlying randomness. This is in contrast to the commonly stated misconception that life is impossible because randomness would never produce such complexity. Because the randomness of systems does not bear on their potential for complexity, there is nothing that argues against the possibility of life arising, increasing in complexity, and forming cooperative entities. In fact, self-organization, or the spontaneous formation of organized structures, is an important area of study in physics.

There are systems that are unpredictable, such as the weather, but even these systems have a well-defined order in which this chaos transpires. So, complex life may be built into the structure of the laws of the universe. How this occurs and what sets this structure is why evolutionary biology is an active area of research. The experimental facts are pretty clear that evolution occurred. Evolution—for all its seeming randomness—is actually an example of order emerging in a system that is driven by an input of energy.

Now, understanding the formation of complex, organized structures— such as life—using the laws of physics in no way precludes God. I believe the right way to look at this is that, even though God is not necessarily in the process of evolution, God's active role is not precluded either. Recall our metaphor of the child in the womb. The physical world is called forth from the fullness of reality and imbued with the properties required to call forth life. In this context, evolution is a peek into God's kitchen; for me, it boils down to understanding the recipe. The laws of physics and the laws of biology are the physical architecture of God's dish. And we understand the way God works by understanding the elements of God's creation.

One aspect of this is a better understanding of complexity and complex systems. I mentioned above that many sciences were in the business of finding reductionist explanation of phenomena; this is changing. The scientific study of emergent properties and systems as a whole is developing at a rapid pace.

In my area of research, and in recent years, I think science is recognizing the pitfalls of reductionism, which is that—as you get to more complicated scales (we like to call them length-scales or degrees of freedom)—there are properties that emerge that can only exist in that system. Landau and Lifshitz, in a standard contemporary physics textbook on statistical mechanics, write, "Thus, although the motion of systems with a very large number of degrees of freedom obeys the same laws of mechanics as that of systems consisting of a small number of particles, the existence of many degrees of freedom results in laws of a different kind."[14] So, new laws of physics occur because the system has many degrees of freedom. One does have to be careful and realize that this is not the idea bandied by the intelligent design crowd called irreducible complexity. Complexity arises naturally out of physical laws, and does not require a designer—though one is not ruled out. In simple situations like heating a fluid, we understand the laws at the system level; for complex situations like life and its origins, the applicable laws are active, exciting areas of research. And evolution is simply one of the mechanisms that we can and have observed experimentally that give us a window into God's design of physical reality.

Evolution as Genesis

No serious scholar—or average person, for that matter—now denies the actual fact of DNA and heritable genetics; what is at contest for some is the degree to which we can assume the laws we observe in the laboratory are the same that brought about complex life on earth. The authors of Scripture, I contend, were not concerned with the mechanisms of creation, but rather the meaning of creation. And if we understand evolution—as I do—to be in part a striving toward more cooperative, more complex, more communal forms of life, we do see ready analogues in the Scriptures. Though we have already discussed the issues of literal interpretations of the Bible, it is worth briefly revisiting Genesis, as literalists will often become preoccupied with the Genesis account of creation.

On the face of it, it seems quite clear: six very busy, twenty-four-hour days. But digging into the account with a figurative eye, we see that we can accord the Genesis account quite neatly with our sense of increasing complexity. We begin, as we discussed in the last chapter, ex nihilo; we first get plants (Genesis 1:11–12), then we get marine life (Genesis 1:20–22), terrestrial life (1:24–25), and, finally, man (1:26–30). Really, this schematic is the process of evolution in a nutshell. We could even read the creation of lights in the sky—the energy source by which we see—as indicative of the evolution of sight (Genesis 1:14–18), as it occurs prior to the creation of any animal that possesses sight.

We are even given clues to this process of evolutionary development in the second creation narrative in Genesis 2; the Vulgate maintains that God fashions humans *de limo terrae* (2:7). *Limo* here is generally translated as "mud," but has also been translated as "clay" (which, to be sure, accords most closely with the Hebrew sense of the verse). But the word also conveys the sense of slime, a primordial living fossil and member of the eukaryotic phyla. God, surely, could have fashioned humans—in the mind of the Genesis author—out of the slime of the earth, which would have entailed building humans out of less complex organic materials.

But, then as now, *slime* connotes a base, revolting thing that may be meant to serve as an anticipation for the Fall of humanity (indeed, the Catholic Douay-Rheims translations preserve the slimy sense of the word *limns*). What's most important, at least to my mind, is that the only species mentioned directly by the Genesis author are whales, cows, and humans. This indicates a preoccupation with these creatures as being somehow representative of their respective domains; whales are the quintessential sea creature, cows are the quintessential land mammal, and humans are quintessentially important to the author's sense of God's design. But in Genesis, we also get a sense of species continuation, as all organisms God creates are instructed to procreate "after their kind."

But creation—if evolution was to be a part of it—could not have happened in six twenty-four-hour days. Elsewhere in Scripture, we see the authors understanding the situational and metaphorical use of "day." Psalm 89 reads, "For a thousand years in thy sight are as yesterday, which is past" (89:4); this passage even refers to this figurative day in the context of creation. Can this passage suggest that the psalmist understood the figurative nature of the Genesis author's day? Numbers in the Bible are perhaps best understood as figurative, and the length of the day, really, couldn't have been established before the creation of the sun on the fourth day.

We can even see some evidence in Scripture of a consciousness of Mendelian heritability; in Genesis 30:32, after the birth of Joseph, Jacob requests from Laban leave in order to return home after his many years of service. Laban asks Jacob to name his wage for the services he rendered. Jacob replies,

> You shall not give me anything. If you will do this one thing for me, I will again pasture and keep your flock: Let me pass

through your entire flock today, removing from there every speckled and spotted sheep, and every black one among the lambs, and the spotted and speckled among the goats; and such shall be my wages.

But before Jacob can pick over the flock to collect his wages, Laban hides away the sheep and goats matching the description and places them in the care of his sons, who are a three-day trip away from Jacob. Not deterred, Jacob "took green rods of poplar, and of almond, and of plane trees, and pilled them in part: so when the bark was taken off, in the parts that were pilled, there appeared whiteness: but the parts that were whole remained green: and by this means the color was divers. And he put them in the troughs, where the water was poured out: that when the flocks should come to drink, they might have the rods before their eyes, and in the sight of them might conceive. And it came to pass that in the very heat of coition, the sheep beheld the rods, and brought forth spotted, and of diverse colors, and speckled." (Genesis 30:37–39)

The woods mentioned by the Genesis author may well have been used to construct fencing or may have been used (as almond extract was and still is) as an aphrodisiac; I think the former possibility is more likely. Now, the Genesis author is clear that Laban understands the process of heritability of phenotype among his flock—as does Jacob. Sure enough, after an indefinite number of mating cycles, Jacob's share of the flock was increased to the extent that it "enriched [him] exceedingly" (Genesis 30:43).

Biblical exegetes have long understood this passage to underscore a biblical notion of impressive traits—the ability of a pregnant mother to be influenced by her surroundings and impress them upon her offspring. But, if we understand Jacob's use of the pieces of wood figuratively, we can see how Jacob could effect a selective breeding program by which he specifically bred the sheep to emphasize dark coloration—a recessive trait. Only rams of a specific phenotype were permitted sexual access to the ewes—which itself conveyed the underlying genotype—in order to maximize the number of individuals that would eventually belong to him.

In a Mendelian table for the coloration of ovines, the expression of the genotype for melanism would be recessive (i.e., aa), while the expression of whiteness would be dominant (i.e., AA, Aa, Aa). But 75 percent of the population of this flock would carry the recessive gene. Therefore, after one generation of random pairing, the flock would be one-quarter composed of individuals bearing only the dominant allele, half composed of individuals bearing the recessive gene, and one quarter composed of individuals expressing the recessive trait. Within six generations of selective breeding, a population that did not originally possess any individuals of the recessive phenotype could be artificially selected to express close to three-quarters membership by animals that possessed that phenotype.

Now, certainly Jacob and the Genesis author both lacked the ability to describe this process theoretically, but, as individuals well versed in animal husbandry, they may well have understood the process intuitively. After all, the ability to selectively breed for a given trait predates Mendel's experiments and description of the probability of outcomes. And perhaps reading this story as an allegory of genetic heritability belies the author's intent, which was surely to demonstrate God's favor in Jacob's craft. But the implication is clear, or at least imaginable: Jacob could have stewarded the genetic profile of his flock to reflect a desired outcome, and he could have done it using the techniques of husbandry available to him at his time.

Evolution and Salvation History

So, how are we to understand Scripture in a way that complements and even enhances what we can observe empirically? I think here the idea of salvation history becomes most helpful. Salvation is a profoundly evolutionary idea—one that stewards humans (crafted and animated, as they were, from baser elements of the earth, such as slime) and provides for them the means of transcending their circumstance and developing a greater, more complex relationship to the steward.

If we—as I contend we must—understand physical systems to develop toward complexity under the right conditions, then salvation as a key tenet of both faith and evolutionary processes should be expected. And, if natural selection is the process whereby that development is effected, then we should expect to see allegories in Scripture that convey understandings about salvation and human development in terms that could also be applicable to evolutionary processes. In John, Jesus presents us with an image of vineyard cultivation as an allegory for the process of salvation. Jesus says,

> I am the true grapevine, and my Father is the gardener. He cuts off every branch of mine that doesn't produce fruit, and he prunes the branches that do bear fruit so they will produce even more. You have already been pruned and purified by the message I have given you. Remain in me, and I will remain in you. For a branch cannot produce fruit if it is severed from the vine, and you cannot be fruitful unless you remain in me. Yes, I am the vine; you are the branches. Those who remain in me, and I in them, will produce much fruit. For apart from me you can do nothing. (John 15:1–5)

Jesus is referring by analogy to the process of shearing away unproductive branches of a tree to facilitate fruit production. The practice involves facilitating the production of fruit by removing unproductive elements of the organism, thus resulting in a more productive organism overall. We also see variants of this idea in Jesus's parable of the vine in Matthew 7:15–20 and Luke 6:43–45; the New Testament authors were using the vine imagery of the Old Testament authors, who describe both David's line and Israel more generally as vines that branch out and grow more complex with time (e.g., Psalm 80:8—16; Isaiah 5:1-7; Jeremiah 2:21; Ezekiel 15:1-8, 17:5-10, 19:10-14; and Hosea 10:1). But this image looks quite similar to the image of speciation by natural selection; that the Tree of Life and the tree of life could look so much like each other should be reason to pause.

In a sense, Jesus is also talking about the competition inherent to natural selection as biologists would understand it. Natural selection will remove unproductive branches from the evolutionary tree by means of extinction and genetic obsolescence—and salvation works the same way. Only by pruning the dead ends of development can we clear the way for healthy, robust, competitive organisms—both in an evolutionary and a salvific sense.

Conclusion

Both evolution by natural selection and Scripture make it clear that we are not done evolving—in either a physical or spiritual sense, respectively. We see that organisms are able to adapt to new circumstances and environmental changes, and it is altogether likely that we will continue to adapt to our dynamic environment (we are, after all, composed of the same organic stuff as the rest of the animal kingdom).

Evolution is not a completed project simply because we appear to sit at its apex as the most successful species the world has ever known. Likewise, the kingdom of God and Christ's thousand-year reign have not come to pass. But if we understand both the process of evolution and the process of salvation to work as two engines of the same vehicle, we can pose questions about what will come next. It seems clear that both evolution by natural selection and salvation select for increasing community and cooperation.

The waxing into community undergone by life on this planet has been nothing short of striking. Evolution by natural selection suggests that we all started out as DNA that figured out how to replicate itself. To anthropomorphize this molecule for a moment, let it decide to construct a membrane; on a long enough timeline, this DNA develops the means to self-organize these phospholipids in order to create that membrane. Along, in sequence, comes all the cytoplasm, the organelles, and the means of phagocytosis. Before you know it, you have a fully functional cell that wouldn't look at all out of place on a slide a few doors down from my office in Rowland Hall. Given a bit more time, natural selection continues to favor cooperative behavior—your first multicellular organisms. Eventually, you have specialization of organs that results in increasingly complex organisms, just think about the extraordinarily complex, cooperative living environment that is our body.

We are a collection of cells conditioned to survive only as a collective. A few more billion years after the first organism, and you have such extremely complex organisms that they have figured out this process; they have looked into God's cookbook and discerned much of the recipe for life.

The evolution of complex relationships is also the story of Scripture. Scripture speaks in one voice with respect to the importance of community. It is only by collective cooperation that we can share the promise of salvation, and it is only by mutualism and charity that we can realize our full potential. Given the clear parallels between evolution in Scripture and science, why must conflict and concern carry the day? Why do some see the need to couple our understanding of creation to a God who needs magic to intervene in physical processes to create us—as opposed to a God who uses the physical laws of God's own making in order to create?

I am inclined to suggest that, if God is truly incompatible with the evolutionary science, then this would suggest that God—or, in this case, a god, having been reduced back into the god of the gaps—needs magic in order to create. I think that folks resist incorporating evolution into their vision of creation because of the metaphors they hold for creation itself.

So I encourage us to return to and to ruminate on my maternal metaphor of the child in the womb.

The maternal metaphor points to an understanding of God's action in the world that is integrated into and works through physical laws. With this understanding of God, then no part of evolution by natural selection can preclude a God who is constantly, intimately engaged in this world. In fact, God's creation by means of evolution by natural selection is a reasonable consequence of God's desire for a relationship with us, God's loving us, and, especially, God's offer of salvation to us. In a world that has consistent physical laws, we are most free to respond to God's call for relationship. I will address this point further in the following chapters, but I think that a world of consistent physical laws is one of the greatest gifts from God.

We will continue to grow and change. The question is how? If we turn to our contemporary mythology—that of comic books—we can see visions of our evolutionary future. The X-Men—Stan Lee's allegory of the civil rights movement—cause us to ponder how we ought to deal politically with the concept of difference. But on a more fundamental level, the X-Men bring to mind only physical evolution; our Scripture and our spiral journey of faith call us to consider spiritual evolution.

Only by breaking the mold of God as just another superhero can we understand the fullness of God's design and freely enter into a relationship with God. A critical faith is one that asks whether we are simply static in our faith or whether we are working toward spiritual evolution. While physical evolution is a useful analogy, it is incomplete on its own to serve as a comprehensive metaphor. Rather, working in an evolutionary sense toward ever-increasing union with God requires that we understand the ever-changing nature of our spiritual existence and celebrate the ways in which God's actions manifest in the physical world.

Chapter 6

The Universe Between Our Ears:
God and the Science of Consciousness

God is love.

—1 John 4:8

On April 2, 2013, President Barack Obama announced the beginning of a collaborative research initiative called Brain Research through Advancing Innovative Neurotechnologies, known through its telling acronym as the BRAIN Initiative. This research promises to take modern neuroscience over the horizon and to the next frontier. Already in 2014, the halls of my home department at the University of California, Irvine, are abuzz with breathless talk about the brain. We stand at the threshold of an exciting time: the science of the twenty-first century promises a much deeper understanding of that most mysterious of organs; one hundred years from now we will have a better understanding of the gelatinous gray matter that resides between our ears.

One of the most exciting elements of this new research is our ever-growing understanding of the plasticity of the brain. And on the cutting edge of this research is our improving understanding of the ways in which habit encodes itself into the very hardwiring of our brain. Smokers continue to smoke despite overwhelming scientific evidence and popular consensus of the harmful effects of this habit. These individuals persist largely because their brains have been effectively rewired to that addiction. Drinkers drink for the same reason, and every morning I sit down with my copy of the *Los Angeles Times* and eat my Cheerios and drink a

Diet Coke for the same reason. My morning ritual has become encoded into my brain by virtue of anticipation, execution, and repetition.

It was on one of these mornings, as I was getting my morning fix, that I flipped open my *LA Times*. "This really gets my goat," I muttered while indignantly cramming a spoonful of Cheerios into my mouth. "What a thing to go and put out there."

"Hmm?" was my wife's cursory response; she was busy at her own morning habitus.

"Oh, the *Times* has a piece on God and the brain. I just find these claims frustrating."

"Science at the table, hon," she said, reminding me of our agreement to keep contentious issues off the table, so to speak.

"I know, I know...but this isn't science."

My wife smiled and asked me, "Then what's the problem?"

The problem, I explained, was that this piece began with very elegant science; a researcher had recently written a book on the neuroscience of religious experience.

Religious visionaries evidently exhibited increased cortical activity in similar, predictable ways. Scientists reproduced these effects by stimulating the same neural pathways. This result of the research was fascinating. The problem I had was with the conclusions expressed in the article. Essentially, the claim was made that the fact that we could replicate religious experience by stimulating parts of the brain was irrefutable evidence that all religious experience was illusionary, and, therefore, God was unnecessary and likely nonexistent.

"Conclusions ought not to outstrip the evidence that support them."

"Well, maybe one day you can write a book about those questions."

Well, this is that book. A fundamental underlying assumption of this book—the fact that physics and evolutionary biology do very little to prove or disprove the existence of God—is equally applicable to the burgeoning field of neuroscience.

Truth be told, the data that suggest that all religious experience is reducible to neurological impulses do not negate the veracity of religious experience. After all, we have a very solid understanding of the neuroscience of hunger; we can observe neural activities associated with hunger and—in some lower-order animals—we can trigger neurons to mimic that sensation. The result is that we can make a test subject feel hungry even though he or she has just eaten. But—and this point is crucial—no one concludes against the existence and reality of hunger simply because we understand the neurology and can replicate that neurology artificially. Just because we have the map doesn't negate the existence of the road.

But equally important as the underlying assumption is the main thesis of the book: as much as science is not provisioned to address the question of God's existence, questions raised by science are still useful for our exploration of our relationship to and our understanding of God. When we understand God as the fullness of reality, then, by definition, physical reality is contained as part of that fullness. The previous chapters on creation and evolution illustrate the power of our exploration of the physical world to provide insights into God's methods in a relatively clear fashion for two reasons. First, these questions explicitly addressed the nature of physical reality; and second, in the context of the questions, the boundaries between physical and nonphysical reality were relatively clear.

As we move on to questions of mind, miracles, and free will, the boundaries between the physical and nonphysical—as presented in both science and philosophy—are less clear. One could very easily defend the consistent, evident position that the only reality is physical reality. Such a focus would provide satisfactory explorations into the above-mentioned subjects, albeit from a very particular perspective. I find this perspective, however, to be an overly confining premise. A priori, I see no reason to exclude the possibility of nonphysical reality simply because science is not equipped to study it.

To me, it is much more fruitful to at least consider the possibility of a fullness of reality that goes beyond the purely physical, and ask the question: What can we know about this fullness of reality? As we consider the fullness of reality, it is important to remember that the scientific method is our most powerful tool to assess physical reality and to make predictions about that reality. And, ultimately, we expect to be able to figure out the mechanisms by which physical reality transpires.

Therefore, an understanding of the fullness of reality must be in accord with scientific understanding. Also, even though the scientific method cannot directly assess or make predictions about nonphysical reality, there may be cases where understandings predicated on physical reality naturally lead to understandings of the fullness of reality.

Therefore, as we reflect in the rest of the book on questions that touch on how and to what degree we access and interact with nonphysical reality, I will draw on perspectives from science, Scripture, human experience, philosophy, and even social sciences. Each of these fields can sustain postulations about the nature of the nonphysical and its interaction with the physical. Asking key questions about this interaction can allow our current understanding of the sciences to broaden and deepen our faith.

But the way the sciences frame questions about the world we inhabit cannot presently sustain inquiries into the nonphysical; in order to allow the sciences to supplement our faith, we must employ an interpretive framework. Now, this necessity cuts both ways; on the one hand, the sciences cannot undermine religious faith because faith is predicated on sensitivity to the nonphysical; on the other hand, scientists who make definitive statements about the existence or nonexistence of God using the tools provided by the scientific method are at risk of making a logical misstep and misunderstanding the nature of their evidence. Such hypotheses and conclusions, by definition, are not supported by empirically based *physical* data, unless one first confines God to a physical being, a concept we have already rejected.

Because we live in an era of scientific authority—that is, we as a society have invested scientific explorations with a unique explanatory power—a scientist who makes these pronouncements lends the credibility of his or her method to conclusions that the method cannot support. Just as in the fields of cosmology and evolutionary biology, neuroscience can provide the how, the when, the where, and the what. It cannot begin to entertain questions about the why.

Love and Consciousness: Gift from God and Wonder of the Brain

Christians are often struck by the profundity of the simple passage in John's first epistle: "God is love." Such a sentiment brings us comfort and reinforces the special position we humans occupy in the divine cosmogony—the potential for a relationship with the fullness of reality. Love, as a concept, is one of those richly textured emotions that we can all understand but cannot define with anything approaching precision. If humans share an element of the divine—in the form of the breath of God—then our ability to love is certainly related to God's capacity to love us. What, then, are we to do if we reduce love in humans to a series of chemical reactions in the brain? Does that imply anything about God's capacity to love us? If our ability to feel love is but a series of natural processes and chemical conditions, what can we say about the love of something as transcendent as the fullness of reality for a part of physical reality?

The challenge with a purely reductionist view of emotion, I think, is that it misses the fact that emotion might emerge from more than one underlying system. Consequently, emotions such as love may emerge purely from physical processes within us, but also involve concepts that go well beyond the purely physical aspects.

At a minimum, this points to the difference between our finite love and God's infinite love. God's love is conceptually more majestic, more numinous, and more inexplicable than human love. Because God loves us in this way, and because we aspire to love God in the same fashion, to focus just on the reduction of love to a series of neural reactions to external stimuli seems too limiting to capture the affective intensity of love as a concept. But everything hinges on the definitions we employ to describe love, consciousness, and the elemental bases of these phenomena.

The value of the new neuroscience is rich indeed, and it promises to further enrich our understanding of the brain as physical mechanisms that power our perception and our consciousness. Neuroscience can even tell us about the evolutionary history of religious sensitivity; there appears to be a definitive evolutionary point at which the human mind—under the power of natural selection—began to be predisposed both to religious belief and abstract thinking; indeed, it seems that these two capacities are linked in lockstep.

It seems that under environmental pressures caused by the increasing complexity of communal living, it became evolutionarily advantageous to believe in an extraworldly judge to whom all transgressors must answer. Belief in a deity, then, fortified the social structure and provided a sort of self-control that facilitated smooth social interaction. We could usefully term this sensibility *religious belief*. We can even identify the discrete elements of a given neurology that play host to religious phenomena: the prefrontal cortex of Homo sapiens is proportionally much larger than that of any other primate; when adjusted for the relative size differential between hominid populations, our prefrontal cortex would be 200 percent larger than any other primate's (and would use much more energy relative to other brain functions).

Is the prefrontal cortex the original locus of religion? Was the evolutionary sensitivity to religious experiences a first step in understanding God's call for us to enter into a relationship with God? We can guess that these elements of the brain are the physical mechanisms that put us on the path to a relationship with the divine, and future research will no doubt refine these views. But, like every other branch of the sciences, neuroscience can do nothing to undercut the absolute and autonomous existence of a God and can only provide an indication for the way God works. Again, even if we know how something works, where its work is located, and when it began to work, the knowing of these parameters does not negate the work being done, and recognizing their material and historical underpinnings does nothing to address the question of why this works.

The brain is a staggering organ. On the one hand, the brain is a curious gift from our evolutionary history. The question of the human brain is a chicken-and-egg scenario: Did human society develop as a consequence of the brain or did human society occasion the development of the brain? We still don't have a good answer, but we know how to frame the question. We can begin by observing the ponderous complexity of the physical brain. In one cubic millimeter of brain tissue, there exist four linear miles of neurons. That is, if we laid in a line all the neurons from this cubic millimeter, chosen at random, it would stretch from Jersey City through the Holland Tunnel, traverse Canal Street in Manhattan, proceed over the Manhattan Bridge, and stretch to Prospect Park in Brooklyn. The average brain occupies a volume of 1,260 cubic centimeters, and weighs about 1.4 kilograms. Best estimates of the total number of neurons range from about eighty-six billion to about one hundred billion, with the lower end being closer to the average.

The density of neural matter, brain-to-body ratio, energy demands, and gross architecture of the human brain all scale almost perfectly from other primate brains. That is, relative to body size, humans have about as much gray matter as chimpanzees. What differs between the human brain and that of other primates is the allocation of these neurons; humans have vastly more energy expenditure for centers associated with cognition, perception, higher-order thinking, problem solving, and complex behavior. The brain uses a full 20 percent of the total energy required to power our bodies—a vast amount that far outstrips the energy consumption of other animal brains. However, these tidy figures, as impressive as they are, merely scratch the surface of the universe we have between our ears. The brain is the most complex, dynamic system yet considered by science; there is simply so much we do not yet know about how the brain works and how the brain developed.

We don't know the contours of the future of neuroscience yet, and we can only imagine the complexity of the field in its final, well-developed form. But, I see at least two paths forward in our understanding of the brain that will allow us to explore the frontiers of neuroscience. The first path forward will depend on the ever-increasing sensitivity and accuracy of our measurement tools. MRI, CT scans, EEG, and other tools will continue, we expect, to become ever more refined, ever more delicate, and ever more nuanced. Indeed, our estimates of the number of neurons in the brain itself depend totally on the metric being employed; we don't know because the instruments we use to gauge the number are not sensitive enough to their task! As technology increases, and the means of discovery improve, so too shall our understanding of the brain. Science always enjoys the biggest breakthroughs when we develop new tools for measuring things.

The second path forward will be an oblique approach based on an analogy. In the past fifty years—and, really, the past twenty—our understanding of computers has furnished an analogue to our study of the brain. To be sure, our neurology and our computers use different means of information signaling. A computer is composed of silicon chips; the human brain employs fluids with ionic species dissolved into it. The former uses electrons to transfer signals; the latter employs ionic species to generate voltage differences that travel the length of an axon. Though on the surface they are both electrical systems, their components operate according to two different sets of physics. But the architecture of the former can tell us about the architecture of the latter. The Einstein of neuroscience is likely to be a computer scientist: machines may one day acquire a type of consciousness.

But we're not there yet.

No matter how much our understanding of neuroscience develops, one of the most interesting questions will be the nature of consciousness. Currently, the ways in which our brain suggests to us the absolute actuality of a conscious self are a matter for debate. What is not debatable—in all the halls of all the science faculties in all the world—is the significance of the complexity of the brain, and the challenge it presents for scientific study. As we consider the question of consciousness, it is imperative to remember that just as persons of science can overstep their bounds, so can persons of faith. Scripture, for instance, does not provide us with insights about our neurology according to the means we currently possess to understand it; neither does science address questions of significance and meaning.

I think it is useful to step back and consider the analogy of a creator that I advanced in chapter four. We are conducting our scientific experiments within the child in the womb of the mother. We are subjecting creation to examination and sustained consideration. But there is no experiment that we can conduct that will allow us to step outside of our circumstance, that will allow us to transcend our situation, that will negate our subjective context as existing within that system. We cannot, I contend, pose scientific questions from outside a system. We cannot conduct an experiment that would provide definitive proof of the existence of that pregnant mother, and no experiment that we can conduct and execute will conclude the nonexistence of that mother. We have only finite, limited reality at our disposal, not the fullness of reality.

Love, Consciousness, and Mind in Scripture

The Bible does not furnish its readers with any understanding of the mind as an abstract concept. Consciousness and thought are simply necessary preconditions to enjoying human status. And this is borne out by considering the anatomical conceptualizations according to which the authors of Scripture labored. The heart, not the brain, was the poetical site of consciousness. When Moses demanded the release from bondage of the Hebrews, God was said to have "hardened Pharaoh's heart" (Exodus 9:12). The organ that God hardened here was the בֵל, the lev, or the organ that pumps blood and thereby sustains life. But this organ also served as the locus of thought and emotion. This organ was the locus of the core of a person—and in this sense it accords most closely with our own poetic understanding of the heart (for example, one can get to the heart of the matter, or construct a chair of heartwood, etc.). The internality suggested by the word heart could stand in for mind or will in a way that could accord with our notion of consciousness.

The heart, in Scripture, is the very core of a person—his or her thoughts, opinions, memories, and emotions. The entirety of inner life transpires within the heart, and the agency of an actor is an outflowing of the power of the heart. But at its core, this anatomical model would suggest—to a literalist—that inferiority is seated at the heart. To be sure, the heart is an important organ, and it is the centerpiece of the circulatory system. But as modern biology, anatomy, and medicine tell us, the heart is not individually responsible for the formation of consciousness.

The בֵל of biblical Hebrew carries into the Septuagint as "καρδιά," literally *heart*, and into the Vulgate as "cor," "cordis," again, literally *heart*. This latter word is related more generally to the sense of body and viscera (in the total sense) in the form of the *corpus*.

These translations miss an important aspect of the Hebrew original; by doubling the final consonant, viz. בֵלֵל, the word invariably refers to *heart* in the sense of *mind*. When the author of Jeremiah writes, "The heart is deceitful above all things, and desperately sick; who can understand it?" (17:9), we could understand the use either as heart in a poetic sense or as mind. But when the author of Isaiah writes "My heart [בֵל] falters, fear makes me tremble; the twilight I longed for has become a horror to me" (21:4), we must understand this heart to refer to the mind. Even though we may still translate the subject noun as *heart*, we must understand the sense to make reference to *mind*. Our own language can support the Hebrew wordplay, but to translate both words so slavishly misses an important distinction that these Hebrew authors were making by their word choice.

We see other uses of heart as a synonym for what we would call mind in Job 12:3; in his lamentation, Job says to his friends, "I also have a heart [בֵל] as well as you: for who is ignorant of these things, which you know?" Now, does the author of Job believe that understanding originates in the heart, or is *heart* in this case used as a metaphor for internal understanding? I'm not sure the distinction is important. What is important is that the Hebrew authors of Scripture conceived of what we would call mind or intellect in visceral terms—nothing approaching an approximation of the abstraction of what we would call mind.

A literalist would be forced to believe that thoughts originate in the heart; I contend that no such slavish literalist actually exists. You see, the authors of the Old Testament held an anatomical notion that would not be comprehensible to a modern neuroscientist; that is not to say their anatomy is wrong. Rather, it is figurative, metaphorical, and poetic. We know from neuroscience that the seat of the self, the original locus of personality, is an invention of the mind, which is itself a product of complex neural operations that transpire within the brain. Should we expect scriptural authors to have known that? I think not.

But, like many other features of experience, faith, and reason, we find that the Old Testament preserves a bodily or corporeal understanding of phenomena rather than a cerebral or abstract understanding, which we typically find in the New Testament. The implications of this distinction are telling; authors will devise and deploy metaphors intelligible to the culture for which and in which they are writing. The metaphorical palette available to the authors of the Old Testament was tactile, not abstract.

We should expect—and indeed we find—that different metaphors were used in the New Testament to communicate the more ethereal religious sensibility of the incipient Christian faith. The difference in metaphors bespeaks a changing understanding of religiosity and a changing demography of the faithful. The culture that produced the New Testament was equal parts Semitic and Greek—a combination that caused a new conceptual palette. Much of what we know and love about the Christian faith arises from this combinational process.

In the New Testament, Paul communicates an understanding of the individuated self that would appear to accord with modern notions of selfhood. Paul's use of the term *psyche* (Greek: ψυχή) is telling. *Psyche,* according to Paul's usage, stands for both mind and soul; the term does the double work of referring to both the material base of understanding and perception (mind) and the religious sense of nonmaterial personhood (soul). The material base builds to the immaterial, though; the metaphysical, thinking mind is an extension of the physical.

This *psyche* of the self is used throughout 1 Corinthians and Romans as denoting a self that is both aware and conscious, and thereby signals some understanding of what we could call self-consciousness. But this self-consciousness is incomplete outside of its expression within a community of believers. "Now you are the body of Christ," writes Paul, "and each one of you is a part of it" (1 Corinthians 12:27). The community of faith, then, is for Paul the perfection of the articulation of self; each person, who possesses a thinking *psyche,* has a position within that community. For Paul, there is no autonomous or absolute self until there is a reference to the absolute; we do not exist as selves but in relation to the mystical body of Christ.

Paul also deploys a term specifically for soul, *pneuma* (Greek: πνεῦμα literally *breath*), which further distinguishes the *psyche* of the mind from the *psyche* of the soul. The Vulgate renders this same word *spiritus*—literally and originally "breath." The *pneuma* to which Paul refers intends to translate the "breath of life" from Genesis. "God formed the man of dust from the ground and breathed into his nostrils the breath of life, and the man became a living creature" (2:7). The Genesis redactor places this narrative after the initial creation narrative provided by the first chapter of Genesis, wherein God creates man "after our likeness" (1:27).

What is God's likeness? Are our minds after the likeness of God—that is, intellect, moral sense, will, and so on? Are our physical forms—that is, is God corporeal? Does the Genesis author imply some combination of the two? I am inclined toward the first proposition: our likeness to God is our capacity for reason and inductive thought, our ability to empathize with others and suspend self-interest, our means of predicting outcomes according to a logical sequence, and our very minds themselves.

But in Scripture, one character especially appears to possess consciousness.

The authors of Scripture are unequivocal that God possesses consciousness. The problem here, as I see it, is that we as readers of Scripture expect the authors to be univocal on the matter. Truth is, writers committed Scripture to writing over a thousand-year period—and that time lapse by necessity occasions different and developing perceptions of the divine. "In the beginning," writes the Genesis author, preparing to tell a story about a God who exists in the plural, has particular interest in one family in one area of the Middle East, and who seems to exist as a personal God in competition with other gods ("you shall have no other god before Me," per Exodus 20:3). By the time a reader reaches the New Testament, this God is alone the one God, who shall stand in judgment of the "quick and the dead" (Acts 10:42, 2 Timothy 4:1, 1 Peter 4:5). The ways in which our authors communicated their experiences of God developed from describing an entity whose existence is not mutually exclusive to that of other deities to an entity that is both all-powerful and all knowing. Humans come to recognize God as not only omnipotent but also omnipresent.

Omnipresence seems to suggest a God who thinks in a very different way than we do. As nothing would be external to God's perception—that is, God could perceive everything past, present, and future simultaneously—one might argue that no object could be the focus of God's attention; indeed, no object would need to serve as a relative referent to God. If we appreciate consciousness as simultaneous consciousness of self and external objects beheld in perception, then an omnipresent God would have no need to think. But I would suggest that this syllogism is specious—and doubly so if God is the fullness of reality.

First, I am not convinced of the categorical necessity of external referents to thinking. I can very well imagine meditative thought on abstract concepts that have no concrete basis in observable reality. Second, if God is indeed the fullness of reality, and if God's fullness in this case encapsulates both observable and nonobservable phenomena and physical and metaphysical realities, then reference to objects outside of God does not make sense. All instances of divine perception would be self-perception. Certainly, I am capable of introspection and certainly able to reflect upon myself without any reference to the external world—though usually only for extremely short times before the external intrudes! And, as I understand it, when I am dreaming, the brain is in a strongly self-referential mode without connection to a separate externality.

As I suggested in chapter two, we should resist the temptation to anthropomorphize God. An omnipotent God would resist simple personhood such as we can imagine. Rather, as the fullness of reality, God cannot possibly be conscious in the way we are conscious; God's consciousness, by definition, is a perfect and complete consciousness. God exists only in the middle voice. In Latin, as in English, only the active voice and the passive voice remain fully developed. One can do something (active), and something can be done to one (passive); in Greek, however, there is a third voice—a reflexive voice—according to which something can be done to one by one. That is, a self can be acted upon by itself. That is God in a grammatical nutshell. As the fullness of reality, any consciousness God possesses is self-consciousness.

This reflection on the consciousness of God as seen through Scripture has led to a concept of God's consciousness as something beyond our consciousness. But what do we make of our own consciousness? Is it a gift from the divine or a purely physical manifestation? There is a sense in which reducing consciousness to a series of neurological states, impulses, and conditions in humans could occasion some concern on the part of persons who wish to view consciousness as a gift from the divine. At its simplest level, as with evolution, I do not see an inherent contradiction between consciousness that emerges from physical processes and consciousness as a gift from God. God, according to my belief, presents the physical world as a gift, so all aspects of it are a gift as well. But what, after all, is this gift?

Consciousness and Its Metrics

Consciousness is a difficult concept. I am not a neuroscientist, so what follow are ruminations on my reading and reflections on subjects relating to the mind. As near as I can tell, we have, on the one hand, a narrow definition of consciousness as an awareness of who we are—a self-awareness, if you like. This is a soft self. This definition would consider as conscious all beings that can understand themselves as unique individuals. If this is our definition, then we must allow that creatures other than human beings share a form of consciousness. Rats can pass the mirror test; my dog responds to its name; chimpanzees can paint self-portraits. And this narrow sense of consciousness will most probably be completely explained by neuroscience eventually. We will identify the processes and mechanisms by which organisms are able to self-reflect.

On the other hand, we have a fuller sense of self that the narrow definition cannot encapsulate. A wide definition of consciousness would recognize oneself as an agent. A hard self is absolutely autonomous such that the self continues to exist even without external relationships. When you put this book down, you, yourself (barring an unforeseen catastrophe), will continue to exist without necessary recourse to relationship with me. It is that hard self that the physical sciences may not be able to explain, as it may be inherently a manifestation of the nonphysical. Because we cannot, according to the limitations of science, yet pose empirical questions about nonphysical reality, such a reality is not testable in the traditional scientific sense. Herein we might find the soul.

Even within a purely physical model of consciousness, it seems clear that consciousness is greater than an assemblage of firing neurons wired together by axons and dendrites. The truth is much more complex. Consciousness seems to be an emergent property of the physical brain. And if consciousness is the result of complex neural interactions that build from the physical into the metaphysical, how far might these structures extend?

We might fruitfully call this emergent property—a system greater than the sum of its parts—a soul. Those who adopt the philosophical position that consciousness is nothing more than a consequence of the brain would certainly agree that the brain is amazingly complex; those who place consciousness outside the physical brain would certainly agree that the brain is crucially central to cognition. But in both camps we see an agreement that the brain and the mind exist in a complicated relationship to each other. The question remains open for people of faith: To what degree do our physical attributes, our magnificent brains, participate in the nonphysical aspects of the fullness of reality?

The assumption that we participate in the nonphysical is reflected in our Scripture—human beings, after all, share the "breath of life" that escaped from God and entered into our nostrils at the moment of creation (Genesis 2:7). Exegetes throughout the Christian era have interpreted the gift of the breath of life as the very moment of the soul's creation. That is, God's breath is the soul we seem to possess, which itself is suggested by the very reality we experience. Our thoughts, our prayers, our hopes, our fears—all seem not to be located within a viscous, gelatinous brain but instead seem more at home among the ether; we cannot feel ourselves thinking.

From a scientific perspective, the brain presents a unique challenge. The instruments that we can use to measure thought are increasing in sophistication and becoming ever more precise. It may indeed be the case that one day we are able to identify with irrefutable accuracy the way in which we think—it may all be explicable if we use the right metrics and tools. But the brain is incredibly complex, variegated, individualized, impressionable, and plastic; studying the brain might be perennially frustrated barring an equally complex, variegated, individualized, impressionable, and plastic approach to the study of systems. Currently, our approach of building up an understanding of the brain from its individual parts— despite our sophisticated utensils to do so—has failed to capture the full complexity of even a single thought. The brain, and consciousness more generally, may be so much more than the sum of its constituent parts that models predicting brain behavior or attempting to mimic it (i.e., computers) fail precisely because this sum outweighs its component parts.

Our metrics and tools for measuring the brain have been until quite recently somewhat crude and rudimentary. One of the earliest attempts to associate the brain with behavior occurred in the nineteenth century with the rise of phrenology. In 1819, Franz Joseph Gall, a German organologist (a specialist on bodily systems), published an overview of his theory.

His fivefold hypothesis maintained that the brain served as the principal organ of the mind, which is an aggregate of suborgans, each given a specific function and faculty. These suborgans are located on the outer layer of the brain. The size of these suborgans is relative to the specific strength of that function or faculty in a given person—like a muscle increases in size when it is exercised, so too do these suborgans grow in size when they are exercised. Because the skull ossifies over the brain, the relative size of these suborgans is reflected in the topography of the skull itself; one need only measure the skull to get a sense of what lies beneath. By measuring these areas in relation to one another, the phrenologist could compile a personality profile. In constellation, in the aggregate, these data were seen as significant.

Now we know all of this is poppycock, but that did not prevent phrenology from being used in criminal proceedings and marriage screenings, in addition to other predictive uses. Very often, this "science" erred toward overtly racist understandings of human faculties: savages were savage because they possessed savage features—but the same savages served as the criteria of adjudgment for savageness. The tautology is evident in hindsight. We know now that Gall's methodology, his metrics, and even the theoretical underpinnings of his field were tainted by the racism of his era—and were completely and totally without scientific merit. So phrenology joined the rubbish bin of science history, along with Mesmer's animal magnetism, and J. J. Becher's phlogiston theory—embarrassing footnotes to scientific progress.

Even though we know that the methods phrenology employed were unscientific, this pseudoscience advanced the notion that the brain was the locus of personality and consciousness—the mind, in short. It also popularized the theory that there were suborgans of the brain; that is, certain areas of the brain were dedicated over and above others for certain behaviors and faculties. Now, as very often happens, pseudoscience precipitates actual science—every now and again, a blind squirrel will find a nut. Alchemy lead to the development of chemistry; astrological prognostication provided a nurturing cradle for astronomy. And phrenology provided to neuroscience the aggregate brain—a model of the brain that holds that certain areas are responsible for certain behaviors, functions, and faculties.

Over the course of the nineteenth century, research into the brain really got underway. Two physicians in particular, Paul Broca, a French surgeon and anatomist, and Carl Wernicke, a German neuropathologist, both pioneered research into the speech centers of the brain. Working separately, the two researchers uncovered areas dedicated to the formation of speech (Broca's area in the frontal lobe of the left hemisphere of the brain) and to the understanding of speech (Wernicke's area in the superior temporal gyrus in the left hemisphere of the brain). Owing to the rudimentary nature of surgery, diagnostics, and neuroscience at the time, the two researchers did not have a ready supply of living patients to examine. Their methodology, as morbid as it seems, involved examining the brains of deceased stroke victims, who had for a while survived their ordeal but were left impaired by the catastrophe.

Based on their work, the idea that the site of language could be segregated to one portion of the brain emerged. This is a striking result, to my mind. Language facility is central to our experience as humans, and the notion that language resides in a regular, predictable, individual neighborhood of the brain seems counterintuitive; so much of our perception and our experience is filtered through our ability to linguistically describe and linguistically comprehend it that one would imagine a much greater allocation of resources to its execution.

In the early twentieth century, a neurosurgeon and neuropathologist named Wilder Penfield (a fellow Princeton man) dedicated his life to mapping mental processes to various regions of the brain. He devised the aptly named Penfield homunculus, a graphic representation of the respective areas of the brain that controlled parts of the body. This graphic—also called the sensory homunculus and the cortical homunculus—provides a map of the hemispheric brain overlaid by parts of the body. It is a model of the body within the brain. The thinking goes that these parts of the brain are responsible for the movement and sensory perception of various parts of the body.

This model has been instrumental in the diagnosis and treatment of phantom limb syndrome and paralysis. If, owing to a tragic accident, one were to lose a foot, the next closest neighbors to the neurons responsible for the foot are those responsible for the genitals; in many cases, manipulation of the genitals can satisfy phantom pain perceived in the patient's foot. The neural wiring for the hand resides in close proximity to that of the face; it is possible to prick the spectral finger of an amputee by applying the stimulus to the face. This suggests that the brain can rewire itself to accommodate changes in its condition. These advances point to a brain that observes predictable rules regarding the placement and function of behaviors and faculties.

But these regions and areas in the brain exist in constellation with others—such that the web of neurons in the brain allocates neural work to regions that are not exclusively dedicated to such work. Take, for example, the life of Phineas Gage. On September 13, 1848, Phineas Gage, a New Hampshire railroad man, was blasting rock in order to lay track in the vicinity of Cavendish, Vermont. The Rutland & Burlington Railroad intended to pass through there, and Gage was setting dynamite into a deep hole in a rocky outcropping. He laid the charge into the hole and then tamped it into position within the rock using a tamping iron, a three-and-a-half-foot-long metal rod about an inch and a half wide. Something went wrong and the tamping iron produced a spark, igniting the dynamite and expelling the iron from the borehole like a bullet. The tamping iron passed directly through Gage's head, entering the left cheek just under his eye between the maxilla and the mandible, traveling behind the eye, and exiting through the top of his head. The thirteen-pound tamping iron was found eighty feet behind the spot where Gage fell, covered in blood and gore.

Gage landed on his back, convulsed a few times, and remained conscious for the entirety of the ordeal. Within minutes he was speaking, sitting upright, and walking under his own power. Gage survived both bacterial and fungal infections during his recuperation in the care of Dr. John M. Harlow. Within a month, he ended his convalescence and attempted to get his job back. Never without his tamping iron thenceforth, he began to travel widely, and he died in San Francisco in 1860.

By all accounts, Phineas Gage was able to lead a relatively normal life after his incident, working as a teamster in Chile and as a farmhand in California. But the accident had resulted in a complete change in personality. The tamping iron had passed through the frontal cortex of his left hemisphere, destroying it almost completely. In the process of diagnostic discovery, his doctor inserted a finger to feel around in Gage's head, and determined that Gage was missing much of his brain. Twenty years after the event, Dr. Harlow wrote of these changes:

> The equilibrium or balance, so to speak, between his intellectual faculties and animal propensities, seems to have been destroyed. He is fitful, irreverent, indulging at times in the grossest profanity (which was not previously his custom), manifesting but Little deference for his fellows, impatient of restraint or advice when it conflicts with his desires, at times pertinaciously obstinate, yet capricious and vacillating, devising many plans of future operations, which are no sooner arranged than they are abandoned in turn for others appearing more feasible. A child in his intellectual capacity and manifestations, he has the animal passions of a strong man. Previous to his injury, although untrained in

the schools, he possessed a well-balanced mind, and was looked upon by those who knew him as a shrewd, smart businessman, very energetic and persistent in executing all his plans of operation. In this regard his mind was radically changed, so decidedly that his friends and acquaintances said he was "no longer Gage."[15]

The profundity of the changes in Gage's personality is debatable, but all sources agree that his personality was fundamentally altered as a result of this experience. He was able to hold employment after his accident—blind and afflicted with ptosis in the left eye—and it seems that he was not totally debilitated, but he was somehow different. Gage's experience indicates the great flexibility of neural architecture; even in the face of cataclysm, these structures realign—sometimes imperfectly—to produce the self that we experience.

New neuroscience is beginning to shed light on what might have happened to Phineas Gage on a neurological level. The brain exists in a dynamic equilibrium; many regions and areas play their part in creating the material base of a mind. The loss of any one of these parts alters the system. The brain is occasionally able to compensate for some of these maladies owing to its incredible plasticity. Nevertheless, the brain builds to a sum that is greater than the whole of its parts because of the amazing ways in which the individual components conspire to build into an integrated unit. As Gage reminds us, these manifold components form a delicate balance that is subject to specific conditions; one piece goes missing, the edifice itself changes. The brain, in no small way, exhibits emergent properties—and therein, perhaps, we find the breath of life.

Emergent Properties and Neuroscience: The Divine Connection

Our exploration of the Scripture and science of the mind and brain raises a number of interesting questions. Is consciousness integrated into our gray matter or separate? Do we have a mind distinct from a soul? And does God think? Can God love? At a minimum, a sufficiently complex system generates consciousness—we are proof of that. A sufficiently complex system generates love—we are proof of that as well. Because humans, as the beings who possess the most complex brain known to science, have both consciousness and the capacity for love, it follows that an even more complex system—the fullness of reality—generates the fullness of consciousness and love. This logical proposition is, to my mind, reasonable. In his Gifford lectures of 1985, which were subsequently published as a book entitled Infinite in all Directions, Freeman Dyson, a physicist at the Institute of Advanced Studies in Princeton, New Jersey, argued:

> The universe shows evidence of the operations of mind on three levels. The first level is elementary physical processes, as we see them when we study atoms in the laboratory. The second level is our direct human experience of our own consciousness. The third level is the universe as a whole. Atoms in the laboratory are weird stuff. It appears that mind, as manifested by the capacity to make choices, is to some extent inherent in every atom. The universe as a whole is also weird, with laws of nature that make it hospitable to the growth of mind. I do not make any clear distinction between mind and God. God is what mind becomes when it has passed beyond the scale of our comprehension. I am thinking that atoms and humans and God may have minds that differ in degree but not in kind. We stand, in a manner of speaking, midway between the unpredictability of atoms and the unpredictability of God. Atoms are small pieces of our mental apparatus, and we are small pieces of God's mental apparatus. Our minds may receive inputs equally from atoms and from God.[16]

Dyson is advancing a fractal argument; as one proceeds to larger and larger scales, one notes the recurrent patterns that the scales adopt, and one cannot but be struck by the apparent symmetry of the arrangement.

The heart of the matter is really whether we are satisfied with the reductionist impulse. If we are focusing on the trees, we are sure to miss the forest. We should, I think, understand the emergent properties at work. Put simply, the recognition of an emergent property requires the analysis of the entire system. The dynamics of that system, and the behaviors observable within that system, exist by virtue of the fact that there is a system—and go beyond the behavior of the individual elements. The system under consideration is an interconnected one, and the outcomes of the system are difficult to predict owing to the number of interactions within that system.

My own research focuses on emergent properties. One such example is the flow behavior of foams. Now, foam is an interesting material. Foam is composed of different states of matter. At its core, foam, such as shaving cream, is composed of gas bubbles trapped inside of liquid walls. The liquid walls hold together because of their surface tension. And this same surface tension holds the bubbles together. On the molecular level, every building block of that shaving cream is either a liquid or a gas, and so they are free to flow or fluctuate according to the physics that govern fluid dynamics. But the foam system does not.

If you were to squirt a handful of Barbasol shaving cream into your hand, you would be able to manipulate that dollop according to the physics that govern a solid. In many senses, it is a solid. But the material is even more complicated. If the common, grade-school definitions suggest that a liquid is a substance that is free to flow and a solid is a substance that is not free to flow, then foam is both. Foam flows when subjected to sufficiently large forces—that's why it doesn't hurt when you spread it across your face; and foam will resist flow for small forces and deformations—you can shake it in your hand and it will hold its shape. But—and this is the weird thing about emergent properties—until you know about the structure (i.e., that a foam is composed of gas bubbles suspended within liquid walls) there is nothing about the properties of the molecules that you can use to predict the solid behavior. The molecules of the foam are in a well-defined state: they are either a gas or a liquid. Solidness emerges from the larger scale structure of the liquid-suspended gas (i.e., the bubbles).

We in physics call foam a complex fluid because it is multiphase (that is, its components exist in more than one phase, in this case liquid and gas). Understanding the solid and fluid behavior of the full foam, on the one hand, is trivial; the foam is solid when the bubbles are in each other's way and they can't move, so they hold their shape. The foam is liquid when you do something to make the bubbles move around each other (like spreading it in your hands). Assembling the molecules into a foam produces a particular structure that determines the interactions between the bubbles. By virtue of this spatial structuring and the bubble interactions, you've made a material with solid and liquid properties out of a collection of gas bubbles.

Foam is a collection of bubbles that interact strongly with one another. This collection is, at its fundamental basis, molecules that would otherwise observe the physics that govern liquids and gases, or single bubbles with solid-like properties and no real resemblance to a fluid. But observe the physics of the collection and it is either an oscillating solid or a flowing liquid. A single soap bubble, by definition, can't have collective motion. And so the elemental properties of this blob of shaving cream behave differently simply because they are part of a system.

Now, there are many materials that have this basic structural behavior with different microscopic structures.[17] Consider a pile of sand. The physics on the scale of the entire pile (the macroscopic behavior) are the same as our foam. But, on a smaller scale, things are different. The pile is composed of numerous individual grains, which are dry, solid particles with air in between them, instead of bubbles of gas with liquid between them. And yet, the pile of sand will hold its shape—more or less—and you can make it flow. Again, the basic principle is that particles get in each other's way, which induces solid-like behavior. When the particles can move, the system exhibits liquid-like behavior.

We study multiple examples of complex materials because in physics we are trying to understand the emergent properties of each system and determine how they translate between systems with different constituent parts. A fundamental scientific question is, "How similar are the complexes of foam and sand?" Macroscopically, they behave almost identically: they are both composed of particles that get in each other's way and induce certain similar movements. Even so, the microscopies are totally different: the foam's "molecules" are liquids and the sand's "molecules" are solids. When bubbles slide past each other, the resistance is provided by the fluid between them (known as viscosity), but as sand particles move past each other, it is the familiar friction between solid particles that provides the resistance. In so many ways, the behaviors of the constituent elements of the system are different, but these systems appear to have similar macroscopic behaviors. It is reasonable to say that similar emergent properties arise from very different microscopic physics.

The brain also has emergent properties. As a minimum, consciousness and love are the result of the emergent properties of a complex system. For humans, the fundamental elements of the complex system are likely to be interacting neurons and chemical responses to pheromones—but neither love nor consciousness is contained in a single neuron, a single chemical, or a single region in the brain. Because love and consciousness are fundamentally emergent properties, as with the foam and the sand, there is no reason to assume that consciousness and love are intrinsic to the microscopic details. The fact that the brain is a collection of neurons and host to a specific brain chemistry is relevant, but not totalizing. It is more likely that many different complex systems could produce the same basic emergent behaviors of love and consciousness.

This raises important scientific and philosophical questions. To be sure, love and consciousness must be the result of complex interactions of elements in the brain rather than simply the nature of elemental chemicals and neurons. I cannot imagine that we will ever discover that consciousness is somehow other than a condition of systems within the brain, or even the entire brain. It could indeed be that consciousness only lies in a portion of the brain. Perhaps some parts of the brain are not necessary to it. But the sum of the elements of the system builds to a greater quantity than the individual elements—because of the emergent properties and their existence as a system.

Like my analogy to the foam and the sand, dynamics emerge in complex systems to a large degree because of their structure and the interactions that this structure produces. The microscopic pieces can matter, but only to the degree that they determine the range of structures and interactions that are possible. We can still be special, unique, individual people even in a scientific understanding of love and consciousness, but we should not hold the mistaken belief that neurological activity is the only possible source of love and consciousness. And, as people of faith, we should recognize that we may well find the soul in the emergent properties of the brain. If such is the case, there is no reason to think that this reality is any less a gift from God than traditional conceptions of the soul.

Conclusion: Looking up the Macroscope

We in the sciences are beset with a fundamental limitation. When we seek to pose questions about the nature of the system of which we are a part, we hit a roadblock. Remember, there is no experiment that you can mount from our position inside the fetus developing in the womb of the mother that also encompasses the mother. Similarly, there is no means by which a molecule within the foam system described above can ascertain that it exists within a foam that has very different properties. That molecule—to anthropomorphize it for a moment—is allowed only experiments that are tied to that of which it is a part. It can't go outside.

How do we know foam is a solid? We apply a force from the outside of it and measure its response. The properties of that system are inherent to that system as a whole, and our molecule cannot step outside. If we only exist inside the system—in this case, the fullness of reality—how do we do that equivalent experiment? Put simply, we can't. How do we know that God—as the fullness of reality—is conscious? We don't—at least in strict science. Science can do nothing to support or undermine such a proposition. In other words, we cannot step outside our reality to conduct experiments on it as we can with the systems we observe. But this does not mean that we have no other ways to access the fullness of reality.

Now, imagine the level of a bubble in the foam—a part of the full reality that mirrors the full foam, to some degree. The bubble can get a sense of the full behavior of the foam by how it interacts with its neighbors. By analogy, we can look at our own neurology and understand that there is something special there. We are creatures who can consider creation abstractly. The capacity for abstract thought in ourselves should suggest a capacity for abstraction more generally, owing to the fractal properties that allow systems to reflect their constituent pieces.

Consciousness need not be simply confined to neurobiological processes; to limit consciousness strictly to biochemical bases is sloppy science; doing so does not consider the nature of consciousness as an emergent property. The consciousness we experience is probably inherent to the complexity of the manifold brain—not just a collateral and incidental consequence of the fact the brain is assembled of neurons.

Therefore, consciousness is a phenomenon that one would expect at many levels of complexity.

That the fullness of reality would possess a consciousness isn't surprising; since you have it in the microcosm, you should expect it in the macrocosm. That is to say, God can still be personal—in a manner of speaking—as the fullness of reality. The sciences can support our belief in a loving, conscious God because, as the fullness of reality, God encompasses the fullness of complexity. Given the scientific fact that complexity at the level of the brain exhibits love and consciousness, it strikes me that the most reasonable conclusion is that the fullness of complexity will exhibit the fullness of love. And this returns us full circle to John's first epistle: "God is love."

Now, the fullness of love is not something we can encapsulate with finite language. If we are to take our consciousness—as an emergent property defined by its complexity—as a road map for the external world, then we should understand that our emotions (love, anger, joy, etc.) are themselves natural features of the universe, emerging from the physical laws laid down by the fullness of reality. We can experience and explore these in part, but never in full. This is one reason that our love of God and our relationship with God is always a journey.

We of faith often ponder questions of theodicy—from whence evil, if creation is good? How can a kind and loving God allow atrocities to transpire? This topic deserves significantly more attention than can be provided in this book. But I would suggest, as much as it might hurt to hear, that God's love—as infinitely more complex than our own—reflects the complexity of God's role as the fullness of reality. And though I would never suggest that God wills evil or intends for us to suffer, I would suggest that our free will certainly flows from God's love, as complex as it is. And with free will built into the system, evil as a result of human agency seems to be unavoidable and is certainly consistent with the Genesis account of the Fall. In the end, we may not be able to get any better an answer regarding why bad things happen to good people than Job did. Who are we to try to understand fully the complexity of the fullness of love that has caused God to order creation the way God has?

Chapter Seven

Mirabile Dictu: Scientific Law, Probabilities, and the Miraculous

They say miracles are past; and we have our philosophical persons, to make modern and familiar, things supernatural and causeless.

—Lafeu, in William Shakespeare's *All's Well that Ends Well*,
Act II, scene 3

To me every hour of the light and dark is a miracle, / Every cubic inch of space is a miracle, / Every square yard of the surface of the earth is spread with the same, / Every foot of the interior swarms with the same.

—Walt Whitman, "Miracles," *Leaves of Grass*

Nothing is too wonderful to be true if it be consistent with the laws of nature.
—Michael Faraday

Soccer is one of those games that some sad sadist many misty moons ago configured as an all-weather sport. As I trudged through the snow that blanketed the late-autumn Connecticut countryside, I half cursed my decision to play. Wearing multiple layers, I wondered whether it was worth it. I, after all, had elected this abuse. It was 5:30 a.m., and the old platitude was true: it is always coldest and darkest immediately before the sun rises.

You see, the game of soccer was conceived and nurtured in Europe—where the milder weather is infinitely more conducive to late-autumn play. Indeed, the juvenile and professional levels in America configure soccer as a late-spring or early-autumn sport—owing, no doubt, to the very real concern all sane humans share for hypothermia. The high school and college games, however, insensibly preserve the temporal inheritance of their cradle.

As the temperature rose steadily with the rising sun, my thoughts defrosted enough to recall the coming glory of the pitch. I played left wing at Fairfield College Preparatory, Prep for short, and we were preparing to play one of our crosstown rivals—either Notre Dame or St. Joseph's. The anticipation of victory helped me to push through the burn of the chilling cold. *One more mile*, I thought, *might make the difference...one more mile.*

Before every game, our coach would lead our cheer: "Hail Mary! Queen of victory!"

To which we would chant in unison, "Pray for us!"

Thinking back on this chant, I believe this prayer sought neither favor nor intercession—perhaps ironically; to be sure, we wanted the Mother of Christ to intercede on our behalf and help us to win. But on another level, I think this chant was an exercise in intimidation; we certainly hoped that the opposing team would hear our entreaties. Ultimately, as often as this petition for intercession worked, just as often it did not work. We did not win every game.

Now, had my faith been based on the satisfaction of these petitions—by my prayers being answered by physical manifestations of divine favor—it surely would have been shaken by anything less than an undefeated season. What, after all, is the point of praying for outcomes that are only half-likely to transpire? I think back now—the preponderance of my prayer life in high school, to an embarrassing degree, was spent asking for stuff (e.g., good grades, making the varsity team, college admission, etc.). But as my faith seasoned and matured, as I continued on my spiral journey of faith, I realized that these prayers focused less on outcomes I hoped would transpire and more on changing myself in order to effect those outcomes—and then on accepting those outcomes, regardless of how they came about.

Fundamentally, a prayer is a conversation with God—a profound point of access to the infinite fullness of reality. This prayer does not, however, compel God to intercede as we desire. Unlike a regular superhero, whom we expect to swoop in and save the day, God, as the ultimate superhero, acts in far more profound ways. You see, God's action in the world is fundamentally not predicated on arbitrary violations of physical laws—neither for positive nor punitive reasons. Rather, praying for intercession, to my mind, is about entreating intercession from the fullness of reality to support one's choices through God's grace.

All these prayers for beneficial outcomes—in my high school career, for my extramural activities, for my college applications, and others—had the net effect of keeping me focused on what was important to generate the outcome I desired. Also, these prayers prepared me to accept the outcome, whatever that might be. Was I the beneficiary of God's grace? I believe so, but not necessarily a grace that led to victories in soccer. My regular practice of prayer in high school, even if it was immature prayer at times, laid the groundwork for continued prayer later in life that has continued to evolve.

As I recall, I don't even think our soccer prayer was ever about winning. It was a more general request, humbly beseeching Mary to pray for us. Sports are exciting, challenging, diversionary activities; they require great skill and superlative effort, to be sure. But the best team is not always the victor. So despite my best efforts—and I gave my best effort all the time—and despite our relentless preparation—and we prepared relentlessly—we eventually had to accept reality as it was, not as we would have liked it to be.

My team and I played hard in that game against our fellow Catholics—each entreating exceptional attention from the same God—until the very last whistle. The team never acquiesced. Nevertheless, we lost. But a miracle did indeed transpire, though the favorable result we hoped for did not. You see, the miracle we witnessed that day was a commitment to do our best, no matter what. And that miracle was indeed satisfying.

Prayer and miracles are inextricably linked with each other. Prayers of intercession play a prominent role in both public and private veneration. After all, Jesus tells us to "ask and you shall receive" (Matthew 7:7). Athletes and actors regularly give credit to God for their accomplishments. And yet one of the most obvious challenges with prayers of intercession is how often obvious miracles fail to emerge. In the face of this, people of faith often fall back on the concept—or, rather, the complaint— that "the Lord works in mysterious ways" (cf. Romans 11:33). The question of miracles seems so fundamental to matters of faith, yet how can we ever consider reconciling miracles and science? How can we achieve the goal of this book and ask: How can the sciences enhance our understanding of miracles?

We need to address two central issues if we are to move toward a more rational understanding of miracles. (The other option is to just get rid of the word *miracle* and start over, but the word is so much a part of the faith experience, I will argue it is worth retaining, but redefining.) First, if a miracle is defined as the suspension of physical laws, and if physical laws were established by God, then a miracle is an oxymoron; God's laws are inviolate. I certainly accept that God is active in the world, and *in principle*, God could violate physical law, but *there is no need* for God to violate physical law. If we are to believe that God acts in the world—as I do—then it is reasonable to use the word *miracle* to describe such action. But we must revisit our definition of miracles such that we dispense with a magical understanding of the miraculous.

Second, the capricious nature of magical miracles suggests a God who plays favorites in ways that do not make theological sense to me. Now, even though my experience has led me to believe firmly that God is active in this world, I cannot accept a God that picks and chooses favorites in a destructive and petty way. Such a capricious God is not a God that Jesus would call "Abba." There must be something more to how God acts. Therefore, just as Odysseus navigated the twin dangers of Scylla and Charybdis on his famous sea voyage, our concept of miracles must navigate the middle course between the twin dangers of magic and capriciousness. In so doing, we will find ourselves closer to the loving God who is active in the world, available to conduct relationships with all people, and who elects to violate no physical law in order to preserve our freedom of action.

There is a third issue underlying any consideration of miracles. Why such a fascination with miracles? Once, while in deep conversation about matters of faith and science, a good friend (a colleague who shall remain nameless) told me he was a naturalist. A naturalist, he clarified after I asked him to explain, is a person who "takes the world as it is." Now, he meant to imply that there was no grander order than what we can measure with our scientific method, but, interestingly, I find this formulation an apt paraphrase of God's response to Job's troubles. God tells Job—and, by proxy, God tells us—to accept the world as it is.

I believe our fascination with miracles, at its very core, is deeply tied to our desire that the world be different from what it actually is—and, consequently, our failure to take the world as it is. Now, the result of this preoccupation is not necessarily negative, being—as it is—the engine that drives us toward progress. It can, however, be a debilitating trap of wishful thinking, which either deludes us into dangerous behaviors or harms our faith when God fails to deliver the intercession we requested.

The challenge for this chapter is to revisit the vast history with regard to miracles and address some central questions. What is physical law, and why consider it inviolate? Is there meaning to God's action in a world of regular and reliable physical law? What does action by a loving God, as opposed to a capricious god, look like? To do this, we will start by exploring the definition of miracles; ask why we even focus on miracles in the religious experience; explore some of the past concerns regarding miracles; and ultimately suggest a definition of *miracle* based on personal transformation. This will lead us directly into the topic of the next chapter, free will, and our ability to choose transformation.

What on Earth Is a Miracle, for Heaven's Sake?

The concept of a miracle, I think, has in a sense been cheapened by our cavalier use of the term; we solicit divine intercession somewhat blithely; we attribute simply improbable outcomes to divine intervention. It is a miracle I made it to work on time; Mike Trout made a miraculous catch; we speak of the miracle of modern medicine.

Really, we are entirely too imprecise with our use of this term. God doesn't care about the Super Bowl. God isn't concerned with your bank account. God's concerns are universal, they are inclusive, and they are entirely benevolent. By asking God to intercede on our behalf with a suspension of the natural order, I believe we have not only misunderstood the nature of God's interaction with the world, but we have stretched an already elastic terminology to its cracking point.

I do not mean to castigate common parlance here; rather, I simply hope to illustrate the many ways in which we use this terminology. The question of definition here is paramount; how we define *miracle* will determine whether or not a given understanding of the miraculous will accord with scientific understandings of phenomena. In its broadest contours, the traditional definition of *miracle* refers to God's agency in the world that results in beneficial outcomes. The *Oxford English Dictionary* defines *miracle* as, "A marvellous event not ascribable to human power or the operation of any natural force and therefore attributed to supernatural, esp. divine, agency; esp. an act (e.g., of healing) demonstrating control over nature and serving as evidence that the agent is either divine or divinely favoured." According to a definition such as this one, it is the divine entity that is responsible for the commission of miracles, and it is from God that they flow.

The above definition is an idea with a rich history. Consider the famous medieval theologian. Thomas Aquinas: "[Miracles are] those things... which are done by divine power apart from the order generally followed in things." This definition draws from a previous definition that Aquinas gives for nature. Moving to the eighteenth century, the philosopher David Hume defines a miracle as "a transgression of a law of nature by a particular volition of the Deity, or by the interposition of some invisible agent."

Jumping to the twentieth century, the philosopher J. L. Mackie defines a miracle as "a violation of a natural law...by divine or supernatural intervention...when the world is not left to itself, when something distinct from the natural order as a whole intrudes into it." Finally, the contemporary Oxford philosopher Richard Swinburne defines a miracle as "a violation of the laws of nature, that is, a nonrepeatable exception to the operation of these laws, brought about by God." So, according to each of these thinkers, an outcome can be deemed miraculous if and only if it involves the suspension of natural, physical, or scientific laws.

But the definition of *miracle* as a capricious suspension of physical laws by means of divine agency has its gradients. C. S. Lewis, in his aptly titled book *Miracles*, uses the word *miracle* "to mean an interference with nature by supernatural power." But this interference, he maintains, is not a violation of physical law per se; he maintains that "miracles...are [not] contradictions or outrages [of nature]." Rather, he uses *miracle* to mean that "left to her own resources, [nature] could never produce" those initial conditions nor those outcomes. God, then, employs physical law to achieve his will.

Lewis is erecting a subtle distinction between initial conditions and the determinant operation of physical laws. Lewis raises the possibility of

God acting through physical laws, but maintains that a miracle is consti-
tuted when God leverages God's power to effect God's will by condi-
tioning those initial conditions and guiding the operation of physical laws
to accord with God's desired outcomes.

Lewis's formulation is closer to my proposal. I propose we take it one
step further and dispense with the requirement of an initial condition
that is outside of nature's resources. The dynamics of physical systems are
sufficiently complex—with all the subtleties of quantum uncertainty and
chaos—that if God desired to impact physical outcomes using physical
laws, then I suggest there is no experiment we could do that would invali-
date this hypothesis. Any physical process, by definition, would still be
explicable by physical laws, and would be governed by the laws of probability. Asking the question of whether God acts in a particular system or
not is always a matter of faith—and moving from the consideration of the
physical to the nonphysical.

It is illustrative to consider the etymology of the word here, as it demonstrates that the original meaning is rather different than our current usage.
Our word "miracle" descends from the Old French word *miracle*, which
itself was given to the same elasticity of meaning borne by our contemporary usage. Old French speakers in turn derived this word from Latin
miraculum, a noun meaning "a wonderful, strange, or marvelous thing,"
or, in a delightfully more abstract sense, "wonderfulness" or "marvelous-
ness" itself. Ultimately, the word appears to have originally been a nominalization from the Latin verb *miror*, a deponent verb of the first conju-
gation, meaning "to wonder at" or "to marvel at." I believe that it is this
original meaning of *wonder* that is key to understanding miracles.

In Jerome's Vulgate, the word *miraculum* appears only a handful of
times, and it only appears in the Old Testament. But a related word is used
where we now read *miracle*. Jerome employs the terms *signum,* meaning
"sign " *prodigium,* meaning "prodigy, wonder," and *virtue,* meaning

"strength," as words that fall within the general category of *miraculum*. All of these ideas—sign, wonder, portent, prodigy, power, strength— originate in the Hebrew notion of "נֵס," which translates literally as *flag* or *banner,* but figuratively means *sign* or *miracle.* Thus, we ought to conceive of the word *miracle* not so much that God tinkers with the world, but rather that God demonstrates action in the world by means of explicit announcement. These actions inspire wonder, but there is no sense that the announcement has to violate physical law.

But what is a physical law, and why would we even care if it is violated or not? We explore this in more depth later in the chapter, but, briefly, a physical law refers to the fundamental principles that govern the behavior of matter and energy in our universe; historically, philosophers and scientists deemed these physical laws or natural laws. It is important to reiterate that I do not suggest that God *cannot* violate physical law. Instead, my understanding of God is that God *chooses* not to violate physical law in order to preserve two of the greatest gifts God gives us: reason and free will. It is this belief that requires a rethinking of miracles.

The concept of miracle—configured to refer to a momentary or ongoing suspension of physical law—would be little more than magic. A miracle of this sort makes the most sense for a god of the gaps, and can only occupy a tenuous position. As science explains more of the world, this type of miracle becomes harder to accept. In fact, it is far more miraculous, to my mind, that reality behaves systematically and predictably. I find much more evidence of a creator in my ability to understand and measure God's design than I would if that design were not consistent and absolute. Miracles as magic actually contradict the type of creator exhibited in Scripture—a creator that wishes to engage us in relationship.

Think back to the metaphor for the fullness of reality that I offered in chapter four: creation as gestation (the expectant mother is in the act of creation while pregnant). God, as the fullness of reality, creates immanently, within God. Creator and created are no longer separate. The concept of miracle as magic—or the very suspension of physical law—is rooted in the image of creator as separate from creation, creator as artisan. This artisanal model of creation invites a God that intervenes in creation in ways that violate the physical laws set down at creation. The creator as fullness of reality invites a God that interacts with physical reality while preserving its integrity, and our freedom—miracles, but no magic.

What on Earth Is a Miracle For?

The concept of miracle is a powerful one, and one should take care before arbitrarily demanding a redefinition of the concept. One question we must ask is why are miracles such a strong element of the faith experience? Is our new definition consistent with this experience? If we assess the notion of what miracles are intended to achieve, does this lead naturally to the reframing of miracles that I propose?

In the prescientific world, miracles, I think, performed an important function as proofs, in a logical sense, of the power of God to act in the world. People had experiences of the divine, and they translated these experiences according to the vernacular explanation available to them: namely, miracles. Jesus himself says, "Believe me when I say that I am in the Father and the Father is in me; or at least believe on the evidence of the miracles themselves" (John 10:38 and 14:11).

These accounts of the miraculous date from a time during which miracles were accepted because the understanding of the world included them; miracles, for the authors of Scripture, are an exhibition of proof for the actual existence of the divine, and they accordingly did very important work in an early Christian worldview. Miracles are the signs that our exploration of the linguistic roots of the word pointed to. And it is the sign that is the key, not the magic.

A problem with miracles develops when we hold fast to the magical aspect of miracles as proof of God's actions. Too often we want the magical aspects of miracles to perform the labor of proof; we want magic to dispel our doubts. These are natural, commodious, and quite commendable ends. But when these miracles require magical violations of physical law, this dependence on miracles can be a crutch for a crippled faith. Were the magical outcomes on which we predicate our faith to be destabilized, so too would be our faith.

Therefore, the problem with miracles as proof, really, is our focus on the magical aspect of miracles. Instead, we need to ask the real questions: What was God's intent or action in the world that was interpreted by those experiencing it as being a miracle? What was the real sign or wonder that was the source of the miracle?

As the sciences become ever more refined, and as our explanatory models become ever more sophisticated, and as our predictions become ever more accurate, miracles as magic become increasingly impossible. Indeed, as our understanding waxes, the possibility for miracles of the magical type wanes. To be sure, the world operates according to well-understood and dependable physical laws. And theologians from Augustine to Karl Barth have, increasingly, had to revise their view of the miraculous. For example, one approach to the subject, as inexplicable phenomena have become explicable, is to treat miracles as a question of probabilities. I am suggesting we make the next logical step and recognize miracles as God's action in the world, shedding the unnecessary constraint of miracles as magic. Like our image of God and our interpretations of Scripture, if we cling too tightly to the sands of our notion of miracle as magic, the grains will slip through our fingers.

The Practice of Science and Physical Law

To understand why miracle as a suspension of physical law has caused consternation on the part of empiricist philosophers and natural theologians—not to mention scientists—it is worth discussing just what we mean by physical law, and how science as a discipline leads to the uncovering of physical laws. At its best, science has shown us that if it appears physical laws have been violated, then we probably misunderstand the physical laws, or we are witnessing a natural phenomenon transpiring according to a law we do not currently know or understand. Ascribing the violation of physical law to divine intervention reduces God into the role of a magician, bestowing favor capriciously and violating God's own rules to do it. This God—more accurately, god—would be just another super-hero, subject to the same debunking that has befallen ancient nature gods and modern, science-inspired comic book protagonists, and not the ultimate superhero I propose God truly is.

We may not understand physical laws fully at this time, but the practice of the sciences assumes that underlying all physical processes are principles and laws that are both fixed and knowable through the scientific process. Often, these physical laws—being the fundamental principles of the sciences—are elegant, simple verbal or mathematical formulations. We in the sciences talk in shorthand about these laws. Though it is true we have nothing approaching a complete set of physical laws, the practice of science has resulted in a body of laws, theories, and principles that are so well confirmed that we are confident that they are inviolate—and equally confident that these laws govern the behavior of matter and energy throughout all of physical reality.

We have confirmed these laws based on three elements of the scientific process: First, scientific laws are always subject to rigorous testing. Scientific laws are the product of repeated experimental observation; at a certain point, their validity is beyond doubt. A scientific law summarizes a vast collection of empirically observed facts into a simple, exclusive statement.

Second, all of the predictive potential in the sciences is predicated on the refinement and reality of our laws. A principle is considered to be a physical law precisely because all relevant experimental observations conform to the predictions of the physical law. Once a law has been repeatedly verified—and never falsified—the physical law supports a robust predictive capacity. Third, and finally, by definition, a scientific law must be falsifiable by experimentation, but must have never been falsified—despite a wide range of experiments.

That physical laws must be falsifiable in principle but never falsified is an interesting feature of science. When data suggest that a given highly confirmed scientific law is false, before rejecting the law, scientists must carefully scrutinize other options. Almost always, this leads to new and exciting knowledge, while at the same time preserving the physical law that was apparently violated. Therefore, because of the reiterative experimental process to which these laws are subject, very rarely is a fundamental scientific law falsified once it has been confirmed. It may be expanded and better understood, but the principle remains fundamentally true. What is important here is that scientific laws must be subject to the potential of falsifiability; they must be subject to empirical research.

Once discovered, physical laws tend to stand the test of time. Consider the laws governing the conservation of energy; you see, the total amount of energy in an isolated system does not diminish—indeed, it cannot change. Energy, according to the first law of thermodynamics, can neither be created nor destroyed in such a system, but it can change forms. Therefore, the chemical energy of coal can be converted to the thermal energy of exhaust gases, the thermal energy of exhaust gases can raise the temperature of water in a boiler, the thermal energy of that steam converts to the mechanical energy of a turbine, and the mechanical energy of a turbine converts to the electrical energy of a generator.

Now, because energy is changing form, if you focus on too small a system, the total amount of energy will appear to diminish because of inefficiencies (i.e., the loss of energy to kinetic sound energy, light energy, frictional thermal energy, etc.). But as long as you keep track of all forms of energy and consider a large enough system, the total amount of energy intrinsic to the coal at the initial stage is accountable throughout the process, and energy is conserved.

As scientists started to probe the smallest scales of matter, a handful of scientists noticed that, in certain processes of radioactive decay, energy appeared not to be conserved. Now, this was alarming because energy conservation had long served as a cornerstone of physics. Was all of physics prior to that moment wrong? Not necessarily, but in order to preserve the conservation of energy, scientists proposed that an almost undetectable particle must exist. Scientists labored to discover this mystery particle—and preserve energy conservation—making calculations and experimenting carefully. Eventually, Frederick Reines discovered this particle—which had been named the neutrino by Enrico Fermi—and preserved energy conservation. He won the Nobel Prize for that one!

So, scientific laws can tell you what things you can't see might look like—such as the neutrino. They can also tell you about the parameters of possibility. Like most scientists, I have been approached by all manner of excited folks selling their perpetual motion machines. I politely tell these people that their projects are featherbrained impossibilities without even looking at the schematics they provide. How? Because, owing to the second law of thermodynamics, it is impossible to make a machine that outputs more energy than the machine receives as input. Were such a device to exist, it would effectively result in free energy.

Free energy is pretty attractive to most people, and so people have spent countless hours trying to design a machine that generates excess energy. But no matter how innovative their design, no matter how complicated their schematics, no matter how elegant their mathematics, no matter how well they claim to understand the principles underpinning their project, the second law of thermodynamics stands directly in their path to success. So as I sweep their letters into the circular filing cabinet and mark their e-mails as spam after responding to them, I think how nice it is to have an inviolate second law of thermodynamics on my side.

Philosophy and Physical Law

If physical law is inviolate, can we account for God's agency in the world by means of physical law? If indeed God is agentive in the world, as I believe God is, and if indeed God elects not to subvert physical law, as I suggest is the case, then perhaps the physical laws that govern our observations of nature are the very channels by which grace flows. Though many philosophers focused on miracles as violations of physical law, the idea that these so-called miracles are actually rooted in physical law also has a long history.

In the early fifth century, Augustine argued, "We say that all portents are contrary to nature, but they are not so. For how is that which happens by the will of God contrary to nature, since the will of so mighty a Creator is certainly the nature of each created thing? A portent, therefore, happens not contrary to nature, but contrary to what we know as nature."[18] God's will, for Augustine, was the steward of outcomes in nature; God, then, was the hand guiding these events.

Signs and wonders were certainly known through the Scriptures, but their nature was debatable even in Augustine's time; were miracles examples of the suspension of physical law, or were miracles simply God's use of physical laws to demonstrate God's agency in the world? Augustine seems to argue for the latter. But, really, Augustine's conclusion is predicated on a particularly strong statement regarding God's interaction with the world. Because God is so powerful, his rhetorical question suggests, God's will alone is the true nature of all things. Therefore, nothing can transpire contrary to God's will, and thus all miracles must be explicable by natural philosophy on some level.

Augustine's conceptualization of the miraculous takes into account the incomplete nature of human knowledge—perhaps expectedly so, given his formulation of original sin. Furthermore, all entities have a nature that might not be totally understood to us as observers and, therefore, what appears to be contrary to nature is actually wholly explicable by the nature of the thing under observation.

It is interesting to ask how other philosophers have dealt with this question. Baruch Spinoza, a sixteenth-century Dutch philosopher, empiricist, and lens grinder, expressed a similar—if more overtly hostile—opinion on miracles. The problem, for Spinoza, is that if indeed God is the author of creation, then the laws that govern the physical world are themselves God's laws. It is an "evident absurdity," Spinoza believes, to suggest that God would ever act against God's own nature. Spinoza maintains,

> Nothing, then, comes to pass in nature in contravention to [nature's] universal laws, nay, everything agrees with them and follows from them, for whatsoever comes to pass, comes to pass by the will and eternal decree of God; that is, as we have just pointed out, whatever comes to pass, comes to pass according to laws and rules which involve eternal necessity and truth; nature, therefore, always observes laws and rules which involve eternal necessity and truth, although they may not all be known to us, and therefore she keeps a fixed and immutable order.[19]

Spinoza does, however, allow for the provisionality of interpretation. The underlying causes of events that seem miraculous are only so given our incomplete understanding of their causes. All phenomena in nature have an explicable, material, empirically discernible base—even those that seem to contravene our understanding of nature.

Voltaire, writing one hundred years later, voiced a similar argument more succinctly: "A miracle is the violation of mathematical, divine, immutable, eternal laws. By the very exposition itself, a miracle is a contradiction in terms: a law cannot at the same time be immutable and violated."[20] For

Spinoza and Voltaire, a miracle is a logical impossibility: because God's will is nature itself, and because God's will cannot be violated owing to God's omnipotence, it follows that miracles, defined as the suspension of physical laws, are a categorical absurdity.

David Hume, an eighteenth-century Scottish philosopher, also supports the impossibility of miracles that violate physical laws; he writes, "A miracle is a violation of the laws of nature; and as a firm and unalterable experience has established these laws, the proof against a miracle, from the very nature of the fact, is as entire as any argument from experience can possibly be imagined."[21]

Miracles, pace Hume, are singular impossibilities, as "Nothing is esteemed a miracle, if it ever happens in the common course of nature." Nature—not violations thereof—is the evidentiary underpinning of empirical observation. And because the laws that govern nature are sacrosanct, the actuality of miraculous occurrences is impossible. John Stuart Mill extends Hume's reasoning: "We cannot admit a proposition as a law of nature, and yet believe a fact in real contradiction to it. We must disbelieve the alleged fact, or believe that we are mistaken in admitting the supposed law."[22]

Both of these formulations take for granted the inviolability of physical laws. Indeed, if we are to assert that physical laws are inviolate—and they must be for them to have any predictive power—then we must accept that any violation of these laws must either: (1) be mistaken, (2) render invalid the law itself, or (3) be indicative of a new, yet-to-be-understood physical law that supersedes the initial violated law.

For philosophers and natural philosophers, the concern about miracles as violations of physical law has led to various conclusions. For example, we already saw that Augustine offers the possibility that God acts through physical laws, while others simply conclude that miracles are impossible. Another approach, as naturalistic explanations of phenomena have

waxed into certainty, is to reduce God's actions in the world from violations of physical laws to a question of probabilities. This is the relative of
the current-day miraculous sports win from behind, or the lucky lottery
ticket.

Hume notes the probabilistic nature of events as a significant reason for
reticence when considering the validity of miracles:

> A wise man...proportions his belief to the evidence He considers
> which side is supported by the greater number of experiments:
> To that side he inclines, with doubt and hesitation; and when
> at last he fixes his judgment, the evidence exceeds not what
> we properly call probability. All probability, then, supposes an
> opposition of experiments and observations, where the one side
> is found to overbalance the other, and to produce a degree of
> evidence, proportioned to the superiority.[23]

This view of miracle suggests that when considering the miraculous nature
of a proposed miracle, we must consider the likelihood of the event's
occurrence in accordance with that scientific probability.

An oncologist might give a one in fifty chance of a patient's survival;
if that patient survives, is it miraculous? There was, from the outset, a
chance for a happy resolution, but that outcome was not guaranteed and
was overwhelmingly improbable—but it was possible. Therefore, it is by
means of probability that we proportion our belief to the evidence.

Albert Einstein notes a similar condition for miracles when he discusses
the possibility of a personal God. Science, he maintains, establishes general
rules to "determine the reciprocal connection of objects and events in
time," and human observers impute significance to the outcomes of these
events.[24] So rather than God existing, for Einstein, in a personal, affective sense, it is instead human understanding that imputes onto natural
phenomena a type of religious significance.

Paul Tillich, the German Protestant theologian, dissents from this perspective, but still maintains that likelihood and unlikelihood are satisfactory criteria according to which we might judge the miraculousness of a given event.[25] The likelihood of a favorable outcome—be it small or large—seems to be a necessary consideration when interpreting an event as miraculous.

The British mathematician John Edensor Littlewood also considers probability when determining whether a given event could be usefully called a miracle.

Littlewood maintains that humans experience about one event per second, and, over the course of a month, a given human will have experienced about one million events. Defining the word *miracle* as an outcome whose probability is one in a million, Littlewood's law maintains that this given person—indeed, all persons—will experience a miracle, per his formulation, at the rate of about one a month. That is, every human being is the beneficiary of the probabilistic nature of outcomes, insofar as we are constantly experiencing statistically unlikely events.

Now, Littlewood continues by saying that these "miracles" wouldn't seem miraculous—being on the extraordinarily minute scale of a one-second-long event—but that they would be statistically unlikely at a probability of about one in a million.

A shoelace becoming untied under normal wear and tear, as long as it carries a probability of one in a million, constitutes a miracle according to Littlewood's law.

From a probabilistic view of miracles, God's action in the world is simply a matter for statisticians to consider. However, I would suggest that even this probabilistic view severely limits God's actions and misses the point of miracles. As much as it might agree with the everyday use of the word as discussed at the beginning of this chapter, treating miracles as unlikely events tends to miss an important issue. Statistically unlikely beneficial outcomes would be evidence of a capricious God—not at all the behavior of a just and merciful judge.

Why should God have tipped the odds for the Seahawks in Super Bowl XLVIII, but reserved favor from the unimaginable suffering of the Holocaust? Why would God have stacked the deck in my favor when I found my keys this morning, but stacked the deck against the thousands victimized by the 2008 financial crisis? How could a kind, loving, infinitely beneficent creator shepherd my eldest daughter to her freshman year at Salve Regina, but forget to recall the covenant God established in Genesis 9:15 in the aftermath of Hurricane Katrina? The truth is, even though God's method of dispensation is fundamentally unknowable to us, I doubt God plays dice and only acts in unlikely ways. As Job reminds us, Providence is a knife that cuts both ways, and it slices both abundance and dearth in a like manner. God's actions must mean something more.

I think we need to deal frankly with the distinction between phenomena and significance. The description of a given outcome as miraculous is always propositional: one either believes God to have acted in your life—whether through an unlikely event or an everyday event—or one does not. To accept a given outcome as consonant both with physical law and religious interpretation requires that one interpret that outcome as God's action.

John Hick, the eminent British American evangelical theologian and philosopher, suggests precisely this way out of the quagmire of miracles. He writes, "If 'miracle' is defined as a breach of physical law, one can declare a priori that there are no miracles. It does not follow, however, that there are no miracles in the religious sense of the term, for the principle that nothing happens in conflict with physical law does not entail that there are no unusual and striking events evoking and mediating a vivid awareness of God."[26] I would carry Hick's statement further: an event need not be unusual or striking to evoke an awareness of God; I am often struck by God's majesty when considering the smallest, most inconsequential things.

Because physical laws are a posteriori generalizations formulated to describe what has actually happened, we need not resort to the understanding of miracle as an example of impossibility or unlikelihood. It is the experience and interpretation of a given event as religiously significant that allows us to frame it in miraculous terms. An important feature of this argument is that miracles do not serve as the foundation of religious faith, but, rather, presuppose religious faith.

"The religious response," continues Hick, "which senses the purpose of God in the inexplicable coincidence or the improbable and unexpected occurrence, makes an event a miracle."[27] Religion, then, provides the channels through which faithful experiencers of unlikely events may voice their apprehension of the divine—regardless of the physical reality that lies beneath the putative miracle.

So, if physical law is inviolate, and if all our apprehensions of the miraculous are rooted in physical laws, we can expand our understanding of miracle. Einstein points us in one direction: "There are only two ways to live your life: one is as though nothing is a miracle; the other is as though everything is a miracle"; we see echoes of this in Charles Alexander Eastman's recollections of his boyhood: "The logical man must either deny all miracles or none." If indeed, as Walt Whitman would have us believe, everything is miraculous, then we need to frankly admit the commonplace nature of miracles. We live our lives deeply implicated and inextricably enmeshed in a miracle. Miracles exist all around us, and it is for us to impute their miraculous significance onto them.

The events that we deem miraculous require an initial religious perspective. As I said in the book's introduction, religious experience is, in its very nature, individual. Individual experience is the original locus of faith, and these experiences are, ipso facto, unrepeatable. Taken together, our shared religious experience moves beyond individual experience and becomes communal. Therefore, a religious community can view an event as miraculously significant.

By definition, we cannot subject these experiences to anything like the scientific method because they are interpretations of experiences that are generally nonrepeatable. Religious experiences can be true and evident; they simply cannot be subjected to the explanatory power of science owing to their very subjectivity.

Though these events are not subject to scientific inquiry, this does not mean that we shouldn't approach miracles without critical analysis. Even Jesus provides guidance on distinguishing true and false religious experience: Are they consistent with God's love for us? Therefore, even though ultimately I am not in a position to judge your religious experiences any more than you are in a position to judge mine, I do suggest that we ought to submit our experiences to critical assessment. Only then can we ascertain their truth. I would suggest that true miracles always move us to a deeper, more loving relationship with God and the rest of humanity. In this regard, miracles occur every day, only they occur in our hearts and minds and not in our wishes or hopes about the external world.

Conclusion: Toward a Satisfactory Definition of the Miraculous

Now, you may be dissatisfied with this definition of miracle—a scientifically explicable event, the significance of which is determined ex post facto. But as I have said throughout the book, the sciences have the potential to enhance our religious faith and aid us as we make positive spiritual growth. The thrust of our definition should aim to communicate the agency of God rather than depend on violations of physical law. Moreover, God's agency ought not to simply be taken to effect only outcomes that are unlikely; instead, I suggest we interpret miracles to be occasions when people accept the offer from God to enter into full participation with reality.

Again, it is useful to return to the maternal metaphor of creation immanent in God. If indeed God sustains that creation by means of physical laws, then God's agency in the world is evidenced by every falling stone, every rolling Newtonian ball, and every shining star. God did not simply provide to Moses the Ten Commandments in order to guide our moral conduct; God did not only clarify God's expectations of us in the other laws of the Torah; God also stitched God's law into the very fabric of existence. The reality we inhabit is a tapestry woven on the loom of space-time according to a pattern established by God. This natural order—flowing, as it does, from God—is inviolable. That the entire natural universe behaves in accordance with predictable, knowable laws is far more miraculous than momentary suspensions of that order. And, accordingly, the regular behavior of the cosmos, both celestial and mundane, whispers the will of God.

If God is indeed the fullness of reality, and if indeed this reality is composed of both physical and nonphysical elements, we should expect an interaction between the physical and nonphysical that is consistent with physical laws. I recognize that this represents a problem for the strict naturalist, as it involves the nonphysical, but it is central to a faith based on relationship with God. In this worldview, miracles as examples of magical violations of physical law are not possible; a regular, predictable universe does not allow them. But if we view miracles as integrated into our world system as God's actions, then miracles are not only possible, they are rather probable—and, indeed, we see it every day in every observation we make and in every experience of God that we have.

I admit that even with the understanding of miracles as I propose it, we must still deal with the reality of physical suffering. I cannot pretend to know why the natural order seems to favor the physical comforts of some at the expense of others, but I do believe that we can trust that God's love is infinite. In the end, we are asked both to take the world as it is and to enter into relationship with God out of our free choice. In a strange way, I take comfort in the notion that true evil—the harm done by humans to humans—can only flow from human agency and free will. Evil is not of God. We are free to choose to commit these deeds or to resist them but, ultimately, the responsibility lies with us.

So, how are we to understand stories of miraculous occurrences that we find in Scripture? I have suggested earlier that we need to avoid focusing on the magical elements, and instead, look for the transformative and relational elements. It is useful to consider an example; and for this, consider the story of Balaam in the book of Numbers.

The Israelites had wandered in the desert for close to forty years, and their conquest now aimed at the kingdom of Moab. The Israelites had already enjoyed great success in this campaign owing to the favor of God, and Moab was their next step toward subjugating the whole of Canaan. Balak, the king of Moab, sends his retainers and the elders of Midian to Balaam—a sorcerer and conjurer of some repute—to enjoin him to curse the Israelites and their imminent attack. Balaam replies that he is only able to do what God has commanded, and Balak increases the price he offered to convince Balaam. God relents and allows Balaam to go out to curse the Israelites, but commands that Balaam only say what God wills him to say.

Balaam departs, riding on a donkey, to curse the Israelites from a promontory. On the way, an angel appears to the donkey, which becomes startled and refuses to move. Angrily, Balaam beats the donkey severely. Righting the beast, Balaam attempts to continue, but the angel appears again, spooking the donkey, which collides with a rocky outcropping, crushing Balaam's foot. Again, Balaam violently beats the donkey. Setting the donkey on the path for a third time, Balaam attempts to continue, only to be frustrated while, in a steep gorge of some kind, the angel appears to the donkey, which refuses to move forward at all. This final insult occasions Balaam's most violent beating.

As Balaam is beating the donkey, the donkey begins to speak: "What have I done to you, that you strike me these three times? Am I not your donkey, which you have ridden all your life to this day? Have I been in the habit of treating you this way?" To the donkey's question—and seemingly unsurprised by his talking donkey—Balaam responds simply, "No." At that moment, God causes Balaam to see the angel standing before the donkey. Balaam promptly prostrates himself and worships the angel, who informs Balaam that, had his donkey continued on the path, the angel would have killed him. Balaam's path is perverse and reckless, the angel maintains, and so it must be obstructed (Numbers 22:1—39).

Now, at face value, this miracle is absurd. To be sure, Christ reminds us that "through God all things are possible" (Matthew 19:26), but a talking donkey strains credulity. Indeed, a donkey that talks would seem to violate the natural order governing equines—which are famously taciturn, except in myth, fable, fairy tale, and the movie *Shrek*. But I would argue that this story is an account of an actual miracle—just not the obvious physical miracle of a talking donkey.

Whether or not Balaam heard a donkey talking is irrelevant. But the crux of this account is that Balaam had a set of experiences that caused him to perceive reality differently than he would have otherwise perceived it—and that these experiences were the result of God's actions. In the end, Balaam still could have chosen a different path despite these experiences—due to free will, the subject of the next chapter—but he elected to embrace these experiences. In a similar manner, God's interaction with reality leads to Abram's choice to risk it all and become Abraham (Genesis 17:5), Saul's change of heart (1 Samuel 10:9), and the scales to fall from Paul's eyes (Acts 9:18). God opens the opportunity for people to change their circumstances by entering into relationship with the fullness of reality. Therein lies the miraculous.

Things do not end well for Balaam: though, as a result of this experience, he confers a blessing on the Israelites rather than cursing them (as Balak would have had him do), he nevertheless tells Balak how to make the Israelites curse themselves—by means of worldly temptation. When, eventually, the Israelites are victorious against the Moabites and Midianites, Balaam is put to the sword along with the rest. But Balaam is unique as a Gentile prophet, and his miracle—his sign, his wonder—was not his impossible talking donkey; rather, Balaam experienced the divine by means of his change of heart. That was his miracle.

So, if we turn the definition of miracle on its head, we see that a miracle starts as a private occurrence—by which one is transformed in their relationship to God—and then expands into the communal sphere through the actions of the recipient that were engendered by this transformation. Now, it is not my place, nor the purpose of this chapter, to suggest what really did or did not happen from a physical point of view for each and every miracle in Scripture—or for miracles attributed to God since then. But I do want to emphasize that when we focus on miracles as violations of physical law, I believe this distracts us from the real point of the miraculous experience.

For example, when looked at closely, the heart of all of Jesus's miracles is not the physical occurrence. We may be surprised or troubled by the physical aspects of his miracles, but our scientific concerns tend to obscure what shocked the people of his time: the performance of miracles on the Sabbath, the forgiveness of sins, the elicitation of a deeper faith—in summary, the transformation of individuals and communities that results in a deeper relationship with God. These are the wonders and signs that made the actions miraculous and worth recording.

In no way do I want to suggest that God never acts to engender positive physical outcomes for people. It is not my place to judge if a particular turn of fortune was the direct outcome of God's actions. This is for individuals who experience the event to decide. But, I need to emphasize that my view of miracles has two related implications. First, if God is causing particular physical outcomes, it is occurring in a way that would not appear to violate physical law. Second, this view of miracles raises an interesting open question—how do nonphysical reality and physical reality actually interact? This is a question for which I do not have any answer. But one thing I do believe, the Resurrection is one example of God's interaction with the world that is properly considered a miracle, even by my definition. As I will explore in chapter nine, the question of life after death is fundamentally an issue of our transformation from a life based in physical reality to a new life in full union with God, the fullness of reality. This transformation is the ultimate realization of the daily transformations generated by God's interactions in our life, and it is not a violation of physical law as it is first and foremost a transcendent, or mystical, experience that goes beyond the purely physical.

To my mind, the formulation of miracles in terms of God's interaction with us and our transformation due to that interaction is a useful starting point for reflecting on how the nonphysical and physical aspects of reality interact, and it is a far more potent understanding of miracles than would otherwise be suggested by a God who violates physical laws. A God who violates physics is the magical god of the gaps, the mundane superhero that contravenes physical law by simply saving the day; if God is the ultimate superhero—as the fullness of reality—then any miraculous action on God's part would make use of the physical reality. That physical reality is intelligible and explicable at all seems to be a better proof of God than examples of physical law being contravened.

If we are free to elect to take God's invitation to join in full relationship with God, then we can reframe the concept of *miracle* as one of personal transformation that enables this relationship to occur. It is indeed miraculous that the fullness of reality would desire a relationship with us, and it is even more contrary to expectation that God would call us to this relationship. Jesus tells us, "Unless you see signs and wonders, you believe not" (John 4:48). These signs and wonders, I believe, are the personal religious experiences that urge us toward communion with God, the sensitivities and sensibilities that impel us to understand the fullness of God's reality, and the laws that constrain the conduct of heaven and earth.

Chapter 8

God's Dice: Free Will, Determinism, and Compatibility

The heart of man plans his way, but the Lord establishes his steps.

—Proverbs 16:9

Man can do what he wills; but he cannot will what he wills.
  —Arthur Schopenhauer, *On the Freedom of the Will* (1839)

[God] does not throw dice!
  —Albert Einstein, letter to Max Born, December 4, 1926

Stress is a choice, so do not choose it.
—Kimberly Dennin, to her father while writing this book, 2014

Love is a choice, so choose it.
  —Michael Dennin, while writing this book, 2014

I often call myself a cradle Catholic—a member of the Catholic Church from infancy—but I have a confession to make. That's not strictly true. Sure, I have participated in the sacraments according to the normal schedule: I was baptized as an infant, catechized prior to my First Communion and confirmation as a teen, confessed to a priest, and married in the church. But I didn't really choose to fully engage my relationship with God and my community until I was a graduate student.

This might sound odd: I can count on one hand the number of Sundays that I have missed the Mass. It's the way that I structure my week; it brings me comfort in its familiarity. I've always been partial to the pomp and circumstance of the Mass; I feel refreshed by the intellectual challenge presented in a really good homily; I've never failed to be struck by the timeless themes of Scripture. But—and I don't think this is uncommon for many religious persons—I never had a moment of conversion akin to Methodist founder John Wesley's Aldersgate experience of a "heart strangely warmed." High Church traditions—such as Eastern Orthodoxy, Catholicism, and some confessions in the Anglican Communion—don't necessarily require experiences such as these. Though I'm somewhat ambivalent about the necessity of a "heart strangely warmed," I can tell you that my version of such an experience was the result of making a choice.

Even as an undergraduate at Princeton, I was an observant Catholic: I went to Mass and participated in the community and outreach. But if someone asked me why I did so—as some of my more secular-minded colleagues did—I would have provided an answer largely based on habit. I went to Mass, participated in community and outreach, and worked toward the sacraments because I always had; it felt right. There was no challenge or real growth.

That all changed in graduate school. Exercising my usual habits, I became involved in the community at St. Mark's, the university parish at the University of California, Santa Barbara. The focus of the parish was ministering to the Catholic community at UCSB; the parish was run by the Paulist Fathers (it is now administered by the Los Angeles Archdiocese), and the pastor was the inimitable Fr. Ken.

Until that point, my faith had always been very intellectual and fundamentally personal. To be sure, my experience at a Jesuit high school had deepened my understanding of both faith and myself as a religious person, but it had not challenged my growth as a person in the context of a community. Fr. Ken, however, had other ideas.

Fr. Ken had invited me to take a leadership position on the parish council—a committee that helped the pastor to administrate the community. Bear in mind, I was a graduate student and therefore beset with the responsibilities of a scholar. Additionally, Fr. Ken and the parish leadership took seriously the job of spiritual directors for the community. They did not hesitate to challenge us on areas where we needed to grow. I did not like being challenged, and found the call to growth very discomforting.

After a few months, I offered my resignation—and I was ready to quit participation in the local parish altogether. My excuse to myself was the time commitment, but the reality was the desire to avoid challenges to who I was and how I behaved. Fr. Ken wouldn't hear of it. "You have a choice," he said. "We can't compel you. But you need to step back and figure out what's important to you."

I had to weigh the balance: Would I remain individualistic in my faith, and thereby work in solitude? Or would I invite the community into my heart and, in the process, grow as a person? In the end, I choose to break from my usual mold of resisting personal challenges, and I persisted. And the decision was solidified in early spring—as part of a Lenten spiritual direction program.

All of us, at one time or another, have probably been asked to take a personality test. In grade school and high school, I took many of these tests to ascertain my ideal future vocation, to determine my ideal college major, to figure out my options for school, among many, many other diagnoses. I had always found these examinations to be utterly useless. But in preparation for this retreat, we had all taken a diagnostic examination about our values and aspirations in faith. My cynicism no doubt colored my expectations of this examination.

As part of the spiritual direction program, we had all taken the Hall-Tonna Values exam, a questionnaire created by Brian P. Hall, a professor of counseling and pastoral care at Santa Clara University. This questionnaire seemed innocuous enough: It begins with what seems to be a generic personality test. The taker is then prompted to categorize experiences based on levels of interpersonal awareness. Ultimately, it assesses what is important to a person. And my results resonated so well with my current situation—my need for community and my desire to learn to accept the hard work of personal growth.

Now, this might not seem like a Wesleyan moment of deep revelation, and on one level I agree. But, understand, I was ready to make the choice to leave this parish. If my past was any predictor of the future, that is the choice I would have made—the easy choice. But at a crucial moment, I made the harder choice. I made a choice to do something different and differently. I chose to embrace community and partake fully in the spiritual direction. In retrospect, this was also my choice to enter fully into a relationship with my God. And it was through the combination of the free choice to embrace this change and my employment of the tools provided by spiritual direction that I was able to change as a person.

Every day I am greeted by fortunate circumstances that are themselves direct consequences of that decision I made in graduate school—I met my wife, Jeni, at St. Mark's. Our three beautiful daughters are a direct result of my decision to live for others in the context of community. The ramifications ripple through the waters of my whole life. And I write this book as a direct result of this experience. I made the choice to do something different and differently. I exercised my free choice to effect a desired goal by God's grace.

Everywhere we turn, with everyone we meet, at any time it seems as though there's a decision to make. These decisions are variously simple (what route to take to work in the morning?) or complex (how should I vote in the next election?). Each of these decisions, however, is both radically individual and circumscribed by situation and circumstance. Similarly, the choice I made to live my spiritual life for the lives of others was simultaneously freely willed and dependent on my particular circumstance.

There is an underlying tension, I think, in most of world literature; it seems a defensible generalization to note that much—if not all—literature is concerned with the exercise of free will. Is our life predetermined or do we have radical choice?

Every great work of literature that I can recall features (or is wholly predicated on) a rumination on or consideration of questions of fate, destiny, and choice. Are outcomes fated, or is destiny firmly in hand and actionable by choice? I would argue that this question of free will occupies an even greater proportion of human contemplation than the question of God's existence; it is crucially central to our everyday experience.

We as humans feel an ever-present tension; we feel both complete control and lack of control. But at the end of the day, at least we have—if nothing else—the illusion of choice. We certainly have opportunities, and we can make decisions according to those opportunities. Yet, at the same time, on some grand scale, we feel at times as though life is out of our control.

The topic of free will is extraordinarily rich and complex; not only does the tension between free will and determinism, on some level, preoccupy much of human literature, the tension has long been considered by theologians, philosophers, social scientists, and physical scientists. How can we explain the possibility of free will in a reality that—our sciences would suggest—is fundamentally deterministic? In the sciences, when we have full knowledge of the initial conditions of a given system, then—to an extremely accurate degree—we can predict all future behavior of that system. We scientists call that determinism; theologians, with reference to salvation, might call it predestination.

We certainly structure society in accordance with radical free will. We have laws, we publicize those laws, and if you break those laws—except for a few extenuating circumstances—we interpret this as an act of volition and, ultimately, we send you to prison. The fact that we assume there is choice is intrinsic to the fact that we are making a rule. Were there not choice, there would be no need for a rule. But at the same time, we are constrained in our decision making—whether by social convention, by the limits of possibility, or by reality itself. We perceive these limits, usually, and operate within them. So, from a certain perspective, our choice is illusory—or at least delimited.

Is our choice merely an illusion—or, worse, a delusion? While we can discount our experiences as conditioned by circumstance, while we can query our perceptions as culturally coded, while we can second-guess the validity of our actions, we cannot but be struck by the fundamental reality of our agency. Perhaps even more striking are the examples of people who decide to change their lives—as I did as a UCSB graduate student—and then follow through on that choice by successfully changing their lives. Likewise, the examples of people beset by largely identical circumstances enjoying different life trajectories are, to me, examples of free will at work. Examples of people making the choice to change their lives leads me to conclude that, on some level, free will must exist. The question is: What on earth does that mean, for heaven's sake?

At this point in my life, I understand free will as the ability to choose to do something different or differently than your past would suggest. As we are too aware, choice is not always enough to enact the change we desire. Circumstances do matter. Therefore, often, a critical component of this choice is the election of a new regime that can turn the choice into habit—especially if there is an external support structure associated with the new regime. This election of a new regime is the intersection of free will as choice and religious practice as habituation that opens us up to a relationship with God.

Reflex, instinct, and rapid response are all features of human agency, but they do not negate the possibility of free will. If every choice we had to make was subject to deliberation, we would be paralyzed by infinitude. We clearly do not function that way. Obviously, a large amount of our responses are automated—and they need to be, lest we fail to function quickly enough. We are beings that are both automated and automating; we are both subject to determinism and availed of free will; we are both constrained and agentive.

A useful analogy here, I think, would be an example of an athlete, an artist, or a musician when compared to a person who wants to become an athlete, an artist, or a musician. Training is absolutely crucial to any higher-order physical expression. A learner develops reflexive muscle memory, hones the intellect that governs the theory behind the action, and practices until these become second nature. Free will, in a sense, is the ability to accustom oneself to a new behavior.

Free will in the context of faith makes clear what our goals should be. The practices and rituals of any religion are not ends in themselves. Prayer, the sacraments, the Mass—these are not the endpoints of faith. Meditation, charity, community building—these are not the endpoints of faith. These are the tools that allow us to enter into a free relationship with God; the relationship is the end goal, and this relationship with God leads to deeper and more authentic relationships with the people in our lives. It's not the works that make a person religious; rather, the works serve to condition you to higher religious awareness and the works flow from your choice to have a relationship with God. On the other hand, we see how the choice is coupled with the hard work of making the choice a habit—and it is through the continued practice that we keep the choice alive. As James reminds us, "For just as the body without the spirit is dead, so faith without works is also dead" (2:26).

The central tenet of free will, to my mind, is that we've been given choices—independent of who we are, no matter where we're born, incidental to what our genetics are—and we've been asked to make these choices at some point in our lives. And, regardless of external factors, we can make the decision that we would like to do something different or differently. This places free will not in contrast to determinism but in the context of determinism—a qualified determinism, if you will. In this way, free will and determinism need not be mutually exclusive features of the human condition.

One side of free will is the understanding that we must freely choose to assent to God's grace—just as I did as a graduate student at UCSB. The other side of free will is the understanding that we are subject to preconditions that can make the ascent to a relationship with God more difficult. And the works of religions—spiritual practice toward greater religious sensitivity—are vehicles designed to help get us to our desired destination. Once on the journey, God's grace completes the chosen journey for you. We make the decision to start the journey; God paves the road for us.

I believe that evidence for free will comes in three flavors. We have the individual experience of free will: the choice I made to develop my skills as a soccer player despite nature herself limiting me; the choice I made to embrace my faith in God, despite my natural inclination to take the easy path. Most of us can cite moments at which we made decisions to act outside of our normal behavior. Though this evidence is anecdotal, it is still powerful and highly suggestive of, at the very least, the possibility of free will.

We have psychological experiences that support the existence of free will: prison rehabilitation programs and twelve-step programs are but two examples. In both of these examples, individuals elect to undergo a type of reprogramming. Freely made decisions underpin these experiences, and these experiences are wholly predicated on a robust change in behavior based on a contrite heart and a receptive mind. These enterprises are committed to helping people make better decisions, and if the participant assents, they have a remarkable track record of success.

Finally, we have religious experiences that involved particularly sensitive persons having deep experiences of the fullness of reality that radically transform their lives. Such historical figures as the Buddha, the Old Testament prophets, Jesus Christ, Francis of Assisi, Ignatius of Loyola, Mahatma Gandhi, and Martin Luther King, Jr., among many others, are examples of people who experienced a developmentally profound moment of change that signaled a deep connection to the fullness of reality. We need look no further than Abram's transition into Abraham (Genesis 17:5) and Saul's conversion into Paul (Acts 9) as singular moments of profound religious experience that resulted in a dramatic change in life-style—and ones that resulted in the fundamental reformation of the experiencer as signaled by their name changes.

If we agree that free will is, on some level, the ability to choose to do something different or differently, then I think there are three logical possibilities for free will as a concept. The first is categorical nonexistence. If everything is deterministic—if everything simply reflects the physics that governs it—not only does that negate the possibility of free will, it makes the existence of God somewhat unnecessary. Free will, then, enjoys a place of prominence in relation to our understanding of the divine and the existence of the divine. It is certainly possible that all that's out there is a constellation of physical laws that determine the behaviors of phenomena in reality and nothing more. The fundamental impossibility of free will is certainly a possibility, but I don't think that this option is consistent with our experience as human beings who make choices every day—no matter how those choices are constrained.

The second option is that free will is simply an emergent property of our biological and social conditions, explained by the sciences alone. If such is the case, free will would be real in a fundamentally physical way. This premise does not necessitate recourse to the divine to explain free will. If free will is an emergent property of our biology, this could be the result of God's will as embodied in the physical laws of nature, or it could exist in a reality that does not go beyond our physical reality. Therefore, if science were able to demonstrate that free will is a result of our biology, both divine existence and nonexistence would be logically possible. Right now, our science is unable either to support or eliminate the postulate that free will is an emergent property of our biology, but it is a reasonably logical possibility.

The third possibility for free will fully incorporates understandings intuited by faith and the possibilities afforded by the sciences. It embraces a concept of free will that accepts the reality of the nonphysical when contemplating the fullness of reality. It locates the ability to freely choose to change how we act within our direct participation with the fullness of reality that is God. Free will in this sense goes beyond a purely emergent property of the brain. If we contemplate this type of free will, we need to ask direct questions about the possible interactions between physical and nonphysical reality—and how choice fits within the constraints of a physical world.

I find myself favoring this third possibility—that radical free will exists and is a direct consequence of the nonphysical. Or, to turn this formulation on its head, if radical free will is not a reality, the very concept of God—and especially the concept of a God that loves us and wants to have a relationship with us—probably doesn't make any sense. If we are all mechanisms in a preordained clockwork, what would be the point?

As to the question of free will as emergence, I would not be surprised if this were the case. Systems are often found with amazing properties not present in the underlying physics. Perhaps the most challenging example of emergence is the thermodynamic arrow of time, a concept first advanced by British astronomer Arthur Eddington in 1927.

At the scale of molecules, there is no sense of a direction of time; on the molecular level, systems can move in either direction in time with equal probability. However, form these molecules into a large enough system, and suddenly we have a strong sense to a direction of time. The gas molecules in a room will never spontaneously gather in the corner. But if these molecules start in the corner, they will always spread out and become evenly dispersed. Entropy, the tendency toward disorder in equilibrium, provides the arrow of thermodynamic time.

Try an experiment at home: go into a room with a linoleum or concrete floor, a table, and a cup of coffee in a ceramic mug. Set up a superfast video camera that captures this system. Finally, push the cup of coffee off the table so that it shatters on the floor below. Now, watch the video you have made playing both forward—that is, with time—and backward (against time). Almost as if by instinct, you know that shattered coffee cup gathering back together spontaneously and "falling" back up onto the table is backward. But were you able to zoom in and focus on a single molecule in this video, whether you viewed this video forward or backward would not matter. When viewed in any temporal direction, either forward or backward, the movement of that molecule looks perfectly normal.

The directionality of time is not intrinsic at the microscopic level. Entities at this scale are time symmetric: the theoretical statements that govern their behavior remain true regardless of the directionality of time. But we, at the macroscopic level, experience a flow of time. Eddington believes that this sensitivity to the directionality of time is a consequence of consciousness and reason. But—and this is crucial, I think—time directionality only becomes consequential in the organization of systems; that is to say, the directionality of time only becomes important as systemic complexity increases. This is a classic case of an emergent property, and free will may be a property that emerges when neurons are connected in a sufficiently complex manner.

Now, this might be a perfectly legitimate explanation for free will, but I think that a more likely explanation of free will is our participation in a fuller reality that is not physical. My intuition that we participate in something more than our physical selves flows from my belief in the existence of God as the fullness of reality. I believe that our free will is deeply connected with our sensitivity to and participation in the divine—what we might rightfully call our soul. For me, this is the most likely reality, and I believe science even points us in this direction, though it cannot directly test ideas regarding the nonphysical.

I would suggest that our free will is best understood as the metaphorical breath of God bestowed upon us at creation. If we are indeed made in the image of God, then we, too, must possess the capacity for choice, and these choices must be—to the degree possible—freely actionable. Now, as we will see below, this formulation makes sense when considered alongside our current best models of physical reality. Our choices, like the outcomes of scientific systems, are governed by factors beyond our immediate control, but we are able to elect to change these parameters. I think our ability to choose—despite or perhaps because of the limited choice palette we find available—is strong evidence in favor of divine interaction, especially when we define free will as the ability to choose to do something different or differently.

Some of the most exciting and novel fields in physics point toward this qualified determinism—this compatibility between free will and determinism. But in order to understand how the sciences can enhance our faith and give us a glimpse into the fullness of this reality, we need to confront some heady scientific concepts.

Quantum mechanics is among the most misused and misunderstood features of modern physics. Its features appeal to the esoteric—wave-particle dualities, wave functions, and uncertainty principles...the list of abstruse and enigmatic phrases is long. It is for this reason that quantum mechanics is often pressed into the service of questionable New Age spiritism; but quantum mechanics—divorced of its pop-culture associations—is currently the best model we have for predicting phenomena on the smallest scale we can currently imagine. For that reason, a more robust understanding of quantum mechanics provides a glimpse into the fabric of God's tapestry.

Agency and Determinism in Scripture

Free will and determinism may often seem to be mutually exclusive propositions. Theologically, the contrast between free will and determinism is generally placed in the context of salvation. If God has predetermined the salvation of the elect, for instance, where does that leave the potential for free will? If we are radically free agents—free to choose to accept God's grace—then how, logically, can God predetermine that outcome? Before focusing on the scientific issues, a brief overview of the histories of free will and theological determinism, called predestination, seems prudent.

Western religious traditions, at face value, would seem to support the radical agency suggested by the notion of free will. While God is variously presented by our scriptural authors as omnipotent and omniscient, the Bible is replete with examples of humanity failing to live up to divine expectations. The earliest story we have in the Bible, after the creation narrative, is the story of the Fall (Genesis 3). From this episode, it would seem that God created mankind with the capacity for free will. Free will is also built into the preservation of God's covenant with the Israelites:

> See, I have set before you today life and prosperity, death and adversity. If you obey the commandments of the Lord your God that I am commanding you today, by loving the Lord your God, walking in his ways, and observing his commandments, decrees, and ordinances, then you shall live and become numerous, and the Lord your God will bless you in the land that you are entering to possess. But if your heart turns away, and you will not hear, but are drawn away to worship other gods and serve them, I declare to you today, that you shall surely perish. You shall not live long in the land that you are going over the Jordan to enter and possess. (Deuteronomy 30:15–18)

The intrusion of free will into this relationship is signaled by the use of *if*. There is a conditional and hopeful element to God's promise of favor. The outcome does not seem predetermined, and God here seems to ruminate on the potential of at least two outcomes. Therefore, this *if* is somewhat deliberative, but also designed to serve as type of deterrent remonstrance. God is simply laying out God's arrangement; God is clarifying God's covenant.

But Scripture also plainly reveals a God who is omniscient, omnipotent, and omnipresent; our free will would appear to be constrained by these characteristics of the fullness of reality. We could, in a sense, term this a type of determinism predestination—the only distinction between the determinism of the sciences and the predestination of theology would be the methodology. Now, when I say predestination, I do not intend here to discuss whether we are all fated and destined either to salvation or perdition; I will discuss the afterlife in chapter nine. Rather, I am using predestination to refer to an idea that maintains a sort of teleology of outcomes—an interpretation of the sum total of lived experience as preordained and predetermined by God.

Scripture certainly presents a strong case for the action of God in our decision-making process. This notion is recurrent in Scripture. Jesus reminds us that "no one can come to me unless the Father who sent me draws him. And I will raise him up on the last day" (John 6:44); that is, salvation through Christ is possible through the role of God the Father as instigator. Paul reminds us, "By grace you have been saved through faith. And this is not your own doing; it is the gift of God, not a result of works, so that no one may boast. For we are his workmanship, created in Christ Jesus for good works, which God prepared beforehand, that we should walk in them" (Ephesians 2:8–10). These passages also might suggest a predestinarian regime is at work, where God makes all the decisions. But I contend there is a conceptual difference between God's offer of salvation and God's preordaining salvation.

Augustine was the first to formalize a robust articulation of God's role in salvation as a theological concept; for Augustine, grace was a significant aspect of soteriology. Grace took the form, for Augustine, of a promise of disposition. In a lengthy letter addressed to SS. Prosper and Hilary, subsequently entitled *On the Predestination of the Saints*, Augustine takes aim at the then-current heresy of the Pelagians:

> [God] promised not from the power of our will but from His own predestination. For He promised what He Himself would do, not what men would do. Because, although men do those good things which pertain to God's worship, He Himself makes them to do what He has commanded; it is not they that cause Him to do what He has promised. Otherwise the fulfillment of God's promises would not be in the power of God, but in that of men.[28]

Though the language of predestination is used here, I would argue that the focus really is on God's role and power in salvation.

The Pelagians, contra Augustinian orthodoxy, maintained that humans were not afflicted by original sin and that human will was sufficient to make moral choices without divine aid. Therefore, it was not by grace that a person gained salvation but by free will alone. Augustine did not agree with that interpretation, and at the Council of Carthage in 418, the views of the Pelagians were condemned by the church. Aquinas echoed Augustine in his *Summa Theologiae*. Aquinas argues that God not only elects persons with foreknowledge but also damns persons with foreknowledge. Again, this can be read either as strict predestination or as the decisions by God after we have exercised our free will.

Modern Christians tend to equate predestination as a model of salvation exclusively with John Calvin, but we must recall that, though Calvin made overtures to reading *sola scriptura,* he was the beneficiary of fifteen hundred years of theological consideration of these matters. In his *The*

Institutes of the Christian Religion, Calvin lays out his opinions on salvation theology. Calvin's real contribution to salvation theology was to totalize the system of predestination and attach that salvific principle to the omnipotence of God.

My own perspective may not rival the exegesis of Augustine; nor may it match the systematics of Aquinas; it might not vie with the fire and brimstone of Calvin. But I believe it is consistent with Scripture and motivated by experience and science.

A key element here is one of clarifying terms—perhaps the most important being salvation. Ultimately, whatever your personal view of salvation is, I would expect it to involve a relationship with God. At its core, the problem with strict predestination as a concept is that it seems to be the opposite of a relationship, which implies a free choice on the part of both participants in the relationship. Therefore, I, for one, cannot imagine that God would invest his creation with the potential for salvation only to determine that salvation without any choice on the part of creation.

To me, it seems clear that a relationship to the divine is a necessary feature of salvation. I would suggest that this feature derives from the connections between our physical reality and the fullness of reality. First, free will is the mechanism of choice whereby we can select a closer relationship to God and greater communion with God. But the initiation of the relationship—the call to us—is through the grace of God. Thus, without that grace, the concept of a relationship is not even possible.

Second, all relationships require effort on the part of both participants if they are to succeed. The effort required for our relationship with God to be successful, for true salvation, is beyond our capacity alone. It is through God's contribution to this relationship that we are ultimately saved, but without our free choice to enter that relationship, we can never be saved. And this view of free will automatically implies an ability to participate in, and interact with, the nonphysical—the fullness of reality that is

God—supporting my view that free will requires more than simply emergent physical properties.

Agency and Determinism in Philosophy

As I mentioned above, most—if not all—literature seems to overlay a conceptual struggle between free will and fate. So, too, much philosophy seems preoccupied with this question. In the twentieth century, much of continental philosophy had a decidedly structuralist bent. Prominent in this field was the predominately twentieth-century anthropologist Claude Levi-Strauss, who significantly advanced this view of human agency, or actions. Structuralists maintained that human agency was constrained and conditioned by the situation and circumstance that beset that agent. That is to say, one cannot think a thought that would be unsupported by the culture in which the thinker is thinking.

Humans, these structuralists maintained, operate within structures that govern their every choice and delimit their every possibility. These structures were total and essentially unchanging—and only subject to change at the rate of geological time. They were found in a wide range of human experience. Therefore, Joseph Campbell, a twentieth-century mythologist, could understand all mythology to be variations on a few, ancient themes. Thomas Kuhn, a twentieth-century physicist and philosopher of science, could understand all scientific discoveries to happen according to predictable patterns. Marcel Mauss, a predominately twentieth-century sociologist, could understand all instances of gift giving to be an exercise in reciprocal exchange according to a commodity market. Victor Turner, a twentieth-century cultural anthropologist, could interpret all instances of pilgrimage as representationally related by their transcendence through liminal[29] places. These are all structuralist ideas; the potential of humankind is trapped within the invisible box of culture and cannot extend outside of it.

As the twentieth century wore on, structuralism—owing equally to the rigidity of the conceptualization of these structures and their clumsy, transhistorical nature—fell out of vogue, being replaced with the aptly named theory of poststructuralism.

To view all social phenomena as avatars of a single, governing super-structure ignores important differences between cultures, societies, and positionalities. Critics viewed the eponymous structures of structuralism to be totalizing to an untoward degree. Instead, critics such as Pierre Bourdieu maintained that the structures to which we are subject are themselves the products of negotiation. That is, the structures that dictate the range of possible behavior are themselves established by means of our acculturation.

But—and this is crucially important—the structures of everyday life are not unreal; rather, they exist as unspoken limitations on behavior, percep-tion, and thought. So, we are constrained—physically, morally, epistemo-logically—by the reality that we inhabit. Yet I find much to admire in the notion that we contribute to the structures in which we operate; in a sense, we will them into existence and live with the consequences of them. This process, to my mind, is analogous to the free exercise of radically free will. And if God is the fullness of reality, then our free will exists within the limits of that reality.

Modern thought on determinism and predestination observes this foundational agency. In the sixteenth century, a Dutch theologian named Jacobus Arminius formulated a critique of Calvinist predestination. His formulation, called Arminianism, is the dominant thread of salvation theology currently in place in the United States. Grace, for Arminius, is the mechanism of salvation, but human free will is able to either submit to or resist that grace. Therefore, we are complicit in our salvation. We assent to salvation by means of assenting to grace.

But notice there is nothing in that formulation that violates a level of determinism. Also, nothing in it violates the radical agency of human beings to elect to assent to that determinism. One might call this view *compatibility.* Physical determinism is true (we are each subject to precondition of reality); and free will is true (we are able to choose our actions within that reality).

Thomas Hobbes, an English philosopher writing in the seventeenth century, described the ability to choose our actions as finding "no stop, in doing what he has the will, desire, or inclination to do"[30]; David Hume understood that possibilities were conditioned only by the ability to do other than what was done[31]; Arthur Schopenhauer, a nineteenth-century philosopher, argued, "Man can do what he wills but he cannot will what he wills" (Einstein, in an article published in the *Saturday Evening Post* in 1929, translates this aphorism as "We can do what we wish, but we can only wish what we must"). We are radically free agents, but our means of following our wills can only be in accordance with reality.

The simple fact of the matter is that, if free will exists, our free will is necessarily constrained by reality. We cannot simply will into physical reality something unreal. We cannot force ourselves to apprehend our environment any differently than we do. We can no sooner will ourselves to perceive a blue sweater as red than we can think a thought that is unsupported by our experience and intuition. In a very real way, the parameters of the objective world condition our existence within it. We cannot build a house with our mind alone. As it is written in Proverbs, "The heart of man plans his way, but the Lord establishes his steps." In this, I see both the role of community and God.

How can community help elicit change? No two people in a community have exactly the same experiences. So, though we can only apprehend our own environment, the others in that environment are one window to potential change. Other people bring us into contact with new elements, new ideas, and new experiences. And our relationship with God, the fullness of reality, creates opportunities for growth that would never be possible without that interaction. This is at the heart of grace.

In the fabrication and maintenance of physical reality, we see the omnipotence of the fullness of reality. This is often seen as another constraint on, or problem with, free will. If God is all knowing, then God must know the future—a point regularly made by Scripture, but especially at Isaiah 46:9. But, and this is essential to understand, a God that knows the future, however, is not the same as a God that predestines the future.

I can have full disposal to free will even if God has full disposal to the outcome; the choices can be mine even if God knows what those choices are going to be. If God is truly outside of time and we make our choices in time, then there is a fundamental difference between knowing the outcome and making it happen. So, while free will and omnipotence may seem to be in conceptual conflict, they are by no means incompatible. In fact, the fact that reality constrains free will is itself suggestive of the actuality of the fullness of reality. But in order to see how that might be, we need to see what the sciences can tell us about determinism.

Determinism and Agency in the Sciences

In 1814, Pierre-Simon Laplace, a French mathematician and astronomer, offered a quirky, yet profound, thought experiment. Subsequent interpreters have called this thought experiment Laplace's Demon. Were there to exist, Laplace opined, an infinitely superior intellect who could know the precise location and momentum of every atom in the universe, then we could predict the past and future of every particle of matter using only the laws of Newtonian mechanics. Laplace mused, "We ought...to regard the present state of the universe as the effect of its anterior state and the cause of the one which is to follow. Given for one instant an intelligence which could comprehend all the forces by which nature is animated and the respective situation of the beings [i.e., atoms] who compose it—an intelligence sufficiently vast to submit these data to analysis—it would embrace the same formula of the movements of the greatest bodies of the universe and those of the lightest atom; for [this intellect], nothing would be uncertain and the future, as the past, would be present to its eyes."[32]

For Laplace, as for the scientists of his generation, physical phenomena occurred in space and were governed by time. Laplace and his ilk conceived of time as a linear concatenation of discrete though causally related events. These phenomena were explicable by the laws governing motion, known also as dynamics. To turn this statement on its head, if we have the laws that govern motion down pat, then all motion we observe will accord with those laws. This is causal determinism in its purest, most maximal articulation.

The predictive power of Newtonian mechanics is grounded in the use of mathematics to describe physical events. The outcomes of systems are determined by their physics, and the physics is described by mathematics. So, from the seventeenth century through the nineteenth century, scientists would observe the behavior of phenomena—such as the motion of the planets, the rolling of a ball, the acceleration of free-falling bodies— and describe that system using mathematical laws. These mathematical laws have very accurate predictive power. And these laws are expressed using differential equations, which is just a fancy way of describing the ways a system changes in time in mathematical terms.

Even if this language was not used in your math classes in school, at some point you used algebraic equations, solving for a variable that depends on some other variable. In effect, you do this every time you compute correct change or leave a tip in a restaurant. A differential equation, on the other hand, describes the way a system changes in time. Perhaps the simplest analogy is the money that you put in an interest-bearing account; a principal is given over to the bank, and that bank applies a growth strategy to that principal—in this case, an interest rate. Over time, a differential equation (in this case, one that describes the agreed investment strategy) governs the changes in the value of that principal. The investor can figure out the value of the account based on the mathematics (i.e., the interest rate) supplied to him or her at the moment of the investment. All things being equal, the mathematics predicts the outcomes of the system. Your money, one hopes, increases in time, but either way, once you have that rule for how your money changes in time, you can completely predict how much money you have for all time.

Scientific determinism works in a similar way. Rather than determinism in this case being a statement of teleology—where a system moves deterministically toward an end—scientific determinism suggests that, if you know the initial state of a system and the differential equation that governs that system, you can predict the outcome of that system. Consider a flat surface and a rolling ball. As a college professor, I'll offer my office desk and a cue ball (alas, like many college professors' desks, mine doubles as a filing cabinet, but we can pretend it is clear!). If you roll that ball on my desk—noting the initial position, the rate of acceleration, the momentum of the ball, the spin on that ball, and any other parameters—you could predict the exact location where that ball will hit the wall every time you conduct this experiment. A ball rolling on a desk is a relatively simple system; it obeys Newtonian mechanics—and that is described by a differential equation. The system is deterministic because once you know the initial conditions, you know all subsequent motions. Classical mechanics can predict the outcome almost perfectly.

Now, imagine on one half of the desk you fix, say, seventy-two nails— twelve rows of six nails, like the Plinko game on *The Price is Right*. The nails are now embedded onto the rolling plane. You release the cue ball as before, but now you try to predict which nails the ball will strike. You conduct the experiment a few times and, unsurprisingly, the results seem perfectly random. Perhaps surprisingly, this system is still perfectly explicable by Newtonian mechanics. What has changed is an increased need for an accurate understanding of the system's initial conditions: Where are the pegs placed? Are there any imperfections on the ball?

The system is still governed by a well-defined set of rules; were we to write a computer program, we could include all the rules governing this experiment and mimic it with little difficulty. What will happen, however, is that you can generate fairly accurate predictions only for the first few pegs. For each peg the ball strikes thereafter, the error inherent to the mathematical prediction will grow—not because the physics does not work, but because the description of the initial conditions is slightly off. And with every subsequent peg, the error in the prediction gets amplified.

To make meaningful predictions about this system, we would need to turn to statistics. As the accuracy of our predictions decreases (with every peg strike), so, too, does our need to rely on probability to describe the system. In other words, instead of accurately predicting the specific position for a given ball, we predict the distribution of possible positions for a set of balls.

Returning for a moment to Laplace's Demon, consider that our cue ball was now an atom in a gas cluster. The atom is free to move in three-dimensional space, and you want to track the movement of that atom. Now, instead of the nails being in fixed positions, they are now other atoms equally free to move in the same three-dimensional space. The subject atom will careen and collide with the billions of object atoms in an entirely predictable way. But now there really is no way to accurately ascertain the initial positions of every atom in this system; it's simply impossible given the large number of atoms.

We could write a computer program, give each atom a set of individual rules according to Newtonian mechanics, and let this system run. What we would have shown by this experiment is that, using only the deterministic rules of Newtonian mechanics, you can reproduce the behavior of the gas cluster in a probabilistic sense. It does not really matter that our computer model did not behave exactly as a particular gas cloud did; it behaves like a typical gas cloud. And our computer gas cloud certainly behaves exactly like a real gas cloud does when you measure, say, the average properties as opposed to the details. Therefore, in order to get to a point where we can make meaningful descriptions of this system, we must develop a probabilistic model for outcomes, which we call statistical physics, to predict the average properties. We are still predicting the behavior in time, but now we are doing so in an average sense, not for each individual particle.

What you are observing here is an emergent property. A single cue ball traveling across an unencumbered desk is a very simple system that obeys all tenets of classical mechanics. A single cue ball traveling across a nail bed is a slightly more complex system that still obeys all the tenets of classical mechanics—but in addition exhibits statistical behavior. Atoms in a gas cluster—all free to move throughout space—form an infinitely more complex system that is best described using new properties, such as entropy, that only exist for collections of atoms and do not exist at the level of a single particle. Yet, even here, the individual particles themselves still always observe strict Newtonian mechanics; instead, it is the system for which the new probabilistic properties have emerged.

In physics, we impart the following aphorism to our students: "Don't worry about 'the one,' and don't worry about 'the many'; what's hard is 'the few'—and that's what chemists do." It is an exciting and active area of research to determine at what point (for example, how many particles) a system requires a fully probabilistic description. Observing the transition by studying molecules is extremely challenging (for one thing, they are incredibly small!), so in my research, we approach this question by studying the behavior of bubbles (say, about one millimeter big). We can easily start with one bubble and work our way up to thousands of bubbles. And we can ask, "When do I see these bubbles begin to exhibit the probabilistic behavior of a complex system?"

There is currently an indication that it only takes about twenty to twenty-five bubbles to constitute a complex system in a foam. The goal is to develop the ability to predict the transition from behavior as individuals to behavior as a system, or continuum. This transition point varies from system to system. But one way to define the point of transition is the moment at which the description of the system requires statistical mechanics. We always begin with a system that only requires the classical mechanics of individual particles to describe its behavior; as the complexity of a given system increases, and as predictions become expressed only in statistical terms, the system will begin to begin to exhibit probabilistic behavior and yield only probabilistic results.

This discussion of statistical mechanics highlights the importance in science to distinguish between the terms *deterministic*, *predictable*, and *probabilistic*. In the above examples, everything is considered deterministic because the underlying physics of the individual particles can be described by differential equations that are able to predict the motion given initial conditions. For simple systems, we use the term *predictable* to mean that we can directly predict specific outcomes (e.g., where is the particle, how fast is it going, etc.). Finally, for sufficiently complex systems, the behavior is still deterministic, but we are only able to predict probable outcomes. We can no longer say exactly where a given atom will be, but we can talk about the probability of where it might be and the average of where all the particles are; this is probabilistic behavior.

The field of chaos theory is one area of mathematics that is used to study the transition between fully predictable physics and probabilistic physics in systems that are deterministic. Chaos theory is focused on carefully defining the moment at which a fully predictable system is sufficiently complex that it loses predictability. Now the system remains perfectly deterministic—given the exact initial conditions, the future is determined by the physics, but simply unpredictable—owing to even the slightest error in determining the initial conditions. So, when a butterfly flaps its wings in the Amazon, it contributes a slight change to the initial conditions, which could indeed portend hurricane weather in south Florida. The only problem is that these infinitely complex systems are impossible to accurately predict!

One of the most exciting areas of active research currently going on in physics at the moment is the field of quantum mechanics. Unlike Newtonian mechanics and general relativity, both of which deal in fully deterministic systems (systems in which initial conditions determine everything), quantum mechanics is fundamentally a probabilistic theory of nature. It was as an indictment of quantum mechanics that Einstein coined that immortal phrase: "God does not shoot dice."

Quantum mechanics does not predict a value; rather, it predicts the probability of an event. By way of contrast, Newtonian mechanics can provide an absolute value for where the cue ball will come to rest after rolling across my desk; in fact, Newtonian mechanics can predict the position of the ball at any given moment in time. Quantum mechanics, on the other hand, will only give you possible position values based on the probability of a given object occupying a given position. And in some cases, the possible positions are a discrete set of values. For example, it is natural to think that a ball stuck in a box can be anywhere in that box. Quantum mechanics shows that for a particle in a box, there may be special locations in the box where you will never find that particle. The fact that certain properties of particles occur in discrete values is the quantized nature of quantum mechanics; under the right conditions, the physics restricts the number of possible values of a quantity or states of a system.

In order to think about the differences between classical mechanics and quantum mechanics, we need to let go of our normal methods of trying to describe reality in physical terms. We are accustomed to describing matter according to positions and speeds, but really what we want to do in physics is describe the state of a system. In classical mechanics, you describe the state of a system by determining where it is and how fast it is moving. If I tell you where everything in a given system is and how fast it is moving, then, using the laws of Newtonian mechanics, I can tell you about the future evolution of that system and I know its state.

Quantum mechanics, on the other hand, is a fundamentally different way of looking at reality. My quantum mechanics professor at Princeton opened the class by saying, "In this class we learn how to use quantum mechanics; if you want to discuss what it means, that can only be done over a beer in the pub." Because of our experience in describing things in terms of their positions and speeds, we are not used to the idea that, on some core, fundamental level, the subatomic world of quantum mechanics is fundamentally probabilistic—and that the state of the system is the collection of probabilities, not specific values of position and velocities.

It is difficult to grasp probabilistic uncertainty, but I urge us to think about the potential benefits of embracing that uncertainty. First, even though quantum mechanics makes predictions only in terms of probability, it is extremely successful empirically. The precision of its predictions has been consistently confirmed by observation. Using quantum mechanics, we are able to predict the transition lines and spectra of atoms and molecules using spectroscopy. Using quantum mechanics, we can investigate with extreme precision the wavelength of light. With these tools, we can do precision measurements of the fundamental charge of an electron, the fundamental mass of an electron, the angular momentum of an electron, and so on. We can peer into space armed with the predictions offered by quantum mechanics and determine the elements that make up the atmosphere of faraway planets. Second, the measurement of phenomena on the quantum level might yield significant results for quantum computers and quantum computing. It may be the case that our explorations into uncertainty provide tangible results.

A key feature of quantum mechanics is the concept of measurement. All of the predictive power of quantum mechanics is based on a fundamental structure known as the wave function. It is the wave function that provides the probabilities used to predict measurements. It is interesting to note that even though quantum mechanics only makes predictions in a fundamentally probabilistic fashion, the wave function itself changes in time in a purely deterministic fashion; it obeys a differential equation in the same sense that we discussed in the example of the cue ball on my desk. But at the moment a measurement made, there is a fundamental change in the wave function—and this act of measurement and what it means is still a deep philosophical question. Given the fundamental importance of the wave function and the uncertainty it embodies, it is worth trying to develop a better feel for what it is and what it means.

One consequence of describing reality in terms of the wave function is the famous uncertainty principle. It was Niels Bohr, a Dane, and Werner Heisenberg, a German, who formulated this fundamental principle of quantum mechanics. From 1923 to 1927, Heisenberg served as a research assistant to Bohr at the University of Copenhagen. While there, Bohr and Heisenberg originated key elements of quantum mechanical theory. As was mentioned in chapter two, units on the subatomic level exhibit characteristics of both particles, which have a definite position, and waves, which are extended throughout space. Their contribution maintained that the position of particles could only be described using the wave function.

Imagine throwing a baseball or a softball to your child. Due to the innate human propensity to deduce complex geometry, we can predict, without the aid of Newtonian mechanics, where that ball will be at any given moment. And, should we want to calculate its precise location at any given moment, Newtonian mechanics will give us that value. The key is to know both the position and the velocity of the ball at the instant you throw it; then you can predict the rest of the motion. In Newtonian mechanics, position and velocity are two fundamentally separate quantities.

Now, imagine you wanted to throw an electron; recall, an electron is effectively a single-point particle (diameter is not a particularly useful concept when considering things on that scale). Furthermore, imagine you want to throw this electron at a wall that has two slits in it and measure where the electron hits a screen behind it. Now, this example is one of the most classic problems used to develop some intuition regarding how quantum mechanics works. So, even though this example is not critical to my arguments regarding free will, thinking about an electron passing through two slits is incredibly useful in moving from understanding the words in the two-cookie rule to developing an intuition, or understanding, for the two-cookie rule, where here the fundamentally probabilistic nature of quantum mechanics is the two-cookie rule we are trying to understand. So it is worth spending some time on this example.

As a scientist, you want to predict where the electron will go, or to be more precise, where the electron will be when it gets to the other side of the two slits in the wall. So if Newtonian mechanics described electrons, you need to know the initial position, the initial angle, and speed at which you throw that electron. You would determine if it makes it through either slit, and if so which one, and then from there where it lands on the wall. But because an electron is a purely quantum mechanical entity, our description of it is fundamentally different.

What you have initially is a set of values that exist everywhere in space that tell you the probability of the electron being at that very position. These probabilities are the wave function. Or, more generally, the wave function describes the state of that system. If you are holding that electron in your hand—picture this in your mind—there is a probability peak of one at your hand (probability of one means it is definitely there and not anywhere else) and it is zero everywhere else. The probability it is in your hand is one in this case because you are holding it there. This is what we refer to as the electron being localized in space.

But the truly weird thing is that the wave function simultaneously tells you about the probability of that electron being somewhere and having a particular velocity. In fact, the wave function provides all the information you need about the complete state of the system—an idea that we will return to in the next chapter. For our purposes here, the fact that the wave function describes the entire state of the system means that position and velocity are no longer completely independent concepts.

When a particle is localized in space, its velocity is equally likely to have any value. This is a fundamental property of the description of reality in terms of a wave function and not an accident of how we measure things. This deep connection between the probability of measuring a given value of position and velocity is the core of the Heisenberg uncertainty principle. When you attempt to measure both the position and momentum of a given quantum entity, the conditions of the system—the probabilistic wave function that provides the likelihood of the position of that entity—give probabilities that are intertwined in such a way that the more certain you are of the position, the more uncertain you are of the velocity, and vice versa.

Now you throw the electron at the screen. What quantum mechanics predicts is how the wave function evolves in time given the initial state—in our example, the initial state is an electron localized in space. It's helpful to think of the wave function as ripples on the surface of a body of water. Think of a totally still body of water and then plunk a rock into it. The ripples will start as a single splash where the rock hits (the initial wave function localized in your hand) and spread out across the surface of the water forming peaks and troughs—this is the electron traveling toward the slits. Where there is a peak, the likelihood of finding the electron there will be quite high; where there is a trough, the likelihood of finding the electron there will be quite low. But the wave function, like the ripples on the water, changes in a deterministic fashion as it radiates from the initial state of the event.

So, you've let the electron go; we started with a wave function with one peak—an absolute certainty of its position. As soon as I release that electron toward my slits, the wave function will quickly radiate out. The peaks of the probability wave reflect the likelihood of finding that electron at a given position. Now, until you try to measure again where that electron is—and this is the trick of quantum mechanics—the probabilities radiate in a clearly deterministic way. The Schrödinger equation can tell us exactly what happens to this wave function.

As the probability waves begin to approach the two slits in the wall, some will hit the wall, but some will go through each slit. As they go through the slit, they diffract—that is, spread out. Recall our water wave analogy. As waves approach a hole in a barrier, they spread out once they are on the other side of the barrier. Once on the other side, the waves from each slit will interfere with each other. Again, picture water waves generated by two rocks separated by some distance. When the waves from each rock meet, they combine with each other to form a new set of peaks and troughs. For example, peaks combine to make bigger peaks and a peak and trough can cancel each other out to make a flat region.

This type of interference is exactly how sound-canceling headphones function—as sound is also an example of a wave. The net result will be that on the screen behind the slits there is an interference pattern, a set of peaks and troughs generated by adding the waves from the two slits, which is the probability of the electron hitting places.

Returning to our electron, if you have the ability to measure the impacts on the screen, only one spot will light up. And the wave function for that electron—the probability of having any given position—will have now collapsed again into a single point of certainty. Quantum systems, therefore, possess a fundamentally discontinuous moment—the moment of measurement—that effectively resets the wave function in a way that is not deterministic at all. This is the measurement question in quantum mechanics.

Naturally, the notion that precise measurement—even of the most minute of particles—is not well understood is troubling, even to physicists.

Experimental measurement is the foundation of modern science, after all. The Copenhagen interpretation of quantum mechanics—the formulation of Bohr and Heisenberg that quantum phenomena were strictly probabilistic—was met with resistance from many established physicists. It was the fundamentally probabilistic nature of quantum phenomena that raised Einstein's hackles. It had to be wrong; God does not throw dice, after all.

In response, Einstein attempted to formulate what is called a hidden variable theory. Perhaps, he reckoned, we are just missing some piece that could make quantum systems deterministic. In 1935, Einstein and his colleagues, Boris Podolsky and Nathan Rosen, published the EPR paradox. It was an attempt to argue for a hidden parameter that would do away with the probabilistic uncertainty of quantum mechanics. But, in an uncharacteristic misstep, Einstein was wrong. Both mathematically and through experimental measurements, it has been shown that, indeed, the only possible conclusion is that quantum mechanics is fundamentally probabilistic.

Even more important for our discussion, the wave function appears to be real—and not just a mathematical convenience. This has important philosophical implications, as the wave function also cannot be directly measured. Only the probabilities predicted from the wave function can be measured. Therefore, the wave function is not physical in the practical sense of a phenomenon subject to direct study by our senses, or tools that augment our senses.

So we in the sciences are in this weird and unenviable state. Experimentally, we are pretty sure that an object that lacks any physicality—the wave function—fundamentally constrains the reality we can measure. Rather than being simply an abstraction of the probability of having a given position, it appears to be an unphysical aspect of reality. It's not just in our heads; it's also out in the real world.

The fundamental basis of physical phenomena—all events at the quantum level—is described by a wave function. And, as it turns out, we can measure it, but only obliquely. We can measure the existence of this universal feature of quantum behavior only by testing the probability of the predictions that it makes. As far as we can tell, the wave function fundamentally exists. It fundamentally governs quantum behavior. But it is not physical in the sense of a photon, a quark, an electron, an atom, and it is not energy like heat, radiation, gravity, etc. It's out there as a wave of probability.

So, where does this leave us in the discussion about determinism and free will? Three points, to my mind, bear mention. First, the physics governing the wave function represent a certain degree of constraint to the behavior of matter at the most fundamental of levels. As I mentioned, except for the moments of measurements, the wave function evolves in a deterministic fashion. We should not be surprised by this. I've never seen any indication that the world does not behave according to rules; dilate the scope of human society and we can see that we are all subject to predictable mores and modes of propriety. What is unique about both the wave function and human society is the immaterial, nonphysical nature of them both. Both lack an empirically discernible actuality, and yet both constrain unmitigated free will.

Second, even though the evolution of the wave function is deterministic, the act of measurement is inherently probabilistic. A phrase that is often used to describe measurement in quantum mechanics is that the wave function collapses during the measurement process. There is a sense, then, in which our choice to make or not make measurements control the behavior of an inherently nonphysical aspect of reality. By applying our reason, intuition, and empiricism, do we force the divine into conversation? This remains dangerous philosophical ground because we fundamentally do not understand the process of measurement. But, as an open area of both science and philosophy, we must acknowledge that the measurement issue in quantum mechanics strongly suggests that our understanding of reality is at least sufficiently incomplete to make definitive statements on free will from a purely scientific perspective.

Finally, and perhaps most crucially, the wave function is fundamentally nonphysical, but it clearly impacts experience in physical reality. Again, there is a danger in drawing too many conclusions from this situation. But it does suggest that the assumption that only physical reality is relevant and any nonphysical reality is irrelevant does not make sense from a scientific perspective. Therefore, if God, as I have argued, is the fullness of reality that includes a nonphysical reality, then, to some degree, the existence of the wave function provides a strong motivation to further explore the nature of nonphysical reality.

Conclusion

If we define free will as the ability to choose to do something different or differently, then we have a chance of understanding radical agency within limited determinism. Also, this may solve an interesting conundrum regarding recent scientific research on free will. In the June 2014 issue of Scientific American, Azim Shariff and Kathleen Vohs discuss how studies of free will impact attitudes and actions regarding laws and ethical behavior. When people become aware of neuroscientific underpinnings of behavior, especially ones suggesting that free will is an illusion, two things can occur. On the one hand, the idea of retribution for crimes decreases in favor of prevention (and, dare I say, rehabilitation and change?), but, on the other hand, people's willpower for resisting unethical behavior is also decreased. The first is viewed as a positive for society and the second as a negative. The challenge raised by the authors is: Which direction will society take?

I would suggest that viewing free will in the context of choosing to act different or differently addresses these issues head-on. With regard to rehabilitation versus retribution—that is one of the fundamental teachings of Jesus. Christians are called to choose love over hate, nonviolence over violence and redemption over revenge. These are choices that most people, both believers and nonbelievers, can support, but become meaningless in a world without choice.

If our neuroscience drives us to better embrace these Christian ideals, this is just one more example of science helping our faith grow. If we realize that free will is constrained strongly by our neuroscience and that true choice requires hard work to change behavior, then we are able to embrace the help needed to grow in our faith, and work to build stronger communities across boundaries. From this perspective, we counter the negative effects raised by the authors by redefining free will in a more positive way. In fact, reinventing free will is precisely one of the predictions the authors make, and doing so is completely in line with my proposal that free will is the ability to choose to act different or differently.

But why is it important for humans to possess free will? It is interesting to note that our American superheroes are constantly focused on defending our freedom. How much more, then, should we expect God, as the ultimate superhero, to provide us with and protect our radical free will—the ultimate freedom of choice?

But we, as a society, can appear to be deeply uncomfortable with the notion of the personal change that radical free will engenders.

At times we are blithely and crassly dismissive of rehabilitation and the potential for personal transformation. An ex-con, for instance, is too often defined forever by the experience of incarceration, and, as numerous academic studies demonstrate, often experiences profound prejudice in housing, employment, and life more generally. This, I think, is unfortunate. We seem to be reluctant to acknowledge the potential for transformation inherent to each person by virtue of our human ability to exercise our free will.

We can see this trend in the ways we communicate and refer to literature, as well. When I say the word *Grinch* or *Scrooge*, for instance, the average reader will conjure up a curmudgeonly miser intent on spreading negativity and acting malevolently. But at the very hearts of *How the Grinch Stole Christmas* and *A Christmas Carol* are narratives of profound transformation: the Grinch's heart "grew two sizes that day"; Scrooge becomes a man that knows how to keep Christmas all the year round. These are stories that are about transformation. Yet we persist in equating the names of these characters with their initial state: a Grinch in common parlance is an individual akin to the character's personality at the beginning of the narrative; a Scrooge is a miserly hoarder indifferent to the plight of his fellow man. We resist the thesis of these stories—transformation—because we are wary of the actuality of transformation.

Yet free will is just that: transformation. While we cannot choose our conditions, while we cannot operate from without our circumstance, while we are beholden to reality itself, we can exercise considerable latitude within those parameters—all by means of our free will. And in a religious sense, we can elect to connect with the fullness of reality, and we can accept God's call to communion. That is the essence of free will: the free exercise of choice in the face of given conditions.

Free will includes our understanding of the systems and structures in place and choosing to do something different or differently, and embracing the social structures and practices that help enact the change. And we can determine to use our free will to embrace the fullness of reality as the transcendent agency responsible for our physical reality. Thus, we use our past experience to craft our future experience; we elect to connect with God and accept the call of God. We make the decision to enter into a true relationship with the fullness of reality and welcome God's grace to fuel our transformation.

Chapter 9

Life after Life: The Science of Change

From the beginning of the world they have not heard, nor perceived with the ears: the eye hath not seen, O God, besides you, what things you have prepared for them that wait for you.

—Isaiah 64:4

The path to paradise begins in hell.

—Dante Alighieri, *La Divina Commedia,* "Inferno,"
canto III, 1. 9

Just remember that death is not the end.

—Bob Dylan, "Death Is Not the End,"
Down in the Groove (1988)

I am not unaware that I've lived a charmed life. I was reared in a stable, safe environment by loving parents who provided me with the tools to build a successful life. And the people that I hold most dear have been blessed as well, insofar as I've never had a loved one die tragically. But, like everyone else, I have been touched by death—just as we all must be eventually.

My paternal grandfather died before I was born; I knew of him, but I never knew him. I heard stories about him growing up, and I often gazed at our yellowed, framed photograph of him, wondering about the man.

I was a third-year graduate student at the University of California, Santa Barbara. I had not yet advanced to candidacy, and I was feverishly working toward my examinations. One day, the phone rang; my father's rich, even voice spoke steadily from the other end of the line, "Michael, your grandmother passed last night; you need to come home."

My grandmother's death was not unexpected. In recent years, she had been in poor health. In fact, her health was such that her children moved her from her apartment on Long Island to Connecticut, where she could receive the best care possible.

On the flight over, I reminisced about the woman. The matriarch of a large Irish Catholic family, she would certainly have no shortage of mourners. There would be cousins and uncles and aunts and others—I was sure that I would meet folks that I had never met before, but who shared memories of this woman.

When my father pulled into our driveway, I left the car and walked straightaway to the front door; I had been gone for a while, and I paused to consider whether it would be appropriate to enter the house without knocking. The old Irish saying is true: "You can never go home." In your absence, home becomes something else—familiar and foreign simultaneously.

I opened the door and walked in. Peter, my brother, and Elizabeth, my sister, were sitting with my mother in the den. Elizabeth sprang up, the telltale tracks of her tears on her cheeks, and ran over to me and wrapped her arms around my neck. I embraced her right back and asked, "How you holding up?" In my absence, my sister and my grandmother had grown quite close. I was concerned with how she had taken my grandmother's passing.

She managed to sniffle out, "Oh, you know. It's sad—it really is—but I just take comfort in the fact that she's in a better place."

"Heaven, you mean?"

"Hmm?" she looked at me. "Oh, yes, I'm sure...but I meant Long Island. She always did hate Connecticut."

I chuckled, remembering her frequent complaints about having to relocate. "Yeah, she always preferred Long Island. Guess it's nice she's going back. Where's David?"

My mother answered, "He's up in his room. He'll be thrilled to see you."

I climbed the stairs to David's room. I wondered how he was dealing with the news. It was uncharted terrain for him, and news of her death could play out any number of ways.

I knocked on his door and walked in. "Hey, pal, how's it going?"

"Oh, it's OK," he answered. "Grandma died, though."

"Yeah, I heard. How are you doing with that?"

"It's sad, but I'm also sort of excited."

I had not expected that response. As I've mentioned, David has Down syndrome, and his intellectual development is that of a very bright and clever fourth grader. I was interested to see how a grown man with the innocent mind of a child would react to the impending inevitable.

"Excited, huh?" I replied. "How come?"

"I've never met Grandpa. And now we're taking Grandma to him! I want to meet him."

We were, indeed, burying my grandmother next to my grandfather in their shared plot. Twenty-five years separated the ends of their lives; now mere inches would separate them in death.

I smiled. "Buddy, I'm not sure that's how it works."

"Well, we'll just see."

The funeral was actually held in Connecticut, and when it ended, my parents, my brothers, my sister, and I all piled into a funeral sedan to take part in the procession to the cemetery in Long Island. Unfortunately, it turned out that no one really knew where the cemetery was. Somewhere around the Throgs Neck Bridge, we got lost. We took a right instead of a left and we ended up in Astoria, Queens, on a dead end road at Long Island Sound! It was my aunt who expressed everyone's thoughts: "Well,

I am sure Mom is up in heaven laughing at us for taking her away from Long Island!"

We eventually made it to the cemetery, and, I'm sorry to say—for David's sake—my grandfather was not waiting at the grave for Grandma as he expected.

When we in the United States discuss the afterlife, too often we retain an out-of-date controlling image that influences the way in which we communicate about the possibility of life after death. One only needs to think of my brother's image of a ghostly grandfather greeting a ghostly grandmother, or one can consider Warner Brothers cartoons of the 1940s and 1950s to take my point. Bugs Bunny is repeatedly depicted as ascending into the clouds with a white gown, angel's wings, a halo, and a harp—and his character is made less bold and more transparent to indicate his postmortem spectral quality. Heaven, then, is a place in the clouds into which the soul ascends after death. I suspect that, when pushed, most people do not actually believe in this classical image of heaven as some separate place in the clouds. But these images are so thoroughly embedded in Western art and literature that this image is the reflexive, common understanding of the afterlife—a physical place located in proximity to the mundane plane. It is only with careful and deliberate thought that many people move beyond it.

Even in the well-attested literature about near-death experiences, these classical tropes are readily identifiable. Ascending out of the body and making progress toward a white light, coupled with sensations of warmth and contented resignation, are common to the overwhelming preponderance of near-death experiences. Frequently, these folks will meet loved ones, have conversations with divine figures, and see heaven.

Now, some authorities take the commonalities of these experiences to be indicative of a reality suggested by uniformity; these experiences are so similar precisely because people have experienced the same thing. By this formulation, transcendence into the afterlife is knowable based on the proof of uniformity; we know, they would maintain, that there is an afterlife that accords with traditional Judeo-Christian standards because persons enmeshed in a Judeo-Christian culture have had these extraordinary, but uniform, experiences. But this uncritical interpretation is somewhat problematic.

I think it is more useful to understand the profound commonalities between these experiences as a type of vernacular description. The Judeo-Christian conception of the afterlife is the dominant cultural formulation by which we envision life after death—and, therefore, we communicate these experiences according to these tropes. Rather than being evidence of the actuality of a Bugs Bunny afterlife, these experiences suggest that the ways we communicate about the numinous are surprisingly normative and subject to the dictates of discourse in order to make these experiences explicable to other people.

But I do not doubt the experience; far be it from me to suggest there is something disingenuous about the profundity of these experiences. I do believe these experiences are able to offer some explanation to the ways we perceive of and conceive of the process of death and transcendence. What we see, I think, is that our understanding of the afterlife is informed by the Western traditions that envision the afterlife in physical and spatial terms. Gary Scott Smith, in his 2011 book *Heaven in the American Imagination*, argues that even though American expectations about heaven have changed with the times, the road to salvation has remained remarkably constant—and consistently features Protestant moralities and modalities of conduct. What we see is that our theories about life after death have, unsurprisingly, seeped into the way we experience and communicate about life after death. I contend that if we cling to a caricature of the afterlife—one that does not make sense within the findings and understandings of the sciences—then we risk debasing the afterlife more generally, and therefore destabilizing a foundational cornerstone of most religious faith.

When we strip away the accreted layers that have encrusted debates about the afterlife, what we are left with is a twofold question: First, what, after all, is death?

And second, what does death imply for conceptualizations of eternity? Only after these two questions are addressed can we reasonably consider questions of how an afterlife might be configured.

There are a number of interpretations of death, but it appears as though it is a thoroughly biological phenomenon. All organisms—including so-called eternal organisms, such as endoliths (some of which are ten thousand years old), or bacteria, viruses, and spores that have been revived after a period of stasis (the most recent example, a virus discovered in 2014, appears to have entered cold stasis thirty-four thousand years ago), or clonal colonies (the root systems of which can reach ages of about eighty thousand years)—could, conceivably, be killed. All life seems to be hardwired with the ability to die, and, really, this seems to serve a biological purpose.

Where death is the apparent end of life, reproduction is its beginning. Reproduction introduces variability into a gene pool, and this variability contributes in a positive way to the likelihood of survival of a given species. But, for reproduction to be useful, current biological research suggests that it requires death. We may be born to reproduce, but we reproduce in order to die (sorry, kids).

For Christians, the reality of death is equally ancient. The author of Genesis suggests that the Fall of man caused the introduction of death (Genesis 2:9, 2:16–17, 3:22). But, really, death is as old as life itself. It is simply a biological fact that contributes to our adaptability.

To the second question, which gets to the heart of the matter, death would seem to be the opposite of eternality. Therefore, a nonphysical afterlife is an important concept in many world faiths. The guarantee that the mundane plane is not the only plane of existence occupies a place of crucial centrality in the Judeo-Christian tradition. Death means that we are physically finite; creation, though, is infinite. Therefore, if we are to share in the fruits of creation, as Scripture tells us we must, then we, too, must have a chance for eternal life.

This chapter seeks to advance the argument that the sciences do not contradict a strongly articulated understanding of life after death, but it also seeks to advance a cautionary tale about how we must configure the nature of that afterlife. From a scientific perspective, perdition, in its classic articulation of hell, seems to be an unlikely outcome. Also, our visions of the afterlife—themselves crusty accretions, dusty from their seven-thousand-year history—are far too constraining to accommodate a scientific view of the afterlife.

Therefore, like all other matters pertaining to the infinite and the divine—in God's role as the fullness of reality—finite, delimiting language fails to capture the infinite, limitless nature of nonphysical reality. Now, I am not attempting to demystify transcendence—indeed, death and what happens after death are perhaps questions best considered by theologians rather than physicists. The means of investigating the hypothesis of life after death are nonscientific; as scientists, we are beholden to experimentation, and the experimentation required to glimpse the afterlife is nonrepeatable. At some point, each of us, scientists included, will die, and then, if there is an answer to know, we will know it. I do think, however, that understanding the science behind eternality and persistence—and by coupling these understandings with what we know and can know about neuroscience—provisions us with a fine starting point to imagine the ways in which the afterlife might be possible.

Even more than any other topic in this book, science can rule out certain visions of life after death and point by analogy to the possibilities of the afterlife.

But, ultimately, the question of life after death appears to fundamentally be a question of nonphysical reality. So, by definition, science will be severely limited in the type of information it can provide. Also, I would suggest that, for a subject so steeped in tradition and theology as the afterlife, we must divest ourselves of comfortable familiarities in order to entertain the possibilities presented by a contemplation of the fullness of reality.

The Afterlife of Scripture, Theology, and Tradition

Perhaps unexpectedly so, Scripture is rather taciturn on the subject of the afterlife compared to the relatively ample space given over to considerations of morality, conduct, and behavior. Upon reflection, this may not be surprising. An underlying assumption in the Judeo-Christian tradition is that God stewards our salvation—and, with God's help, we take care of life here on earth. So what we need to learn from Scripture is how best to live our lives. In a sense, one of the central salvific elements of Christ's death and resurrection is the freedom to work in this life to bring about God's will precisely because we can rest secure in the knowledge that we will experience full union with God in the next life. But as with many elemental features of religious faith, the ways that authors communicate images and understandings of the afterlife are subject to their historically contingent moment. When considering the images and understandings of the afterlife in Scripture, I would argue that the authors present us with a story of humanity's evolving understanding of what that afterlife is. As I stated in chapter three, the stories collected in the Bible are very much the history of a subset of humanity's relationship with the fullness of reality. This relationship has been one of constant discovery and growth, and through this history we can learn who we are and who we can be as a people. Therefore, it is not surprising that the views of the afterlife in Scripture reflect a deepening of understanding with time.

Additionally, when we read Scripture and take notice of references its authors made to their understanding of life after life, we must countenance the fact that their references to this state or place hinge on three things: the dominant conceptualization of the afterlife in place at the time of composition; the rhetorical work the authors intended to do by mentioning the afterlife; and the confluence of established paradigms and the negotiation and innovation of those paradigms in history. The audiences for which Scripture was written were told not only about the afterlife they were prepared to hear about, but also about the afterlife they needed to hear. And so, because Scripture was composed at a great variety of historical moments, we should expect to read—and indeed we find—widely disparate accounts of the afterlife.

It is important to understand that recognizing scriptural accounts of the afterlife as representing the story of humanity's deepening understanding does nothing to undermine the belief that Scripture is revealed truth. Even Jesus points out in his teaching that different people are prepared to hear different truths, and this is one reason he uses instructive parables to teach. Jesus taught about the afterlife what his listeners were able to hear—and so did the authors of Scripture. Why, then, wouldn't we expect that God reveals truths about reality in a similarly evolving fashion? In other words, the scriptural accounts of life after death represent an evolving sensibility that is consistent with humanity' coming to a deeper understanding of the fullness of reality. Just as God reveals truth to us through our collective experiences and growth, so too do our scriptural authors convey their understandings of the afterlife in a manner that would best be received by their audience.

I do not think it is a coincidence that all religions at all times in all parts of the world consider questions of what happens after death. Even in the so-called atheistic traditions, such as Buddhism and other Eastern faith traditions, postmortem status seems to be a crucial question. Indeed, it would not be far off the mark to treat the sensitivity to an afterlife as a—or perhaps *the*—defining characteristic of religion. A functional definition of religion could be whether that tradition provides a statement on the possibility of persistence after death. It is the very stuff of religion to provide such a statement.

And, I think, it would be equally defensible to recognize the commonalities intrinsic to these articulations of life after death, though the differences between these articulations are equally telling. As the late Alan Segal argued in his monumental tome appropriately entitled *Life After Death*, conceptualizations of the afterlife are intimately tied to the ways in which various cultures dispose of corpses. Cultures that practice inhumation (burial of the dead) will almost invariably conceive of the afterlife as a chthonic place—that is, the afterlife subsists beneath the surface of the earth. Alternatively, those cultures that practice immolation (burning of the dead) will conceive of the afterlife as a celestial place— that is, the afterlife is a place in the sky. Now, just as there are different categories of people on earth, there are different categories of the afterlife. The Greeks, for instance, buried their dead but burned their heroes; therefore, Hades was the de facto afterlife, but Elysium was reserved for the very special dead.

The Semitic religions of the ancient Near East labored under a tripartite cosmology; *Shamayim*—or "heavens"—is the place of residence for God and other heavenly beings. The mundane plane, ארץ, *eret~:*—literally "land"—denoted the sphere of apprehensible existence. But neither of these spheres was in any sense the afterlife. The heavens themselves were reserved as the abode of God, and the land was the venue in which life itself transpired. The third tier of existence was called קשוה *Sheol,* which translates as "grave" or "pit." The earliest authors of Scripture seem to communicate that this sphere is what we would term an afterlife. It was here that the םיקנע, *rephaim*—an etymologically complex word that seems to mean "shades" or "dead ancestors"—reside. But the authors of Scripture are by no means consistent with this usage.

To be sure, Segal's taxonomic model obtains for all the Near Eastern faith traditions of antiquity. The ancient Canaanites—a cadet branch of whom would go on to write the first five books of our Bible and eventually become known as the Hebrews—certainly had a robust tradition of interment, and we should therefore be unsurprised that their views of the afterlife were chthonic. The earliest mentions of the afterlife in the Bible accord with this sense. For the early Hebrews, visions of the afterlife were pretty bleak. Sheol seems to be the site at which the dead congregated (Genesis 37:35, 42:38, 44:29—31). It seems to be located underneath the earth (Isaiah 7:11; Ezekiel 31:14; Psalm 86:13; Sirach 51:7. It is extremely deep (Proverbs 9:18; Isaiah 57:9), so much so that it marks the greatest possible distance from the *Shumayim* (Job 11:8; Amos 9:2; Psalms 139:8).

So, how did a group of Canaanites transcend their cultural inheritance—their bleak, dreary, chthonic afterlife—and innovate the potential for salvation? Put simply: interaction with others. You see, all of the above references to Sheol as a physical place—akin to the Greek notion of Tartarus—come from the First Temple period. These pre-exilic Hebrews did not have the technology of description to imagine an afterlife that conferred advantage to the deserving dead; rather, it was in the experience of exile that they borrowed these concepts from the invaders that ravaged their religious topography.

The First Temple was ransacked first by the Assyrians around the turn of the eighth century B.C. by Sennacherib (2 Kings 17-19; 2 Chronicles 32:1—23). The temple was then utterly destroyed in 587 B.C. when the Babylonians under Nebuchadnezzar besieged and razed Jerusalem and subsequently deported the Hebrews to the east (2 Kings 25:1—26; Jeremiah 32—52; Lamentations 4—7. 2 Chronicles 36 also deals with this history). These events rearranged the Jewish sacral topography; the holy of holies had been desecrated—God's see on the Temple Mount, called Zion, had been altered fundamentally. And the religious self-conception of the Jews had been altered along with it. After the experience of exile—and the subsequent repatriation of the Jews after the defeat of the Babylonian Empire by Persians led by Cyrus the Great—a very different conceptualization of the afterlife is witnessed in Scripture.

Amid these experiences—or, perhaps, because of them—the authors of Scripture begin to speak of the eventual resurrection of the dead (most especially in the book of Daniel), anticipate the deliverance of a Messiah (witness the later additions to Isaiah, such as chapters 40—55 and 56—66), and inaugurate the later Jewish prophetic tradition—complete with punitive features of an afterlife predicated on perdition (the books of the twelve minor prophets, which constitute the final books of the Old Testament). And this happened when the authors of Scripture began to divorce the physical location known as—Gehenna—in favor of the conceptual explanation of that place.

Gehenna—translated in the King James Version as *hell*—is, as the Louvin Brothers remind us, a real place. To this day, the street running from west to east immediately south of the Wailing Wall in Jerusalem is called Gei Ben-Hinnom Street—literally, the valley of the sons of Hinnom. Gehenna, then as now, is the valley south of Mount Zion, the erstwhile home of both the First and Second Temples. The first mention of Gehenna occurs in the book of Joshua, when the author recounts the drawing of tribal boundaries in the city of Jerusalem: "Then the border went up the Valley of ben Hinnom [סוניה ןב] to the slope of the Jebusite on the south, which is Jerusalem; and the border went up to the top of the mountain which is before the Valley of Hinnom to the west, which is at the end of the valley of Rephaim toward the north" (15:8).

Gehenna—literally, the Valley of Hinnom—is a physical locality that was emplaced into the sacral topography of Jerusalem. The Temple Mount was the site of God's seat on earth, and, not incidentally, the highest point in Jerusalem. It abuts Gehenna, the lowest point in Jerusalem. This idea would have profound consequences for the development of an afterlife in Judeo-Christian thought.

Gehenna, as a physical location, became infamous for the unsavory goings-on to which it played venue. King Ahaz of Judah sacrificed his sons there (2 Chronicles 28:3), as did his grandson, Manasseh (2 Chronicles 33:6). The author of the book of Jeremiah notes that this valley was the site of ritual child sacrifice during the period of the Babylonian siege (7:31–32; 19:2–6; 32:35). In the Jewish imagination of the Second Temple period, Gehenna was firmly ensconced as a metonym for perdition. Gehenna, along with Hades, was the default state of perdition in both the late Second Temple period and in the New Testament. And in the imagination of subsequent generations, Gehenna effectively became hell.

Now, into this multicultural matrix intrudes another cultural player: the conquering Macedonian Greeks led by Alexander the Great. Though the Bible never mentions Alexander explicitly (apart from a single deutero-canonical reference in First Maccabees), later exegetes have attempted to explain the prophecies of Daniel as premonitions of Alexander's conquests (fl. 356–323 B.C.). The Jews of the Second Temple period were drawn into the Hellenic ambit and immersed in the philosophical and religious traditions of ancient Greece. Whereas Israelite religion of the first Temple period did not distinguish between the body and the soul, Jewish religion of the Second Temple period maintained a distinction between body and soul. With the introduction of Hellenism to Jewish religious thought came the advent of a positive afterlife result.

A positive side to the afterlife became increasingly evident in the Hasmonean Kingdom, established in 140 B.C. after Simon Maccabeus—brother of Judas Maccabeus, who died in revolution against the Seleucids in 160 B.C.—successfully gained independence for Palestine. While some scholars interpret this kingdom as a renovation of the kingdom of Israel, its rulers termed themselves (βασιλιάς or *basileos*, the Greek term for king or emperor. That Jewish revolutionaries would establish a political dynasty using Greek terminologies is telling; and, accordingly, we should expect to find Greek influences and Grecisms elsewhere in Jewish culture of that time period.

Among the Hellenistic traditions melded into the Jewish religious tradition of the Second Temple period was Platonism and its religiously inflected cousin, Neoplatonism. Think back to Plato's allegory of the cave that I mentioned in chapter one. Platonism, like many contemporaneous Near Eastern traditions, maintained that that which is really real and truly true is unseen; physical reality is defective in the face of formal reality which is the essence of the perfect and absolute that all manifestations of that thing share. Take, for instance, a chair. Two chairs might be wholly dissimilar with respect to their material, construction, and specific function, but these same two chairs share a quality of chairness that cuts across their dissimilarities and unites them in an ontological sense. Plato avers that this is because there is the form of *chair*—somewhere in the conceptual sphere—that allows us to understand two very dissimilar quantities as similar owing to their sharing an essential quality. So there exists a perfect chair, floating somewhere out in the ether, that bestows on all chairs the quality of chairness.

Taking the ideas of forms to its logical extreme, people arc the same way. According to strict Platonism, we, as physical beings, are defective insofar as we are set in physical reality. A perfect person would not be so limited, but instead be unlimited and infinite. The contribution of Neoplatonism was a method for attaining this perfection by means of philosophical consideration and meditation. Really, Neoplatonism contributed to the Judeo-Christian religious nexus a means and a method for ascending to perfection—that is to say, assenting to salvation.

This novel approach to the afterlife did not meet with universal acclaim, and the Jewish culture of the Levant fractured in the face of Hellenization. And it is in this syncretic admixture of Hebrew, Babylonian, Persian, and Greek cultural forms that the authors of the New Testament labored. According to Jeffrey Russell in his magisterial *A History of Heaven,* Jewish interpretations of the soul had been traditionally associated with the body itself; the soul, for Jews, was an extension of the body. The principle contribution of Hellenistic Neoplatonic thought to Near Eastern religion was the separation of the body and the soul into different substances. The soul, for the Hellenized Jews of the late Second Temple period, was an ascendant property, eligible for transition into a higher plane of existence; in short, with the coming of the Greeks and with the advent of Greek thought, heaven had been invented.

Not everyone agreed with these innovations. According to Josephus, Judaism at the time of Jesus was the site of vituperative contestation— Sadducees, Pharisees, Essenes, Zealots, and early followers of Christ were all negotiating the definitional parameters of Judaism; as often as not, this discourse involved varying ways to account for and interpret the afterlife, which was itself the product of repeated invasions and syncretism over the course of Jewish history.

The Sadducees, for instance, were hard-liners against any type of conditional afterlife or resurrection of the body. The afterlife, for the Sadducees, was strictly the Sheol of the Torah—an interpretation in keeping with their belief that only the Pentateuch was canonical Scripture. They were, however, willing Hellenizers, happy to incorporate the rich intellectual tradition of Greece in matters not pertaining to religion.

The Pharisees, on the other hand, argued in favor of bodily resurrection, but were much more circumspect about Hellenization. The Essenes were a separatist sect that argued for a robust, conditional afterlife that was predestined by God. The Zealots were vehement anti-Hellenizers, who were also violently opposed to Roman political rule. Into this complex, multifaceted religious tapestry appeared a small Jewish cult centered around a crucified prophet named Jesus.

It may be surprising to some readers of this book, but the New Testament is presented out of order; a strict chronology of composition would place the Epistles prior to the Gospels—which would be ordered Mark, Matthew, Luke, and John. Luke and Acts share a compositional author and a compositional date, and the Gospel of John—the latest book in the New Testament—postdates Revelation by about thirty years. Revelation can be securely dated to the reign of Domitian, around 95 A.D. So, how consistent are our scriptural authors in the way they communicate about the afterlife?

Well, as it turns out, not very. Our earliest authors—Paul, the other letter writers, and Mark—tend not to recognize the afterlife as an immediate reward for a life well lived. The author of the Gospel of Mark seems to suggest that the "Kingdom of God" is an apocalyptic vision; instead of being a place separate and distinct to which the recently dead ascend, it is instead a marker of the "world to come" (10:30). This formulation recurs in the Epistles. Similarly, all thirty-two references to the "Kingdom of Heaven" in the New Testament (there are no such formulations in the Old Testament) are found in Matthew; from context, this formulation is functionally identical to Mark's "Kingdom of God," and it is likely an artifact of the Jewish reticence to repeat the *nomina sacra*.

The truth is that neither Paul nor the authors of the synoptic Gospels seem focused on the afterlife as either a state or place to which one transcends after death. Though the early New Testament authors do refer to resurrection frequently and a belief in divine reward is replete, it does not seem as though these authors had a formalized conception of immediate transcendence into the afterlife—nor do they have a concern with it. St. Paul characterizes death as being like sleep:

And we will not have you ignorant, brethren, concerning them that are asleep, that you be not sorrowful, even as others who have no hope. For if we believe that Jesus died, and rose again; even so them who have slept through Jesus, will God bring with him. For this we say unto you in the word of the Lord, that we who are alive, who remain unto the coming of the Lord, shall not prevent them who have slept. (1 Thessalonians 4:12–14)

Rather than enjoying an immediate transition into the afterlife upon death, Paul seems to intimate that the dead observe a period of unconsciousness before their eventual resurrection. Indeed, these notions of the afterlife may be an example of an inaugurated eschatology,[33] whereby dead persons transcend to the afterlife in history—and whether that event occurs at the moment of death or at some future time is not altogether clear.

Now, the transition from a Jewish notion of the afterlife to a Christian notion of the afterlife hinges around the linchpin of Luke and Acts. These two books, like Matthew, postdate the crucifixion by about fifty years. But Luke evidences an understanding of the afterlife as an immediate reward, whereas Matthew does not. Accordingly, in the Gospel of Luke, Jesus is able to say to the penitent thief, "Amen 1 say to you, today you will be with me in Paradise" (23:43), whereas in both Mark and Matthew, the two thieves with whom Christ is crucified simply mock him. So why would the author of Luke display a preoccupation with the afterlife and eternality while Matthew does not? Put simply, it was a matter of audience.

According to Robert Wright in his very fine book entitled *The Evolution of God*, Matthew was written as an evangelistic document for Jews, while Luke was written as an evangelistic document tor Greeks. The Neoplatonic idea of ascent by the disembodiment of the soul by means of death—a welcome prospect for such a flesh-wary worldview as Neoplatonism—would have been comprehensible to Greeks in a vernacular sense. By contrast, the audience of Matthew—if indeed this Gospel was written for Jewish audiences—would not have understood this notion intuitively, laboring as they did under traditional Jewish understandings of the afterlife.

Now, by the turn of the first century A.D., when John of Patmos wrote Revelation and John the Evangelist wrote his Gospel, a strong articulation of realized eschatology—found at its incipient stages in Luke and Acts—is evident. Realized eschatology, whereby the soul of a dead person transcends to the afterlife at the moment of death, is a central tenet of the Johannine tradition, and is found all over both Revelation and the Gospel of John. Jesus's promise of eternal life is manifest to faithful believers at the moment of death. It is this conceptualization that found purchase in the theological imagination of the subsequent two-thousand-year history of the Christian faith.

Patristic authors, such as Tertullian and Augustine; medieval mystics, such as Hildegard of Bingen and Thérèse of Lisieux; and Renaissance poets, such as Dante and Milton, in addition to countless others, have all contributed to our current understanding of the afterlife. John Bunyan reminds us in *The Pilgrim's Progress* that "Death is not welcome to nature, though by it we pass out of this world in to glory." This afterlife, promised by Christ and debated by theologians, is a state or a place set apart from the mundane, and it is only accessible by means of death. Therefore, death occupies a place of central importance to Christian life. The afterlife "cannot be described," according to Jeffrey Russell, "but the human concept of heaven can be. Heaven is not dull; it is not static; it is not monochrome. It is an endless dynamic of joy in which one is ever more oneself as one was meant to be, in which one increasingly realizes one's potential in understanding as well as love and is tilled more and more with wisdom. It is the discovery, sometimes unexpected, of one's deepest self."[34]

Heaven, in crass economic terms, is a guarantee. It is God keeping God's end of the bargain. It is the promise of grandeur and beauty and proximity to the divine, whereupon all mysteries of life, death, and the universe become explained. It is equally a mystery and a means of dispelling mystery. It is paradoxical and totally sensical. And, ultimately, a heaven, such as the one described above, is a matter of faith.

Despite the long history of classic visions of afterlife, I think it is profitable to adopt for our understanding of the afterlife the same interpretive strategy that I advanced for imagining the divine in chapter two and for reading Scripture in chapter three, and challenge ourselves to seek new metaphors and images. Also, I suggest that, in this context, it is more productive to focus on the possibility of life after death than the question of what life after death is like. Because all human language employed to consider God and the fullness of reality is by necessity approximate, we should not be surprised to find that all language employed to describe and imagine the afterlife is equally metaphorical, oblique, and subjective.

In this regard, our metaphor of the child in the mother's womb remains a powerful image for meditation. Death is the transition from life within the child—that is, physical reality—to life within the mother—the fullness of reality. This image accords well with the core tenets suggested by the current understanding of salvation in most Christian faiths—perfect union with God after death. Even so, this formulation does not address the particulars of what that union might be. So, the question remains, can—and if so, how does—science enhance or contribute to our understanding of life after death?

The Science of Heaven

The very week during which I wrote this chapter, the popular National Public Radio show Intelligence featured a two-hour Oxford-style debate, held at the Kaufman Center in New York, resolved "Death Is Not Final." Before the debate commenced, Robert Rosenkranz, an economist and generous philanthropist, explained the reason that he commissioned the debate. Evidently, Rosenkranz had attended a Mass in which "the priest was challenging people to believe in an afterlife," using a "quasi-scientific [argument]."

> [The priest] said, "Imagine a fetus in its mother's womb that's almost ready to be born—nine-month, full-term baby. And you're trying to convey to this baby what's about to happen— that it's going to have an incredibly painful experience going through the birth canal; that its ties to its mother…[are] going to be severed. But not to worry! It's going to be a great life after- wards. There's going to be all kinds of experiences and sensory [stimulation] and development and emotional growth and an incredible world that [it] cannot imagine." And, when you think about that, of course you say, "There's no way to commu- nicate that, there's no way that the baby could understand it," and yet we all know it's true.

The metaphor of birth here represents death. All persons that have had the experience of birth know that the world outside the womb is far richer and preferable to the cloister of pregnancy, but there is no indication that the fetus could understand this truth. There is no empirical experiment that this fetus could do to indicate the truth of this statement. Apart from aligning neatly with the maternal metaphor for the relationship of phys- ical reality (creation) to the fullness of reality (God) that I advanced in chapter four, this metaphor helps us think about death as a moment of transition rather than a finite end.

The *Intelligence* debate, moderated by the estimable John Donvan, was conducted in a respectful, though adversarial, style. For the resolution was Dr. Eben Alexander, a neurosurgeon and author of the book *Proof of Heaven,* wherein he recounts the near-death experience he had while in a meningitis-induced coma in 2008. Also arguing for the resolution was Dr. Raymond Moody, an avuncular medical doctor and philosopher who, in 1975, wrote the book *Life after Life,* in which he coined the term *near-death experience.* Their position was rather simple: near-death experiences offer proof—if not scientific evidence—of the actuality of life after death.

We can, they averred, infer the validity of an afterlife by noting the similarities between the experiences of individuals who have had these experiences. Sensations of ascent and traveling toward a white light are recurrent themes in these experiences, as are meeting with deceased loved ones and, occasionally, being in the presence of a higher power. Notably, these experiences are almost universally serene and positive.

Against the resolution was Sean Carroll, a physicist at the California Institute of Technology in Pasadena, author of *The Particle at the End of the Universe* on the subject of the Higgs-Boson "God particle," and self-described naturalist. Also arguing against the resolution was Steven Novella, a neurologist at Yale School of Medicine, and a self-described skeptic. Their position was equally straightforward: mind, they maintained, is a consequence of the brain. "Mind," said Novella, "is what the brain does." As such, when neural activity ceases, so too does mind. They maintained that examples of near-death experiences are not scientifically verifiable and therefore cannot constitute evidence or proof of life after death. The real substance of this debate was an exploration into the mind-brain problem: Can the conscious mind exist, or continue to exist, in the absence of a physical brain?

Alexander and Moody argued yes; Carroll and Novella argued no. And the entry point of each side was the subject of near-death experiences.

This debate was extremely topical. But my concern with the debate, such as it was structured, is that any person—on either side of the motion "Death Is Not Final"—would attempt to marshal scientific evidence to support or disparage claims to these experiences. "What science says," Carroll said during this debate, "is that life or consciousness is not a substance like water or air. It is a process like fire. When you put out the flame of a candle, the flame doesn't go anywhere, it simply stops." Therefore, on the one hand, there is the assumption by the naturalist camp that the functional aspects of the physical brain are the only source of the mind, and presumably the self. Therefore, with this assumption, there is no room for discussion. Once the brain stops functioning (which is scientifically verifiable), the self stops.

On the other side of the debate, it seems impossible to determine when the near-death experience actually occurs relative to the brain activity. I think we are all aware that perceived time in an unconscious state is essentially impossible to correlate with real time in the physical world. Just think of your dream experiences near waking—or between returning to sleep and the alarm going off again after hitting the very useful snooze button. Given the impossibility of correlating internal and external experience while unconscious, I cannot imagine an experiment that could ever determine the correlation between near-death experiences and brain activity.

We are left with an interesting situation. As important and critical as the mind-brain discussion is, I do not see how a discussion of life after death can be decided by neuroscientific experiments. By definition, these questions require experimentation on the brain—which may or may not encompass the entire self. Our current state of neurological understanding clearly points to a deep connection between brain and self. There is a high probability that many aspects of the self are well-defined emergent properties of the brain, but, by definition, the self-brain issue seems to be one that is fundamentally a philosophical, or theological, issue. So where does that leave us?

In this book, I have talked a lot about the intersection of the physical and nonphysical. On the physical side of things, we have waves and particles. On the nonphysical side of things, we have the fundamental description of reality (the wave function). In a way, even the mathematics that governs the physics behind how these events behave (scientific theories, laws, and models) is an example of a nonphysical reality. Both of these factors—the physical and the nonphysical—are equally real. Both are types of reality.

One would not argue against the existence of subatomic particles simply because one does not have a massive particle accelerator or a detector system handy to measure it. I think we should look at the presence and actuality of the human mind in the same way. The self might indeed be rooted in the physical brain, but in its very existence and in its very implication, it seems to me that it transcends the physical into nonphysical reality.

In chapter six, I discussed the possibility of the existence of a soul by discussing the problem of mind as an emergent property of complex interactions in the brain. An emergent property, recall, occurs in a system of sufficient complexity such that the rules governing the system are more than just the rules governing the parts of the system by virtue of the parts constituting a system. In other words, the whole is greater than the sum of the manifold parts. This is a key point in any discussion of the mind.

To be sure, the mind is rooted in the brain—about this fact there can be little to no doubt. However, because the brain is so complex, and because the constituent parts of the brain interact in such highly specific and variegated ways, the total self created by the brain—the software that is the self-reflective, self-reflexive mind—may be more than the hardware between our ears. Now, I make no pretenses to being a neuroscientist, and so I might be completely wrong about this, but it seems to me that interpreting the cognitive, conscious mind simply according to its component, physical parts signals an overconfidence in reductive materialist explanations of phenomena—but I will agree that a purely reductionist interpretation cannot lead to a consideration of the interaction of the physical and nonphysical.

It is important to recognize that emergence itself is not a solution to the question of an eternal mind or self. Without a full understanding of emergence, as it relates to mind, it is completely reasonable to propose that the emergence of mind is fully contingent on the physical functioning of the neurons. Such an emergent property would be no more robust after death than a mind that can be completely encapsulated in a purely reductionist fashion. However, the reason for discussing the question of emergence is to focus on another type of emergence in which the mind is a reflection of the complex structure of the underlying wave function.

As discussed in the previous chapter on free will, the wave function is the underlying reality that encapsulates everything about the state of a system.

Presumably, this includes the relevant features of reality that produce the mind. No one will doubt that the wave functions of the quantum entities that constitute the mind continue to exist even when the neurons are no longer active. And it is in the context of the eternality of the wave function that I wish to continue our reflection on life after death and the possibility of eternal existence.

Before we proceed, I wish to briefly return to a comment from the *Intelligence* debate. During the debate, Carroll referred to the possibility that quantum mechanics might help resolve the life-after-death quandary: "Scott Aaronson"—a physicist at the Massachusetts Institute of Technology—"says [that], as far as he can tell, quantum mechanics is confusing and consciousness is confusing; so, maybe, they're the same thing." This remark captures the essential danger of invoking quantum mechanics to explain anything that is mysterious. Quantum mechanics remains one of the most successful and least understood branches of physics. Therefore, its misuses in popular culture are too numerous to list here. Nevertheless, quantum mechanics is our current best model to explain the reality that we inhabit; the wave function is intrinsically nonphysical; so it makes sense to reflect on the implications of quantum mechanics for eternal life and the nature of the self.

Eternality in Science

If we arc to imagine the possibility of eternal life, it is useful to consider the more general issue of eternality. Science makes use of eternal properties all the rime. Perhaps the clearest example is that of space-time. Recall my discussion of space-time in chapter four. Einstein's theory of special relativity—that the speed of light in a vacuum is invariant, regardless of the initial motion of the light source—points to the reality that the three dimensions of physical space are combined with a single dimension of time into a four-dimensional manifold. Space-time—more accurately called Minkowski space, after Hermann Minkowski, who first posited this solution—allows physicists to speak simultaneously about where and when events occur.

As we discussed in chapter three, the other salient aspect of space-time is that it simply exists. Our experience of time is due to motion through space-time, but in a very real sense, time itself does not move forward. Now, it is true that our best understanding of the current universe is that it is expanding. So, we do have a sense of beginning and end. But, as I said, one way to understand this expansion is as a bubble of space-time growing out of the vacuum state of space-time. Though the scientific and mathematical proofs that suggest the eternality of space-time get incredibly confusing (even for a seasoned physicist such as myself—and here, even I often invoke the two-cookie rule and accept the math and leave the understanding to later), it is reasonable to describe space-time as fundamentally eternal. The structure may change, stretch, shrink, or bend, but it still remains.

While relativity and quantum mechanics have yet to be integrated to each other—and this is one of the major goals of contemporary physics— space-time, a product bequeathed to us by relativity, serves as the stage on which quantum behaviors transpire. As I described in chapter eight, one of the features of quantum mechanics is that the wave function exists across all space and time. The scientific way to describe this existence would term the wave function a field. The values of the wave function at each point in space and time describe the state of the system, which includes the probability of any given quantum entity—say, an electron—of having a particular position, energy, or any other measurable quantity. The exact value of measurable quantities is only established at the time of measurement.

The wave function does change in time by two methods: According to Schrödinger's equation, the wave function evolves and proceeds deterministically between each measurement, and at the time of measurement, the wave function changes suddenly, depending on the result of the measurement. What is important here is that the nonphysical wave function ripples throughout reality for all time. Though the physical properties of the system may change, the underlying wave function is a constant feature of the system.

There are also physical quantities that exist eternally. Consider the first law of thermodynamics, taught in introductory physics courses by the aphorism "energy cannot be created or destroyed, but it can change forms." Now, this law is only strictly true in closed thermodynamic systems in equilibrium, so there is a very real question as to the status of the energy in an expanding universe. But at a practical level for us, energy cannot be destroyed; only its form changes. Chemical energy stored in TNT is released as kinetic energy when a stick of dynamite is detonated. Potential energy is converted to kinetic energy when a ball drops; when that ball strikes the ground, the compression of the ball converts elastic energy into thermal energy (heat). In all of these systems, energy is conserved—and in a very real sense, the energy is eternal.

The eternality of energy points to an amazing feature of the physical world—the constant ebb and flow of life and death. I suggest that as we contemplate the fullness of reality, we should take seriously that physical reality, too, is an image of God, and that what we observe in the physical world should be applied to our understanding of the fullness of reality. Therefore, for me, our deep experience of death and birth in the physical world is strong evidence for death and rebirth within the fullness of reality. The world around us is full of deaths and births—from the seed that dies in order to become a flower to the deaths of stars that produce the very elements necessary for life itself. In life, we experience metaphorical deaths at all those points of transition. As painful as they often are, they can lead to new lives.

Finally, even Scriptures remind us that from dust we came and to dust we return—and that very dust is integrated into the next generation of life.

The energy that our bodies—along with our brains—use and store is effectively eternal. In a very real sense, the energy our bodies extract from food and from the sun is borrowed; that energy derives from radiant energy that becomes trapped in the very plants that are the basis of the food chain. Energy transactions in the sun produce the light that provides a constant source of energy for the earth—producing a fundamentally nonequilibrium system—fortunately for us! Otherwise our system, planet Earth, would die a cold, quick death. It is the sun's radiant energy—light—that powers this spaceship.

The sun's energy courses through us, but it was born in the belly of a star. The only immutable law of the universe—the only law that will never be threatened by our waxing scientific understanding—is the fundamental mutability of the universe. Transformation is the only constant in an ever changing universe.

Now, finally, I think Yoda said it best: "Luminous beings are we, not this crude matter," as he pinched Luke Skywalker's arm. And in one very real sense he is right.

The physical reactions in our bodies that translate the latent energy of our food into the exploitable energy that powers our mechanical work has the byproduct of low-level radiant energy—in other words, heat. Our bodies are energy conversion furnaces that burn at a constant 98.6 degrees. The exhaust from the energy conservation is radiant light energy, perceptible to us as body heat. That is why people appear as luminous figures when viewed through infrared goggles—what we see is heat, the very light we produce. This light shines like six billion candles in a darkened amphitheater—the very light we humans emit travels from its source throughout the universe. And that light travels for all time and in all directions.

Now, the wave functions of the electrons in our brains and bodies, the energy that we use, and the light that we emit are all perpetual—though they themselves may interact with other matter, engendering additional transformations. They do not cease to exist simply because we do. One might ask: Is this an afterlife? All these things persist after life. Does this allow for a continued—though altered—consciousness after death? I would claim that this is almost certainly not an afterlife for the self. But it does highlight the fundamental nature of transformation, and I would argue that in the presence of these eternal physical transformations, it is completely reasonable to posit that nonphysical transformations occur upon the death of the physical self—and these may allow for the eternal continuation of the self.

The Eternal Self

So, what can the sciences tell us about the possibility of a self persisting in perpetuity? Well, it helps to think about what a self actually is. For some, the self is just the mind, and, according to the most reductionist models of mind, it is produced by the interaction of physical quantities in the brain. Now, consider the literal matter of mind; all brains are composed of cells, which are themselves composed of specifically arrayed molecules, which are themselves composed of atoms—the basic building blocks of which are our ever-present protons, neutrons, and electrons. We are, ourselves, built of the same atomic building blocks as the rest of the universe. Now, if all quantum entities are described by a wave function, then so are the quantum entities that comprise our mind.

We should be unsurprised by this; we are, after all, physical entities who possess physicality and are subject to the same physical realities that beset all other matter in the universe. Just as one can write a wave function using elegant mathematics for a single electron, one can write a wave function for a whole constellation of quantum entities. The mathematics for such a probabilistic expression becomes significantly more complex for every additional quantity under consideration. A simple, back-of-the-envelope calculation suggests that to write the mathematics for the wave function of a single mind would take more page space than all the Bibles printed since 1453—and would likely occupy more page space than every single copy of every single book ever written. Until, of course, one employs the scientist's penchant for developing shorthand mathematics—and you define the wave function of the brain to simply be Ψ!

There are additional scientific challenges faced by writing a wave function for a system as complicated as the brain. As a system becomes more complex, one has to deal with issues of the crossover between quantum behavior and classical behavior and issues of how systems become entangled. The net result is that the scientific challenges to a truly quantum representation of the brain in terms of its wave function are immense.

Despite the complexity of the problem, I would like to propose a relatively simple quantum mechanical example to illustrate why consideration of the wave function as a fundamentally nonphysical aspect of reality might elucidate the possibilities of life after death. At the core of this example is the concept of conserved quantities. We have already mentioned the fact that energy is conserved in closed systems. But there are other important quantities that are conserved in physical processes; among these is electronic charge. Recall that systems can either be positively or negatively charged, or if they have an equal amount of positive and negative charge, the system is neutral, or has zero charge.

An important fundamental process is the interaction between an electron (with negative charge) and a positron (or antielectron, with positive charge) that results in the annihilation of the two particles and the production of light (as two photons). This happens in part because particles and antiparticles are exactly the same in every way except for their charge. So, a positron is the same as an electron, but has positive charge. The electron-positron annihilation conserves the total charge of the system. Beforehand the net charge is zero, and afterward the net charge is zero. One can consider this conservation of charge to be reflected in the continuity of the wave function describing the entire system before and after the annihilation.

As we think about these two particles being annihilated, you could focus on the fact that before annihilation we have two particles and afterward we have two photons. This would be equivalent to focusing on death as being the process in which you initially have functioning neurons and afterward you do not. But from the perspective of the entire system, it is equally valid to describe this as a system that—before and after the interaction—can be represented by a wave function that has zero net charge. The question of there being two particles or two photons is the particular manifestation of the zero charge system. So, by analogy, for a sufficiently complex system, one could imagine that the self is a conserved quantity.

For a situation in which the self is conserved, our view of death would be very different. Before death, measurement of the self would be based on measurements of the functioning neurons, just as before the particle and antiparticle annihilation total charge is measured by measuring each particle separately. After the death, measurement of self takes on a completely different character just as after the particle annihilation, measurement of charge is based on measuring photons.

What is interesting here is that we can posit a type of persistent perpetuity throughout eternity of the underlying quantum description of the mind. The physical manifestation of the underlying wave function will evolve in such a way as to fundamentally alter the composition of the initial, emergent state. But, again, that should not surprise us: even the most rudimentary expressions of life after death assume the afterlife to be qualitatively different from life itself.

I want to be clear that I am not making a claim that this is how self works.

The point of this analogy is twofold. First, our current understanding of quantum mechanics does not preclude the possibility that the wave function of a sufficiently complex system does not exhibit a conserved property that is itself the self. So it strikes me as a reasonable direction to pursue. Second, our return to a discussion of quantum mechanics reminds us that we know of at least one fundamentally nonphysical aspect to reality: the wave function. Even if it is not the source of the eternal self, other nonphysical realities may exist—and the eternal self may be another example of such an eternal nonphysical reality.

These views of the afterlife from a scientific perspective strongly suggest a reality that is very different from the physical reality to which we are accustomed.

This requires us, as people of faith—as we have previously with images of God, views of Scripture, miracles, and free will—to be perfectly honest about the historically conditioned and historically contingent nature of our conceptualization of the afterlife. The afterlife need not be wings, harps, and halos simply because that is the conceptualization of the afterlife we have inherited from our forebears. Hell and heaven—and ancillary states, such as purgatory and limbo—are at some level historical constructs designed to fulfill rhetorical functions specific to the moment in which they were conceived. As with our images of God, these images can serve a useful purpose at times, but, I think, they limit the more amazing feature of our Judeo-Christian traditions—that an all-loving God has declared creation to be fundamentally good (Genesis) and desires us to enter into a full relationship with God (pretty much the subject of the rest of Scripture!).

Conclusion

I stated in the introduction to this book that I certainly believe asking the right questions is more effective at times than arriving at any answers. As we moved through the topics in the book, hopefully you noticed that the more challenging issues had more questions and fewer answers. At the end of the day, the question of life after death remains just that—a question, fundamentally. I have argued that the sciences can point us to the afterlife as a distinct possibility, but they can in no way describe for us the contours of that afterlife. Neither our telescopes nor our microscopes are provisioned to observe such a state, and even if they were, we wouldn't be able to frame a scientific question with an experimental apparatus suitable to address those topics. Really, the afterlife must remain just as ineffable as St. Paul, citing Isaiah, says it must be: "Eye has not seen, nor ear heard, neither have entered into the heart of man the things which God hath prepared for them that love Him" (1 Corinthians 2:9). Short of when each of us eventually does die, there is no scientific experiment that can be designed to study the issue of life after death, and so the question of eternal life can sustain no empirical consideration.

The reader may have noticed that I have focused on the question of whether or not eternal life is possible, and I have not addressed the question of how one achieves eternal life. As my concern with this book is the ways in which science can enhance our understanding of our faith, the issue of moral adjudication—as the religious criterion for access to the afterlife—is not directly relevant. I hope this does not surprise you; science is a worldview that fundamentally does not address moral questions, and while we can point to naturalistic explanations for the reasons we perceive certain actions as moral and others as immoral (as likely as not by means of evolutionary biology), we cannot indicate the morality of actions except in the most general, unsatisfying terms.

However, much like the projects I advanced in chapters two and three, I believe our scientific reflections on the afterlife do lead us to consider critically our core beliefs and challenge us to resist received configurations that we have been taught that, to refer back to St. Paul, are appropriate for the faith of a child. As adults, we are called to move beyond these formulae. At least for Christians, whose Scripture starts with God declaring all creation to be good, all people to be in God's image, and whose Scripture concludes that God so loved the world that we are all part of the mystical body of Christ, and (as St. Paul reminds us) love is the greatest of all, it seems only natural that the fullness of reality is the all-loving, all-knowing, all-saving God that calls us all to a personal relationship.

In this context, it would seem that eternal life in God is something we are offered through God's grace, and we can either accept or reject it by our free will. Though the language may differ from confession to confession, I see this as the core message of Christian salvation, and I believe this is a vision of salvation that is also suggested by our contemplation of a scientific understanding of eternal life: salvation is freely available to those persons who choose to share in the fullness of reality.

Just as free will is the ability to choose to do something different or differently, salvation is conferred by means of continually deepening our relationship with God, who is the fullness of reality. As with any relationship, this involves work and effort to sustain, and it is not my place to tell you the best way for you to deepen your relationship with God. But in the best of worlds, our community of faith fully supports us in building our relationship with God. In the end, the regular superheroes save us from physical threats, but God, the ultimate superhero, transforms our lives.

Ultimately, God calls us to a condition and a state wherein we are not limited by the physical; we experience life after death in the here and now; and we experience the fullness of reality without barriers. And in this state of total immersion in the fullness of reality, in our God, with infinite beneficence, benevolence, and benefaction, we experience true joy. We are God's creation and God loves us. And the sciences indicate the multitude of ways that such is the case.

Scientia et Sapientiae: The Theology of Science

"It is finished."

—John 19:30

The manifestation of the Spirit is given to every man unto profit. To one indeed, by the Spirit, is given the word of wisdom [*sapientia*] and to another, the word of knowledge [*scientio*], according to the same Spirit."

—1 Corinthians 12:7–8

The definition [of "wisdom," *sapientia*, and "knowledge," *scientia*] is to be divided so that the knowledge of things divine shall be called wisdom, and that of things human appropriate to itself the name of knowledge...so as to attribute this knowledge to anything that can be known by man about things human.

—Augustine, *De Trinitate,* lib. XIV, ch. 3

This book has sought to advance a series of starting points whereby we can make an honest attempt to place matters of science and matters of faith into serious, fruitful, and productive dialogue—with the hope that we can close the chasm that has opened between the two epistemologies. As I said above, by premising the interaction of science and faith as a matter of debate, we have sculpted the landscape of this interaction in adversarial terms. None other than Carl Sagan, famed astronomer of the twentieth century and agnostic though he was, reminds us: "Science is not only compatible with spirituality; it is a profound source of spirituality—The notion that science and spirituality are somehow mutually exclusive does a disservice to both."

I agree. You see, this entire book has been animated by a sustained belief that the sciences inform the picture of reality that faith initiates, and, indeed, that we must leverage both ways of knowing into a robust interpretation of the world. If, as atheist and twentieth-century physicist Richard Feynman maintains, "Religion is a culture of faith [and] science is a culture of doubt," then we must be frank about what it is we want our faith to do for us. What are our goals as persons of faith? Do we believe that our Scripture provides us with all that we need to understand the world completely? Or do we, as I believe we do, need to approach our faith with a fundamental premise of humility firmly in place?

I have argued that we of faith must adopt a threefold approach to our relationship to religious matters. First, we must dispense with a magical, physical God—an entity that can be no more than a god of the gaps. If we believe that God is omnipotent, omnipresent, and omniscient—necessary prerequisites for an omnibeneficent and omniprovidential deity—then we cannot confine God in and to the physical world; doing so would reduce the fullness of reality, which God is, into a linguistic box, sealed by our limited powers of imagination. Instead, I contend, we should allow the God of our imagination to be the fullness of reality that the "I am" of Exodus claims to be. "When I was a child," writes Paul, "I spoke as a child, I understood as a child, I thought as a child; when I became a man, I put aside childish things" (1 Corinthians 13:11). St. Paul is right—we need to approach the God that makes the most sense according to our mechanisms for posing questions to reality; we need the God that makes sense to the sciences.

Now, this God, I argue, is more than the cloud-dwelling, grandfatherly gift giver—infinitely more. In fact, if God were to simply be the God of such a controlling image, then we would be more accurate to call such a being a god. I cannot accept a god who, in self-serving and ignoble ways, capriciously bestows favor on his creation. God is not just a superhero; God is the ultimate superhero. God does not exploit and co-opt reality; God is reality; God does not break physical law; God is physical law. Accordingly, I opt for a God, strongly configured, a God of infinite power, presence, and knowledge, who is also infinitely good and infinitely active in the world. In order to accept such a God—as, I believe, all three monotheistic traditions call us to do—we must break the mold that we have become accustomed to using when speaking about God. The study of reality (i.e., science) will never diminish God, the fullness of reality.

Scientific knowledge will, as Paul reminds us, call on us to challenge some of the childish aspects of our faith. It might force us to take God out of that safe, reductive box and stretch our experience of whom God is. This is indeed challenging—embracing the infinite always is. But when we understand God to be the fullness of reality—consisting of both physical and nonphysical aspects—then we reach a point where the sciences cannot not argue against such an entity, and all religious requirements for a strong creator God are satisfied.

Second, we must allow Scripture to speak to us its truth; we should not cling to the facts it cannot convey. By understanding Scripture to communicate truth instead of crass fact, we allow the authors of Scripture to speak to us according to their compositional intent. The literal facts conveyed by Scripture are often untenable, and, I argue, unproblematically so. For, you see, if we read Scripture in the same allegorical mode in which it was written, we have allowed ourselves the opportunity to avail ourselves of the truths its authors hoped to impart—not the facts that they did not. As Augustine reminds us,

> Often a non-Christian knows something about the earth [and] the heavens...and this knowledge he holds with certainty from reason and experience To hear a Christian talk nonsense

about such things—claiming that what he is saying is based on Scripture—[is offensive and disgraceful]. We should do all that we can to avoid such an embarrassing situation, lest the unbeliever see only ignorance in the Christian and laugh to scorn.[35]

The fact is that Scripture conveys timeless, nonnegotiable truths—often in moral terms—and does not pretend to address the facts that science is able to convey. To be sure, Scripture is preoccupied with conveying apprehensions of the divine—not apprehensions of the world. Scripture is about relating experiences of the infinite in finite terms; science is about relating experiences of the finite in finite terms. The two work toward different, though related, ends according to different, though related, means; Scripture allows us to consider the nonphysical, and the sciences can only privilege us to interpretations of the physical.

One is fine to speak about the "moral foundations of science," Einstein reminds us, "but you cannot turn around and speak of the scientific foundations of morality." After all, as Cardinal Baronius reminds us, Scripture can tell us how to go to heaven, but cannot tell us how the heavens go. We should not treat Scripture as an incipient science textbook. Doing so forces us to twist scientific understanding insensibly to accord with an outmoded and superseded cosmology—and potentially forces us to reject the truths of Scripture in the face of its problematic factual underpinning. Reading Scripture according to a literal hermeneutic does a disservice to both the authors and the readers of Scripture, and threatens to, in the words of Cardinal John Henry Newman, "poison the well" of Scripture. St. Paul reminds us that "bad associations spoil useful habits" (1 Corinthians 15:33). Therefore, we must all frankly admit that Scripture can tell us extraordinarily important things about experiences of the divine, moral guidance, and ethical conduct, but it does not convey the facts of cosmology and biology.

Third, and to return to Feynman's dichotomy above, we must be frank and honest about our process of faith. Faith is not the absence of doubt, as Feynman and some faithful would have you believe; rather, true faith, agile faith, dynamic faith is about constant reflection, constant revision, and constant refinement. In that way, the discourse and development of faith is not at all unlike the progress of the sciences.

Instead, it is their terminology and criteria of proof that differ. This is the essence of the spiral journey of faith. I may be reading too far into the formulation to suggest that allowing faith to transpire by means of critical investigation is somehow scientific, but the similarities are striking. You see, doubt is indeed crucial to the enterprise of the sciences, as Feynman suggests, but there is no reason why doubt cannot be leveraged to perform positive spiritual work. Indeed, a faith that does not critically reflect is dead and stultified.

So, we should submit our faith to processes of revision and refinement. And we do this by incorporating understandings about the physical world into our view of the fullness of reality. As St. Paul, Augustine, and Galileo remind us, God has gifted us with reason and the ability to understand the physical world to an amazing degree. Therefore, it is absolutely imperative that people of faith understand science and scientific progress to the greatest extent possible. To the degree that measurements can be defined and experiments be done, science is an incredible tool for posing questions and providing answers. And the sciences are always refining our abilities to provide measurements and conduct experiments. The answers the sciences provide, therefore, are not matters of opinion—one cannot simply not believe in evolution, for instance. The findings of the sciences are facts. But if we allow our spiral journey of faith to take as its ultimate goal a better understanding of the fullness of reality, what we discover is that the findings and explorations of the sciences give us a greater understanding of God.

Now, any approach to faith and science must be one of humility. Humility, to be sure, is often difficult. And a lack of humility is, I believe, what has produced the spirit of conflict that animates discussions between the sciences and faith. There are times that the sciences don't play well with others—and this is due to a level of pride intrinsic to the very idea of objectivity and fact. But it doesn't need to be that way. Most scientists understand and respect the implications and limitations of their data; most scientists recognize the need for humility at some level, and possess the ability to admit that they have made errors. But any scientists who seek to address scientific findings as to the existence or nonexistence of a deity are likely overstepping the bounds of the scientific method. Persons of faith who hear such pronouncements should understand these missteps to be what they are: not science.

The core elements of religious faith are unassailable by the sciences—if, indeed, the sciences can even provide analyses of the mechanisms of these elements.

Recall: the sciences can only ask questions about the parameters of these events—Who? What? When? Where? How?—and never about the implication *of* these events—why? Science is about physical reality; as physical reality is constituent *to* the fullness of reality, understanding what the sciences tell us about physical reality does provide insights into God. But this is a matter of degrees.

By definition, the sciences cannot tell us about nonphysical reality in anything approaching detail; rather, the sciences can indicate that nonphysical reality is indeed real. It is at the intersection of the physical and nonphysical that so many interesting questions stand. What is mind and consciousness? What is the source of free will? Does the self continue after death? If there is more to reality than the purely physical, the answer to these questions will depend on how the physical and nonphysical interact. Perhaps the fact that the wave function is a fundamentally nonphysical entity is a starting point for this exploration.

Therefore, we are at a crossroads: the sciences can point to something nonphysical that is real, however, the sciences cannot provide meaning or significance to that something. It is incumbent upon us—both scientists and persons of faith—to frankly admit these limitations in a humble and charitable way.

But this exhortation to humility cuts both ways: persons of faith need to approach the sciences with an open mind rather than simply reentrenching in the comfort of their worldview. Because persons of faith have allowed themselves to succumb to an addiction to infectious fact, the pride of the sciences has crept into the religious worldview. Persons of faith, especially, should be quick to correct this error; *superbia* (pride) is, after all, one of seven cardinal vices—as communicated by Solomon, Paul, Evagrius Ponticus, Pope Gregory the Great, John Cassian, and Dante Alighieri.

Religious persons are called to humility: "pride goeth before destruction, and a haughty spirit cometh before a fall" (Proverbs 16:18). When religious persons approach the sciences, we should have the confidence to understand that the core of our faith cannot be shaken by the sciences, and we should have the humility necessary to open our minds and hearts to new ways of knowing. And part of this humility is allowing the Scriptures to speak to us in their own voice—not according to our own expectations.

If we allow Scripture to speak to its own allegorical voice instead of attempting to press it into our own mold of clumsy fact, we see that God's creation of the physical from a nonphysical perspective is a central and recurrent theme. A spirit of humility would prevent those of faith from making specific statements of privileged knowledge about that process, but many passages support this view in its broadest contours. Solomon reminds us in Wisdom, "We see the original author by analogy from the greatness and beauty of things created" (13:9). So when we approach the questions regarding the nature of God and the nature of God's creation, we see that Scripture and science do not conflict. The nonphysical—God, the fullness of reality, the vacuum state, space-time, the wave function—constrains physical reality and conditions its manifestation. What we see, then, is a disagreement over the terms employed and the intransigence of hubris.

What we see as well, from the analogy of the fractal, is that patterns of configuration repeat as a given system becomes larger. The macrocosm is reflected in the microcosm. And, therefore, we should be unsurprised by features of our existence—love, consciousness, reason, logic—being reflected on even larger and more profound scales. That we possess a loving consciousness is a very strong suggestion toward the presence of a fuller, loving, conscious reality that cares about us as God's creation. The specific configurations of this loving consciousness are a matter of faith, and are not subject to the interpretative and investigative tool of science. But if the sciences can help us recognize the pattern, our religious sensibilities can put flesh on the bones of that induction.

Now, throughout this book, I have referred to my preferred metaphor of creation: a child in the womb of its mother. Physical reality is the child, which exists in the fullness of reality, which is the mother. If, as I suggest, God is the fullness of reality—encompassing both physical and nonphysical elements of reality—then we find an analogue in the most profoundly radical revelation of the New Testament: the mystical body of Christ.

For me, the mystical body of Christ is first revealed in Acts 9:4, in Saul's conversion on the road to Damascus where he hears Christ cry out, "Saul, Saul, why do you persecute me?" Saul, now Paul, makes this explicit in his preaching on the one body of Christ: "For as the body is one, and hath many members; and all the members of the body, whereas they are many, yet are one body, so also is Christ. For in one Spirit were we all baptized into one body, whether Jews or Gentiles, whether bond or free; and in one Spirit we have all been made to drink" (1 Corinthians 12:12–13).

Pope Pius XII, in his 1943 encyclical *Mystici Corporis Christi,* expresses the notion that all members of the Christian communion share in the divine. This is awe inspiring. Returning to the Genesis story, we see that the idea of all human participation in the fullness of reality starts with our very creation in the image of God. Images of our participation in the divine continue in John's description of *Logos* and Christ's declaration of his presence in even the least of humanity: "As long as you did it to one of these my least brethren, you did it to me" (Matthew 25:40). All of these passages reflect an integrated view of humanity and our connection to the divine.

This understanding of our connection to the fullness of reality challenges us to live in accordance with an authentic relationship with God and to each other. Whether this shared nature is our very souls, our radical agency within the parameters of reality, our sensitivity to the divine, or all of the above, what remains is a profound sense that we, as creation, are intimately connected to the creator. We are, in no small way, the product of the project of God's action; we are attenuated to the divine precisely because we share in the experience of reality's fullness. God speaks through the creation that God brought into existence. Really, it all comes down to whether we are humble enough to listen.

Questions for Reflection

Chapter 0: *Faith and Science*

Consider a time in your life when questions, challenges, or experiences changed your view of God and/or faith. Why did your view change and what aspects of the questions, challenges, or experiences were most important for bringing about the change.

Consider a time in your life when questions, challenges or experiences changed your view of science and/or science provided an answer to your questions. Why did science play a role in those experiences?

Chapter 1: *Fullness of Reality*

Describe specific experiences in life that have led you to believe or not believe in a reality beyond physical reality. In sharing these experiences with other people, what is the most important element of these experiences that you would want them to understand?

Describe specific experiences/stories that others have shared with you or that you have read about that have lead you to believe or not believe in a reality beyond physical reality?

Chapter 2: *Images of God*

How has the image of God changed throughout your life, and what has been the cause of those changes?

When you read about God or have God described to you by other people, what aspect and/or actions of God either lead you to a stronger belief in God or make you doubt God's existence, and why?

Chapter 3: *Approaches to Scripture*

Consider the wide range of the literary tradition (poetry, history, science, religious reflections, philosophy, fiction, biography, etc.), what role do the different styles of literature play in your life and, if the Bible is important to you, how does the style of different sections of the Bible impact its relevance in your life?

What facts of religious traditions do you consider most relevant to your belief in them or your non-belief? What makes these facts particularly important?

CHAPTER 4: *Creation*

For you, what does the phrase "Creator of the Universe" mean, and how does this concept impact your view of God? How does the scientific description of creation impact your view of God?

In the book, I propose an image of creator in terms of a mother and child in the womb. Spend some time reflecting on this image. Does this image resonant with you understanding of a creator? How, if at all, does it impact your image of God?

CHAPTER 5: *Evolution*

If you had to explain evolution to someone in two minutes or less, what are the key aspects of a description of evolution?

In the book, I discuss images of the "Reign of God." How would you describe the Reign of God, and do you see any connections between it and our current understanding of evolution?

CHAPTER 6: *Consciousness/Self*

What do you consider to be the most important aspects of your "self"? Would you describe them as being primarily physical attributes or non-physical ones?

If science was able to accurately describe the physical processes connected to the experiences you think of as love, hate, joy, etc., what, if any, impact would that have on your understanding of the "reality" of these experiences?

CHAPTER 7: *Miracles*

Describe a time that you believe God acted in your life. What about the experience convinced you of God's presence and action?

Reflect on an example of someone else sharing about an experience with God (either someone you have heard speak about it or an experience you read about). What about the story either led you to believe that experience or to doubt that experience?

CHAPTER 8: *Free Will*

Describe a time in your life when you faced an important choice. What tools and experiences did you rely on to make that choice?

Describe a time in your life when you choose to change a behavior. What made that change either successful or not successful?

CHAPTER 9: *Life after Life*

What are specific ways in which you live your life differently because of your understanding of what happens after death?

In many traditions, embracing the mystery of what happens after death is more important than believing in a specific vision of life after death. What would be the impact on your life of letting go of specifics associated with life after death and embracing its mystery?

Further Reading

A significant premise of this book is that the faith journey is just that, a journey. This is a very short list of books that I have found interesting on my own faith journey. This is not intended to be a complete list, but rather, a list that points in certain directions. In this regard, I have generally avoided listing books mentioned in the text itself. Also, this is not intended as an endorsement of every idea in each of these books, but I do believe the reader will find these books thought provoking. In fact, it is precisely where authors of these books make interesting arguments that differ from my views that I expect there is a chance for my own faith to grow and expand.

Books on Science and Religion

Aczel, Amir D. *Why Science Does Not Disprove God.* New York: Harper Collins, 2014.

Cannato, Judy. *Radical Amazement.* Notre Dame, IN: Sorin, 2006.

Collins, C. John. *The God of Miracles.* Wheaton, IL: Crossway, 2000.

Delio, Ilia. *Christ in Evolution.* Maryknoll, NY: Orbis, 2008.

Dowd, Michael. *Thank God for Evolution.* New York: Viking, 2007.

O'Murchu, Diarmuid. *Quantum Theology.* New York: Crossroads, 2004.

General Science Books on Topics in this Book

Ball, Philip. *The Self-Made Tapestry.* Oxford, UK: Oxford University Press, 2001.

Feynman, Richard. *The Character of Physical Law.* Cambridge, MA: MIT Press, 1967.

Hawking, Stephen. *A Brief History of Time.* New York: Random House, 2011.

Krauss, Lawrence M. *The Physics of Star Trek.* New York: Basic, 2007.

Notes

1. Empiricism is essentially the view I described in this paragraph that all knowledge is based on sense experience. Here I am also using it to encompass the view that physical reality is the only reality.

2. As we will find out, quantum mechanics deals with things too small to sense directly, and relativity deals with speeds and quantities of matter well beyond everyday experience.

3. *Empirical,* in the broadest sense, refers to knowledge gained by observation and experiment. In a scientific context, one often requires a stricter criteria that the observations and experiments are *repeatable* by other individuals or groups. This is an important distinction as many religious experiences are, strictly speaking, empirical, because they involve the senses, but not repeatable, as they are a singular occurrence.

4. Ontology and epistemology are two branches of philosophy. Ontology is the broad study of existence and reality, with a focus on the categories of "being" and the relations between these categories. Epistemology is the study of knowledge itself, and different epistemologies are different ways of gaining knowledge. Both of these areas directly impact our exploration of reality, and will be a recurring theme in this book.

5. Syllogisms are relatively simple logical arguments involving two assumptions and a logical conclusion.

6. Ilia Delio, *Christ in Evolution* (New York: Orbis Books, 2008), n.p.

7. Hermeneutics refers to the methods used to interpret written, verbal, and nonverbal communication.

8. The moment in the Bible when Saul, the avid persecutor of Christians, is visited with a vision that leads to his conversion to Paul, the first Apostle to the Gentiles.

9. Galileo Galilei, "Letter to Madame Christina of Lorraine, Grand Duchess of Tuscany," 1615.

10. Daniel Harrington, "The Bible in Catholic Life," *The Catholic Study Bible* (New York: Oxford, 2006), p. 26, col. 2.

11. Irenaeus, *Adversus Haereses,* II.x.2.

12. Augustine, *Confessions,* XII.7.

13. Perhaps the greatest concern with the theory of evolution among its detractors is the creation of new species, or speciation. This is often seen as more challenging

than artificially breeding for new traits within a species. But, contemporary biology has clearly established the ability for natural selection to produce new species.

14. L.D. Landau and E.M. Lifshitz, *Statistical Physics,* 3rd ed. (Burlington, Mass.: Elsevier, 1980), p. 2.

15. John M. Harlow, 1868, pp. 339–340.

16. Freeman Dyson, *Infinite in all Directions,* "Progress in Religion: A Talk by Freeman Dyson," acceptance speech for the Templeton Prize, Washington National Cathedral, May 9, 2000.

17. In the study of materials, we distinguish between the microscopic scale of the atoms and molecules, and the mesoscopic scale of bubbles of gas or grains of sand, and the macroscopic scale of the entire system of bubbles or sand particles.

18. Augustine, *City of God,* Bk. XXI, ch. 8.

19. Baruch Spinoza, *Theological-Political Treatise,* ch. VI.

20. Voltaire, *Philosophical Dictionary,* sv. *miracle.*

21. David Hume, *An Enquiry Concerning Human Understanding,* X.4.

22. John Stuart Mill, *A System of Logic,* Book III, C. 25, §. 2.

23. Hume, *An Enquiry Concerning Human Understanding,* X.4.

24. Albert Einstein, "Science and Religion."

25. Paul Tillich, "Science and Religion: A Discussion with Einstein" in James E. Huchingson, ed., *Religion and the Natural Sciences: The Range of Engagement* (Eugene, Oreg.: Wipf and Stock, 2005), p. 153.

26. John Hick, *The Philosophy of Religion* (New York: Pearson, 1989), p. 39.

27. Hick, ibid.

28. Augustine, *On the Predestination of the Saints,* Book I, ch. 19.

29. This basically refers to the state of confusion that occurs in the middle of an intense ritual experience.

30. Thomas Hobbes, *Leviathan,* ch. 21.

31. See, e.g., "Hume on Free Will," *Stanford Encyclopedia of Philosophy,* http://plato. stanford.edu/entries/hume-freewill/#toc.

32. Pierre-Simon Laplace, *A Philosophical Essay on Probabilities* (London: Wiley, 1902), p. 4.

33. Eschatology is the study of the end of things, or the end times. An "inaugurated eschatology" specifically refers to the fact that Jesus's life, death, and resurrection *inaugurated* the end times—so they are both now but not yet here.

34. Jeffrey Russell, *A History of Heaven* (Princeton, N.J.: Princeton University Press, 1998), pp. 3–4.

35. Quoted in John Ortberg, *Faith and Doubt* (Grand Rapids: Zondervan, 2008), p. 59.